THINKING WITH MY PEN

Speeches from a Life in Diplomacy

Anne Anderson

For Claire
My Daughter
Always my North Star

and

For Frank
My Partner
In Life, Love, and Adventure

CONTENTS

PROLOGUE

A diplomat must value words. Indeed, ideally, should love words. Because a lifetime in diplomacy means a lifetime of testing and weighing words, giving them the precision or ambivalence they need, bending them to the purpose at hand.

I remember the jolt of reading for the first time, in adulthood, WH Auden's poem, "Embassy". A magnificent poem, set in a menacing time. It is 1938, and the world holds its breath as "the conversation of the highly trained" drifts across wide lawns.

Thankfully the diplomats of my generation were spared a World War; we were not called upon to play for such high stakes. But in many conference rooms over many years, Auden's phrase would wander into my thoughts. The "conversation of the highly trained" is always necessary. Language is a diplomat's sword and shield; again and again we come back to words: capturing realities as we see them, advocating for what we believe in, and trying to create bridges between differing perspectives.

Speeches of course are only a small part of a diplomat's output in words. I cannot count the number of reports and submissions I have written over the course of my career, the number of texts drafted. Some of these reports, which seemed very consequential to me at the time, will now have faded into irrelevance. Others, and particularly I suppose the more recent ones, may still have some resonance. (I think of my report the morning after President Trump's election: "What Has Happened to America?". Or my final report before I left Washington in summer 2017: "Clouds Over the Fourth of July".)

But these reports do not belong to me - they are on files in the

Department of Foreign Affairs, governed by departmental rules of confidentiality. And so, when I look back and want to piece together a record of what I did or felt at a particular time, the speeches provide a readier lens. Since by definition they are words shared in public, I can draw on them without restraint.

Accessible as they are, speeches have their limitations as a lens; they will never provide a full window on the soul. When you represent your country, there is no scope for self-indulgence in public utterances: you are bound to calibrate your words. Sometimes things have to be suggested or hinted at, even if you might long to speak more directly. You have to gauge your audience's level of knowledge of the subject matter and their likely receptivity to your message. And there are the same considerations as for all public speakers: Who is sharing the podium? What are the time constraints? What level of formality or informality is appropriate?

The speeches collected here mostly were delivered during my five postings as Ambassador (some were subsequent to my retirement) and mostly date from the past decade. This is partly because these are the only ones I have retained, or are easily retrievable. But it is also the case that the number and type of speeches one delivers is a function of where one is posted and in what capacity. For example, although they were four of the most challenging years of my career, there are few speeches dating from my time as Permanent Representative to the European Union. The explanation? I spent most of those Brussels years buried in conference rooms, in the hand-to-hand combat of dense negotiations, and there was limited time or opportunity for public speaking.

Like most civil servants and diplomats I also have a ghostwriting past. When I served at HQ, or at missions abroad in a more junior capacity, the speeches I drafted were almost always for delivery by others. Over the years, I have prepared speeches for foreign ministers, Taoisigh, Presidents - sometimes the drafts were discarded, sometimes partially used, sometimes used in full. But I wanted to include in this collection only speeches that I wrote myself and were delivered in my own voice.

The first of these criteria - speeches that I fully wrote myself - was also key to the choice. An Ambassador is always supported by an Embassy team, and I was fortunate to count very able and committed officers among my colleagues. There certainly were many speeches - to specialised UN committees, for example, or to highly targeted audiences during my Paris or Washington years - which drew heavily on drafting by members of my team. These speeches do not appear here, not just because of the specificity of the subject matter, but because I wanted to keep the collection true to my own voice.

I have resisted the temptation to revise and polish the texts. During the years as Ambassador, I was always writing to a deadline, always under time pressure, and juggling competing pressures. I may flatter myself that, with more time, I could have summoned up more eloquence and profundity. But that will have to remain untested. The only changes I have made are to remove here and there some passages of thanks or acknowledgment which were very specific to the occasion - so there are occasional excisions, but no amendments or additions.

In deciding which speeches to include, the key criterion was to choose ones which are meaningful to me. Mostly that meant that they should say something about issues that I consider to be important. Sometimes the speeches revolve around a person or context that I want to recall. I have divided them rather arbitrarily into chapters - some could easily have been moved around into different sections. My introduction to each chapter tries to give some context and describe the circumstances in which the speeches were delivered. In a few cases, the introduction sheds some further light on particular references that I chose to leave somewhat oblique at the time of delivery.

The speeches cover quite a spectrum in subject matter. As I look at the overall balance, it strikes me how significant a part the gender-related speeches play. Throughout my diplomatic career, particularly as I rose through the ranks, I had a sense of a dual mandate and dual responsibility - to my country and to my gender. This was reflected in my readiness to respond to speaking invitations. And after I retired, there were regular requests to speak at events focusing on diversity and gender equality. I agreed to many of these requests, primarily because I hoped and believed I could pass on something of my own experience to younger women.

But there was also another consideration that governed my choices about where and on what subjects to speak in retirement. I felt much freer to talk more personally and more directly on gender issues. Talking about contemporary US politics and the Trump Presidency - which naturally enough was a subject on which I was often invited to speak - felt much more fraught. Any honest expression of my views (no matter how much I specified they were entirely personal) had the capacity to create awkwardness for my departmental colleagues still at the coalface. So I was correspondingly reticent about accepting speaking invitations that would bring me into this territory.

The title of this collection "Thinking with My Pen" did not require much reflection; it more or less suggested itself. It pays tribute to the centrality of words, of language, that I mentioned at the outset. And throughout my life, it has been by writing things down, putting a verbal shape on things, that I explore and crystallise what I am thinking and feeling. If I don't write it down, it remains inchoate and ephemeral; when it's captured in words, I have found my moorings. This collection reflects my professional life. But in private life too, my pen has helped bring clarity whenever I was faced with big decisions, and has softened the pain at difficult times.

And I do mean quite literally "with my pen". Anachronistic as it is, that is the mechanics of how I always write. My typing is slow and laboured, and throughout my years as Ambassador my habit was to write out my speeches in longhand - most often at the dining table in the Residence after dinner - and bring them to the office for typing up the next day.

(I plead exonerating circumstances. Way back, doing the Intermediate Certificate, I was one of fifteen pupils in an all-girl secondary school in Rush, County Dublin. None of my fourteen classmates continued to the Leaving Certificate, diverting instead to "Commercial Courses" which would equip them with shorthand and typing skills for future work as secretaries. As I switched schools, I vowed to myself that for the rest of my life I would avoid what I saw as the "typing trap". It took decades to overcome this misguided determination, and I have never quite made up the lost ground.)

A final question: what do I see as the purpose of collecting these speeches? In all honesty, I have to admit to an element of ego - a desire on my part to preserve in some way these words that I crafted and inhabited. But maybe I can also claim the instincts of a history graduate. I still thrill to those words that Herodotus wrote more than two and half thousand years ago explaining why he set out to write his "Histories"…"The purpose is to prevent the traces of human events from being erased by time"…Herodotus of course was a giant, and the events he recorded were momentous. But no matter how small or insignificant our own walk-on part in history may be, there is still the impulse to record and bear witness.

Beyond that, I hope that this collection will give some sense of what constitutes a diplomat's life. It is a calling that is profoundly serious at its core. Representing Ireland to the world is a sacred trust, and we diplomats try to live up to that trust every day. But how rich a life it is, full of variety and opportunity. What paths we travel and people we meet. And how lucky was that twenty-year-old who walked through the doors of Iveagh House in November 1972.

Anne Anderson
June 2020

BEGINNING AT THE END

The four speeches in this section all date from the final months of my career in the Department of Foreign Affairs. It happens that all four are acceptance of award speeches, because people are exceptionally generous at a time one is preparing to say goodbye.

I decided to defy chronology, and place them at the beginning, because I think they help establish a context for what comes later.

The four speeches touch on themes that are amplified elsewhere: relationships with Europe and the US, the fight for gender equality. But in snatches they also provide more personal glimpses - the kind of people my parents were, the influences that shaped me, the values that are important to me.

First, a quick summary of the essentials of my career. I entered the Department of Foreign Affairs in November 1972, at twenty years of age. I served for forty-five years, including twenty-two years as Ambassador in five different postings. I was the first woman Ambassador from Ireland in each of those five posts. I retired in July 2017, at the time the longest-serving diplomat in the history of the Irish Foreign Service.

It was indeed a lengthy journey. Forty-five years of trying to find my way: immense privilege; relentless hard work; all the striving and self-questioning that is part of who I am. Impossible to capture it all in any set of speeches, but perhaps these four come closest to giving a flavour.

The first speech I have chosen for this section is the short address I gave at a Gala dinner of the Ireland Funds in Washington in March 2017. It was an emotional night: the last round of St. Patrick's Day festivities of my career. I was honoured to receive the

Fund's International Leadership Award at this glittering dinner, whose attendance included our then Taoiseach, Enda Kenny, and US Vice President Mike Pence. In many ways, it felt like the culmination of the long career journey.

I was thinking of my parents and the pride they would have taken in this evening; also of my dear daughter Claire and my partner Frank, always my anchors and cheerleaders. I wanted to mention them all. And, beyond diplomatic niceties, I really did want to give expression to how much America means to me.

But I was struggling with another emotion too. In the very early months after Donald Trump's election, as we all tried to find a footing with the new Administration, the Ireland Funds had worked hard to secure the Vice President's attendance. I knew I would speak immediately after Mr Pence, and I was apprehensive. I wanted to show the courtesy due to an important office-holder, and our guest of honour at this dinner. But I needed to find some ways to signal, even in coded language, my lack of sympathy with the values of the new Administration and with the Vice President's well-flagged views on homosexuality.

And so I bit my pen over this short speech. I decided to frame it as a series of moments from my time as Ambassador, which allowed me to weave in my vision of America. I spoke about the "lovely mosaic" of the US and finished with an expression of hope: "I know that, at its heart, this is a country of grace and generosity…a country that we pray will stay true to the essence of who it is and what it has always represented."

But what I will remember most clearly from that evening is something that happened in mid-speech. I had deliberately chosen as one of my moments "the delight of so many groups in America when Ireland adopted the Marriage Equality Referendum 2015…". At that point, most of the people in the room rose to their feet with a round of spontaneous applause. There was no doubt: a message was being passed to the Vice President.

The next two speeches I have grouped together because in their different ways they honour my mother and my father. The first was to a Nollaig na mBan event in Washington in January 2017, when I accepted an award from the Irish-American Partnership. I talked about the gender issues that have shaped my life in such fundamental ways, and of that powerful female chain - generational and global - of which I have always felt myself part. But in the opening passages I tried to conjure up for this Washington audience the kind of person my mother was. Margaret Griffin was uniquely herself, but I also saw her as one of those "women full of intelligence, and capacity and longing, but whose horizons were limited by the double constraints of class and gender".

One of the happiest experiences of my final months as Ambassador was the Civic Reception in my honour hosted in Clonmel by the Tipperary County Council. It was a hometown evening full of kindness and warmth. The Council presented me with a watercolour of Slievenamon which now hangs in our apartment in New York.

I wanted to honour Tipperary that evening, but in doing so I also wanted to honour my parents, and particularly my father. Tom Anderson hailed from Roesboro, just outside Tipperary town. Despite the subsequent transplants in search of better opportunities for his family, my father's heart always remained in his home county. In wrapping up the speech, I talked about that same sense of local identity that is a defining characteristic for so many Irish diplomats… "as 'Knocknagow' has always reminded us, it's all for the honour of the little village".

The fourth speech was made when I accepted a Flax Trust Award on 22 November 2016. The date happened to coincide with the forty-fourth anniversary of my entry to the Department of

Foreign Affairs. I touched on some of the defining events of 2016 and noted how they chimed with some of the defining themes of my own career. And my final paragraph was this: "When this anniversary comes round next year, I will have retired from the Department and who knows what turn my life will have taken. But I do know that these things will abide: the pride in public service, the fundamental belief in the European project, and the fight for gender equality."

And so, while these are finale speeches, I hope they will also act as a kind of prologue. The career and life circumstances change but there is an abiding identity, abiding values, and abiding concerns.

Presentation of International Leadership Award
The Ireland Funds: 25th National Gala, Washington, DC
15th March 2017

I am deeply honoured to be recognised this evening by the Ireland Funds – this organisation which I respect so much, and whose work has transformed so many lives over the past forty years.

Tonight is especially meaningful for me because it is the last Ireland Funds gala I will attend as Ambassador. This summer will bring to an end my forty five years in the Irish Foreign Service, the last twenty two of them as Ambassador in five different posts.

Although my achievements do not compare to those of the other honourees this evening, I share what I have heard them describe as a sense of awe at arriving at this point.

Nothing about this was fore-ordained. My parents came from farming backgrounds in Limerick and Tipperary. My father was a psychiatric nurse and my mother before she married, was a post-office clerk.

I had the opportunities I did because of my parents' ferocious commitment to their children's education, and the enlightened policies of the Irish state. I was a beneficiary of free secondary education and of state grants which made it possible to attend university.

So, when I serve my country, I have a deep sense of giving back. And all these years of representing Ireland have reinforced my pride in who we are – flawed and imperfect, yes, but a country of conscience, resilience, imagination and spirit.

Each of my assignments as Ambassador has inspired me, and left a deep imprint, but my twelve years in the United States have created unique bonds.

The ties are very personal. My beloved daughter, my only child, was born here in Washington in the mid-80s. And my partner, Frank, such a stalwart support to me, is a New Yorker whom I met when I was Ambassador to the United Nations.

But it goes well beyond the personal. As Ireland's Ambassador here, there is a constant, pervasive, sense of how close and multi-faceted the relationship is – not just the solemn ties of history but also the human ties that give such life and depth to the relationship.

Tonight, from the kaleidoscope of experiences over the past few years, I want to summon up just some of the moments that will stay with me.

• Early on, a cold winter day when I made the pilgrimage to the battlefield in Gettysburg, and stood before the Irish monument there, remembering Irish heroism and Irish sacrifice at key moments of American history.

• The visits to so many Irish immigration centres, often meeting elderly people with seamed faces, who shared their stories of decades in this country - still deeply Irish but embracing America as their land of opportunity.

• All the St. Patrick's Day parades, the pride as one walks down that green line on Fifth Avenue, but also the intimacy and spontaneity of the smaller parades – when you see the lovely mosaic of this country: the Irish American redheads but also the African American and Hispanic kids tentatively trying out their Irish dancing steps.

• The slightly surreal, fun-filled moments, like meeting the members of the GAA Club in Anchorage, Alaska, which they assured me was the most northerly GAA club on the planet.

• The moving moments like being at the Special Olympics in Los Angeles – being inspired by the courage and passion of the athletes, and the joy of their families and feeling profoundly grateful to America for having given us this movement.

- The many moments during our 1916 centenary celebrations, from the snow of Notre Dame to the sunshine of New York, from the glamour of the Kennedy Center to the small halls of Butte, Montana – everywhere hearing the interwoven stories of Ireland and America, and the determination to keep that story going.

- The delight of so many groups in America when Ireland adopted the Marriage Equality referendum in May 2015. I was in Minneapolis a couple of weeks later and was presented with a rainbow flag which had flown on their bridge during their referendum.

- The wonderful night in Philadelphia, city of brotherly love, when I was admitted as the first woman member of the Friendly Sons of St. Patrick in that city – another small crack in the glass ceiling, in this case a ceiling that was almost 250 years old.

- As well as all the joy, moments too of great sadness, never more so than the tragedy in Berkeley, when six beautiful young lives were lost, but where the outstretched hands of America helped to hold up the families in their time of grief.

These are some of my moments – this is my love letter to America. I know that, at its heart, this is a country of grace and generosity, a country that has such a special place in the affections of Irish people, and a country that we pray will stay true to the essence of who it is and what it has always represented.

It has been, and is, the greatest privilege of my life to be Ireland's Ambassador here.

And so, my thanks – to the Taoiseach for the confidence he has placed in me as Ambassador, to my accomplished and dedicated Embassy team, and of course to the Ireland Funds for this unforgettable evening.

Acceptance of Award from the Irish-American Partnership
Nollaig na mBan Breakfast,
The University Club, Washington DC
6th January 2017

Nollaig na mBan is a day that has a great resonance for me, one of these touchstone days that triggers a lot of nostalgia and a lot of emotion. It's a day that comes freighted with childhood memories; it's also a kind of stock taking day, a day to reflect on the role of women, the progress and the challenges. I would like this morning to offer a few thoughts, some of them personal, some of them ranging somewhat more broadly.

To begin on a very personal note. When Mary (Sugrue) initially contacted me about this honour, I hadn't known or hadn't remembered, that it came with an award of $10,000 to be devoted to a charitable cause of one's choice in Ireland. While I was still reflecting on an appropriate charity, Mary came up with the idea of a poetry initiative which would have students in Ireland attend workshops with established poets, especially on the themes of Immigration and the Diaspora. I was immensely grateful for the idea, and immediately said yes.

The idea of the award brought together a number of important things for me, including my own love and valuing of poetry, and the concern with immigration which is such an important focus of my work here. But there was also a particular aptness about the association with Nollaig na mBan, because this is a day when many of us remember our mothers, who in a first and fundamental way shaped our sense of what it is to be female.

And her love of poetry was part of what defined my mother. She was born Margaret Griffin, in 1921, the youngest of nine children on a small subsistence farm in Co. Limerick. There was no money for secondary education, let alone university, and she left school at 15 to work as a post office clerk. But while still in her teens and early 20s, living away from home in what were then known as 'digs' – fairly basic boarding houses – in small towns in Ireland, she would go to the local library at night and copy out in copper plate writing the works of some of the great classic poets -Wordsworth, Byron, and others. Then she would come back to her room and learn them off by heart, just for the sheer beauty of the language. I still have one of her poetry notebooks from those days, and I cherish it.

And this was part of the soundtrack of my childhood, the reciting and reading aloud of these poems by my mother. It was this which first attuned my ears to the cadence of language and led to poetry becoming my lifelong bolt-hole. As so often, Seamus Heaney found the perfect, unexpected word: "The Redress of Poetry". At a time of such upheaval and suffering and cruelty in the world, we need this 'redress' more than ever.

If I speak about my mother, it's partly to pay homage to her, and to let you know the personal significance of this award for me, but it's also to honour the generations of Irish women like her who have gone before us. Women full of intelligence, and capacity and longing, but whose horizons and ambitions were limited by the double constraints of class and gender. My mother lived out her life in Ireland, but throughout my time here in the US I have repeatedly and poignantly been reminded of the generations of Irish women who arrived in this country as immigrants. They came and worked as domestics, in garment factories, in mills, in nursing wards, as homemakers – women whose stories have been insufficiently told, whose contributions have been insufficiently recognised.

When, last October, I went to Butte – the legendary Irish mining town in Montana – I was presented by local women with a beautiful book entitled "Motherlode". It's a book which bears witness to the richly textured lives and histories of women in that mining town. I would suggest that Nollaig na mBan is a day to remind ourselves of the motherlode – that rich vein of female experience – which is at the heart of the Irish American story.

I mentioned that, as well as looking back, I also see Nollaig na mBan as a day of audit or stocktaking. As a sort of gendered version of New Year's Day, it's a time to benchmark how women are faring in the world and to assess one's own personal challenges in engaging with these realities.

I am very conscious that I make that audit or assessment from a place of immense privilege. My whole adult life has been spent in the Irish Foreign Service, and this is my fifth posting as Ambassador. And what tremendously satisfying posts they have been: as Ambassador to the UN in Geneva, to the European Union, to France, to the UN in New York, and now here in DC.

I have said before that if I ever write my memoir it will be the very opposite of a "misery memoir" – it will be a celebration of over 40 years of the privilege of serving my country. But to acknowledge and celebrate all the privilege and opportunity does not mean airbrushing the difficulties, the frustrations, the challenges.

I joined the Department of Foreign Affairs in late '72, and in those early years, we were such a small minority of women diplomats in the Irish Foreign Service. We didn't have role models, or mentors, to help us find a path. The "marriage ban" had existed since the foundation of the State, and was swept away only when Ireland joined the then EEC on 1 January 1973. The 'ban' meant that the day you married was the day you exited – or, more accurately, were ejected from – the civil service, public service, Foreign Service.

I got married in 1974, within a couple of years of the abolition of the marriage ban. And so it happened that, when I was posted to Geneva in 1976, I was the first married women diplomat to be posted abroad in the history of the service. In each of the five postings as Ambassador, I was the first Irish woman to hold that post. When I went to Brussels in 2001, I was the first woman Ambassador to the European Union from *any* member State of the Union – this nearly fifty years after the foundation of the EEC.

Being the first brings a considerable ambivalence. Yes, it's good to have the minor footnote in history, or to know you have made another small dent in that glass ceiling. But you don't always relish having to be the one to do the campaigning and crusading. I honestly don't know how much I was a pioneer by temperament and how much by circumstances. I didn't consciously set out to be a crusader, it was just that my sense of justice kept being affronted.

I was involved in quite a few battles in those early years: for equal allowances, for equal rental accommodation, for equal consideration for postings abroad. They weren't always easy or comfortable battles to fight. And years later, as I sat around a tableful of men in Brussels, and presided over 24 male Ambassadors during the Irish Presidency in 2004, I sometimes wondered how it would feel for any one of them if the gender ratio was reversed. Like women everywhere, I often found myself projecting forward to a post-gender professional world: where equality would be so natural, so taken for granted, that no-one would be doing the gender tally around the table. But that world still seems very far away.

There have been immense changes since my early years in the Department. We now have a management team that is strongly committed to gender equality. We have women Ambassadors in countries such as France, Japan, Israel, Mexico, and many more; in fact, almost 30% of our heads of mission are female. There is a gender-consciousness in our training, in our assignments, in our promotion policy.

But there is still a significant distance to travel. Despite the progress, our structures remain very pyramidical; there is one telling statistic: at our most senior level in the Department, we are still 85% male and 15% female.

Moving beyond the world of Irish diplomacy, Nollaig na mBan is also an opportunity for a broader audit.

When I look at Ireland through a gender prism over the past year, there is a lot to feel good about. Just to enumerate a few of those developments. At our general election in February, gender quotas for candidates were applied for the first time and the percentage of women in our lower House of Parliament, the Dáil, went from 15% to 22%. Our commemorations marking the 100th anniversary of the 1916 Easter Rising very consciously brought women back into the frame, rescuing them from the "pervasive invisibility" which had been their lot in earlier narratives of 1916. There was an important grassroots movement in the arts: "Waking the Feminists", and there was also a ground-breaking study of women in academia, which resulted in new targets, designed to secure a more equal place for women in the hierarchy of third level institutions.

Here in the US, there is the fact that for the first time there was a woman candidate from one of the major political parties for election to President. And we saw the strength of her support in the popular vote.

But of course one can upend all of that, and look through the other end of the telescope. In Ireland, the centenary commemorations reminded us of the extent to which the feminist vision which many of the 1916 activists shared (some men as well as women) was sidelined, and even betrayed, over subsequent decades. The fact that, in 2016, only 22% of the Dáil should be female might seem more shocking than reassuring. It is equally disappointing that there is still embedded sexism in the arts and academic worlds, which triggered the developments I mentioned.

In America, there is of course the inescapable fact that the electorate chose not to have a woman President. One could express that choice differently, and it is important not to overstate things – this was obviously a complicated election, with multiple factors at play, and the analysts will argue for a long time about the relative weight to be attributed to different factors. But, however you slice and dice the results, I think that few objective analysts will dispute that sexism was at least to some degree a factor.

There was another important election towards the end of last year, also with a global impact. In October 2016, Antonio Guterres, former Prime Minister of Portugal, was elected as Secretary General of the United Nations. Mr. Guterres is widely admired and respected, and will be a good Secretary General in these turbulent times. But in its 70 year history, the United Nations has never had a woman Secretary General, and there was a strong tide of support for the view that this time it should be a woman. There were a number of women candidates of substance, including Foreign Ministers and heads of UN agencies, but ultimately, Mr. Guterres was preferred.

Of course, we all fully respect electoral outcomes and move forward, and we look forward to working with President-elect Trump and Secretary General Guterres. But it doesn't in any way take from the legitimacy of the outcomes to conduct some thought experiments. In the US election, let us imagine that the genders of the two main candidates had been swapped but everything else stayed the same – experience, temperament, character. Do we think that the outcome would have remained the same? In the UN election, if there had been an unbroken succession of eight female Secretaries General since the foundation of the organisation, and finally in 2016, there were a number of highly qualified male candidates, would we still have emerged with the ninth female Secretary General this time around?

I leave the answers to these questions to each of you but I think it is salutary, as we do our stocktaking, to inject some of these hypotheses into discussion. Let me just say, in summary, that while my Nollaig na mBan audit indeed finds some causes for satisfaction, there is also every incentive to continue the long march.

And if I might conclude on a personal note. At the end of my four year term in July of this year, I will be retiring from the Foreign Service and moving on to whatever the next phase might be – as yet, undecided. But there is one thing I do know: you don't retire from being a woman, you don't retire from having a sense of justice, and you don't retire from having a vision for what a more equal world would look like.

To borrow again a phrase from Seamus Heaney – the title of one of his last collections – we are all part of a "human chain". And today, one thinks particularly of the female chain. I spoke earlier about how Nollaig na mBan puts me in mind of my mother and the generations that have gone before, and of course that chain stretches on to our daughters and those who will follow us. And it's not just generational; it is also a global chain, linking us with women in other parts of the world – in other countries: Nigeria, Sudan, Syria, to name but a few – for whom our lives are ones of unimaginable privilege and whose lives and realities and burdens must always be part of our consciousness.

And so, Nollaig na mBan will always be for me a day for remembering and a day for resolve – trying, as we all do, to fulfil the obligation to remain a strong, weight-bearing link on that precious human chain. But, whatever comes next, because of this award, today will certainly stand out in my memory as one of the happiest and most affirming celebrations of Nollaig na mBan – thank you to Mary and the Irish American Partnership, and thank you all for being here.

Civic Reception in honour of Ambassador Anne Anderson
Clonmel, County Tipperary, 26 May 2017

I want to express my deep appreciation to all the members of Tipperary County Council for the honour being bestowed on me today.

I cannot tell you how gratifying it is to be here; nothing feels quite so special as a hometown honour.

The invitation we all received for tonight's reception suggests that I am being recognised on two counts: the fact that I am the first woman to serve as Irish Ambassador in my various posts – in Geneva, Brussels, Paris, New York and now Washington – and my contribution to Irish-US relations.

It is clearly no coincidence that the invitation has been extended when your Council is under the stewardship of Cathaoirleach Siobhán Ambrose, the third Cathaoirleach of the newly amalgamated Council and the first woman in that post.

Tonight is indeed a night to celebrate the strides being made in terms of improving gender representation in Ireland. Things are undoubtedly getting better, and we are seeing more women in senior positions in our civil service, diplomatic service and public life generally. But we still have a long way to go, and change sometimes seems painfully slow and incremental. With only 22% female representation in the Dáil, and less than 20% female representation in boards of major companies, there is certainly no basis for complacency.

Tipperary, the "premier county", is well-equipped to be a leader in this respect too. Your Council's vision statement has a very strong emphasis on inclusivity and diversity, and I have no doubt that gender equality is fully embraced within those goals. So I hope tonight may provide a further boost to that determination.

Of course you honour me not just as a woman diplomat, but as a Tipperary woman. And that I am.

Let me share a little of the family history.

My father Tom Anderson hailed from Roesboro, just outside Tipperary town. He grew up on a farm there and met my mother when she was working in the post office in Tipperary. He was a psychiatric nurse at St. Luke's hospital here in Clonmel. All four of us children were born in Clonmel, and lived on Slievenamon Road. In 1960, when I was eight years old, my father got a promotion and transferred to St. Canice's Hospital in Kilkenny, and a few years later we moved to north County Dublin.

Even if he lived the latter half of his life outside Tipperary, my father remained a Tipperary man in his blood and bones. That meant, among other things, buying the Clonmel Nationalist unfailingly every week to the end of his days. And my sisters and brother will certainly remember: when any new boyfriend or girlfriend entered the house, there was a ruthless interrogation as to whether he or she had any Tipperary DNA!

My mother came from Limerick and, as I mentioned, met my father when she was a post office clerk in Tipperary town. As well as falling in love with my father, she fell in love with Tipperary. All through our youth, we were treated to her stories of halcyon days in the Galtee Mountains and the Glen of Aherlow. And no one ever cheered more loudly for the Tipperary hurling team – somewhat provocatively during our Kilkenny years!

So there was certainly parental reinforcement of a sense of ourselves as being from Tipperary. But still, one might wonder how it is, so many decades after leaving the County, the sense of connection is still so strong.

Part of the answer is a universal one. It's the human condition: we are all imprinted in a very special way by our earliest memories. Another part of it is being Irish – that sense of place that is such a strong part of the Irish psyche. Think of our writers, so rooted in their home counties: John McGahern in Leitrim, Seamus Heaney in Derry, Colm Toibin in Wexford. And Tipperary exerts the same visceral pull: was any writer ever more rooted in his home county than our own Charles Kickham, whose immortal "Knocknagow" will forever bear witness to the homes and people of Tipperary. That vibrant literary tradition continues, with authors like Donal Ryan continuing to bring recognition and honour to the County.

But in my own case, I think part of the explanation of that sense of connection also lies in my years in the Foreign Service and especially the twelve years spent in America. How many hundreds, thousands, of times have I been asked by Irish Americans, "Where are you from?" And how many times have I answered: "Tipperary". And it rarely stops there: everyone wants to drill down: not just your county but your parish, your town, your townland.

The explanation is fairly obvious.

Irish people when they arrived in their new land of America, as a reaction to the vastness of the country, and the anonymity of huge cities, wanted a specific and local connection to home. It was that thirst for connection that led to the growth of the powerful county associations in America. Although these associations are in many cases well past their heyday, reflecting generational change and the growth of social media, the desire for local and regional identification has in no way abated. And that is what offers opportunity to Irish regions and counties today when they seek to build links across the Atlantic.

This brings me to the second reason for tonight's recognition: the contribution to strengthening the Irish-US relationship.

My work over the past four years has been about helping to shape and advance the political and economic relationship between the two countries. I have of course seen and lived the transition from the Obama to the Trump Administration, with all the changes and challenges this entails. But this evening, I will confine myself to a word about the economic relationship and the opportunities it offers.

As I am sure you all know, investment and trade and tourism between Ireland and the US continues to go from strength to strength. Over 70% of our FDI comes from the US. Our exports are powering ahead, with goods exports last year up 12% from the previous year. Tourism too is growing exponentially: in 2016, Ireland welcomed a record 1.4m US visitors. An amazing 10% of all American visitors to Europe now visit Ireland.

With Brexit on the horizon, it has never been more important to nurture and develop these contacts – to continue to diversify and to decrease our economic dependence on the UK.

Tipperary is certainly on its toes when it comes to scouting out the opportunities. I have been delighted to meet some of your leadership on their visits to the US. You have developed your Diaspora Projects; your five-year Strategic Tourism Marketing Plan; and of course, most importantly, your recently launched marketing programme for inward investment: "Tipperary – the Place; the Time".

In the tourism sector, there is undoubtedly a huge amount of potential still to be realised. Your tourism strategy refers to Tipperary as "the undiscovered heartland of Ireland". And that is an absolutely key word: "undiscovered". All too often, American visitors to Ireland are focused on a relatively short list of top sights. If Tipperary is included, it may be no more than a quick stop at the Rock of Cashel. But more and more people are in search of authenticity, of relatively undiscovered places, of experiences that go beyond the cookie cutter ones. In short, everything that Tipperary offers.

So yes, Tipperary, this is your time.

Let me finish on a more personal note. After more than four decades in the Foreign Service, I will retire at the end of July. It has been my extraordinary good fortune to have had such a fascinating career, to have had the great privilege of representing Ireland abroad, to have served in the most interesting places at the most interesting times.

I leave with a huge sense of pride in my country, but also with a real pride in our Foreign Service, which I believe is among the most committed and dedicated groups of people you will find anywhere. And as I look at our Foreign Service, I am convinced that the diversity of background of our diplomats is hugely enriching, truly among our biggest assets. Irish diplomats come from towns and villages and rural areas all over Ireland; we come from all economic backgrounds; very few of us were born with silver spoons in our mouths.

Of course we faithfully represent our country as a whole, and the values and interests of all its people. But none of us leaves our identity at the door as we enter the Service. My early years on Slievenamon Road, my identity as a Tipperary person, my sense of connection to this beautiful county, have helped shape who I am as a person and a diplomat. One may find elaborate ways of expressing the foreign service calling, but at its core, as "Knocknagow" has always reminded us, it's all "for the honour of the little village".

And so tonight there is a sense of completion of the circle, as I accept with gratitude this honour from my home county.

26th Annual Flax Trust Awards
Hay Adams Hotel, Washington DC
22nd November 2016

It is a true privilege to be here this morning.

It is very special to be introduced by my dear friend Tom Donahue. Tom is a great Irish American and someone for whom I have enormous respect. I will never forget those years back in the mid-80s, when I was a multi-hatted young diplomat at our Embassy here, including being Labour Attaché, and Tom was in that very elevated position of Secretary General of the AFL-CIO. He could not have been kinder and more gracious to me, taking me under his wing and looking out for me at the annual AFL-CIO Conventions. These things leave a mark, and thirty years later I still feel gratitude for that kindness.

I was delighted, as I said, to be invited to accept this award. And today's date – 22 November – is an especially meaningful one. Of course it's meaningful for all Americans and for people around the world: it's forever etched on our memories as the day of President Kennedy's assassination. Like everyone else, I remember exactly the circumstances in which I heard the dreadful news.I was an eleven year old girl, living in North Co. Dublin at the time.

But the date has another significance for me too – just in my personal universe. Nine years after that fateful day in 1963, on 22 November 1972, I walked into the Department of Foreign Affairs to begin my new life as a diplomat. I was a bright eyed twenty year old, barely out of university, and I walked in that door to Iveagh House feeling a mixture of pride, apprehension and uncertainty.

Time is short this morning, and I'm certainly not going to trace the arc of these forty four years. But I wanted to touch briefly on the three defining events of the current year, 2016, and to note how they chime with some of the defining themes of my whole career.

As I have experienced this year, the three defining elements have been our commemorations of the centenary of 1916, the seismic upheaval of the Brexit vote in Britain on 23 June, and the Presidential election here two weeks ago.

Firstly, the centenary commemorations. We always knew that the 1916 centenary would have a special resonance in the US and indeed Irish America rose magnificently to the occasion. We have had over 300 events, right across the US, including of course the wonderful three-week festival at the Kennedy Center: " Ireland 100."

I think we got the balance largely right. There were joyful and celebratory events, but also many occasions to reflect. The themes were: remember, reflect, reimagine. As I have said many times, there was no complacency in our commemorations; we often recalled how far short we have fallen of the vision of 1916, and the need to course correct in certain respects. And of course there is the major unfinished business of Northern Ireland. But consistent with all of that, what I want to recall here this morning is the pride of it all – in telling the story of those 100 years, how far our country has travelled, the opportunities we have created at home, how we have taken our place on the international stage, the contribution we have made to disarmament and peacekeeping, the resilience we have shown.

And that I think is what sustained me throughout the forty four years – no airbrushing the problems or challenges, pride in my country, a belief in the innate decency of Irish people, and a sense of the immense worthwhileness of public service.

Now, the rude shock of Brexit. Of course, as you all know, we're trying to carefully work through all the challenges: what it means for the economic relationship between our two islands, what it means for Northern Ireland and the peace process, for the Common Travel Area and so on. The implications are immense.

But it's at a more personal level that I want to say a word this morning. Europe has defined my whole adult life. I certainly wouldn't be standing before you were it not for the fact that Ireland joined the European Union when it did. We became an EU member, together with Britain, on 1 January '73, five weeks after I joined the Department. Until we joined the EU, Ireland had what was known as the marriage ban – the rule that women had to leave public service on the day they married. The EU made us change that, and made us adopt a whole slew of equality legislation: equal pay, maternity leave and much more.

The 1950s and even 1960s Ireland was still socially a very conservative place. Joining the European Union was like opening our windows wide, allowing fresh air to come in. We saw ourselves in a new way, no longer an island behind an island, but part of a European mainstream. It liberated us psychologically, and unleashed a new energy and new creativity.

I am the first to recognise mistakes that have been made in Europe, and there isn't time to catalogue them here. But now I think we are in a fight for the soul of Europe. And it's so important that we stand and fight against the closing of the European mind, the narrowing of vision, allowing the arithmetic and the bureaucracy to obscure what Europe was founded for and still stands for.

The third defining event of the year was the election two weeks ago. Of course, as for every other country, it is always important to Ireland to have a fruitful partnership with the US Administration, and the Taoiseach has already had good telephone conversations with President-elect Trump and Vice President-elect Pence.

This was a complex election and analysis will continue for a very long time. One of the aspects of that analysis that will most interest me is to what extent sexism was a factor, to what extent women are still held to different, and tougher, standards than men, to what extent the discourse is simply different when it comes to women.

Throughout my career, one of the shaping and motivating factors has been equality for women – whether in my own career, or in my Human Rights work at the UN. I sometimes asked myself whether the glass ceiling was the right term – it so often felt like reinforced concrete.

I'm still asking that question.

The election was a vivid reminder that the long march continues, that there is still quite a distance to be travelled.

When this anniversary comes round next year, I will have retired from the Department and who knows what turn my life will have taken. But I do know that these things will abide: the pride in public service, the fundamental belief in the European project, and the fight for gender equality.

Thank you so much for giving me the opportunity to reflect on them today, and for honouring me with this award, which I will cherish.

REFLECTING ON IRISH FOREIGN POLICY: RELATIONSHIPS WITH EUROPE, THE US, THE UN

The seven speeches I have gathered in this section span some fifteen years: the first in chronological order is a lecture I gave at Louvain University in Belgium in November 2002 "A Union of Values: Issues Confronting the European Union". The last is my acceptance speech of a Lifetime Achievement Award from the American Chamber of Commerce Ireland in November 2017. I begin the chapter with these two bookending speeches, because I find it interesting to read them in conjunction with one another. The five others - dating from 2008, 2010, 2012 and 2013 - follow in the order in which they were delivered.

In re-reading the speeches at this remove, I am struck by the extent to which I continued over the years to grapple with the same recurring themes: the duality of Ireland's relationship with Europe and the US; the need for a strong trans-Atlantic partnership but within which Europe would more assertively find its own voice and its own role; and the imperative for Ireland to maintain a values-driven foreign policy, nationally but also as a committed member of the EU family and as the model UN member we aspire to be.

The address to the American Chamber of Commerce Ireland was on Thanksgiving 2017, a few months after my retirement. The dining room of the Berkeley Court Hotel was full; the attendance included Taoiseach Leo Varadkar and I was delighted to have many of my family members present. My speaking slot was quite brief but, as well as the courtesies of a celebratory occasion, I wanted to say something of substance. Most of my speech focused on the three interwoven and interlocking relationships which have shaped my career: Ireland, Europe, and America. Before concluding, I spoke about the "isolationist trends taking hold in America - the drumbeat of sovereignty that is becoming more insistent".

(I mentioned in the Introduction the constraints I felt in the early aftermath of retirement. I now spoke only for myself and was entitled to express my personal views. But inevitably they would be interpreted in light of my former position, and my continuing loyalty to the Department meant I was guarded in my choice of words.)

The Louvain Lecture of November 2002 allowed me a brief respite from the punishing daily schedule in Brussels. I have described in other contexts how it felt to be Permanent Representative to the European Union: the weight of responsibility, the granularity of the negotiations, the challenge of combining deft diplomatic footwork with mastery of technical detail on a range of sometimes obscure subjects. The work was important and rewarding but it sometimes felt a bit claustrophobic. Among these dense trees, it would be all too easy to lose sight of the wood; I wanted a chance to stand back, look up.

And so I chose the title "A Union of Values" to allow me to explore some larger issues about the values at the core of the European project, and how we project those values. In examining the projection, I came back to the Europe-US relationship: the need for us to define ourselves on our own terms and to play to European values and strengths. Today, eighteen years later, although the US context has radically changed, the EU is still struggling with some of these fundamental challenges.

The issue of values in foreign policy is also the theme running through a wide-ranging speech I gave at the Princess Grace Library in Monaco in February 2008. During my time as Ambassador in

France, I also became on a non-residential basis our first Ambassador to Monaco. HRH Prince Albert came to the Library for my talk, and his presence explains my sign-off sentence... "At the core of it all is the challenge for diplomats - as for princes - to help create a better world. It is that which gives shape and purpose to it all."

During my next career incarnation, when I became Permanent Representative to the United Nations in New York, I was still circling around some of these same issues. The November 2010 speech came during a fairly dark week for Ireland, with a visit of European and IMF teams to assess the state of our banks and consider a bail-out. I tried to put the best face on it, emphasising our underlying strengths and resilience. While the main focus of the speech is on Ireland's role at the United Nations, I touched on a couple of other themes - including how, during the Celtic Tiger years, "it sometimes felt as if the sound of cash registers was drowning out everything else". And, towards the end, I tried to connect our EU and UN identities and the balancing act this sometimes requires.

Throughout the New York years, although I was immersed in my day-to-day role at the Untied Nations, I felt a strong impulse to explain and defend the EU to mostly sceptical US audiences. The EU was struggling, and the US media coverage was almost uniformly negative. Addressing the UN Association in New York in November 2012, I acknowledged the storm battering the EU, and the Eurozone in particular, and tried to make the wider case for the essential "modernity" of the European Union and its place and fit in a multi-polar world.

In the same crusading spirit, I accepted an invitation in February 2013 to participate in a Panel discussion at Columbia University on the "Future of Europe". There were six panelists: three of the well-known names were the billionaire George Soros, former Greek Prime Minister George Papandreou and Nobel Prize-winning economist Joseph Stiglitz. The large auditorium was packed - there was a definite sense that most of the students were there to worship at the feet of Soros rather than listen to the rest of us!

I was fairly sure in advance that Mr Soros would do his usual Cassandra act about the Union, and indeed he did, predicting - as was his wont those days - an early collapse of the Euro that would shake the entire foundations of the Union. What I had not quite anticipated was how negative George Papandreou would be; it brought home to me just how embittering the Greek experience of bail-out was proving. In any event, I felt myself a bit lonely in the stance I took in my intervention and the subsequent panel discussion.

The final speech is my address to the Atlanta Council on International Relations in May 2014, entitled "Ireland, Europe and the US: A Road to Recovery and Renewed Partnership". Now Ambassador to the US, I am back on familiar territory: once again both celebrating and interrogating that triangle of relationships: analysing differences, urging partnership, evoking common challenges.

As I look back on these foreign policy speeches from the vantage point of 2020, I am conscious of a relative absence: China intrudes only lightly and sporadically. This partly reflects my career path; I never served in an Asian post abroad or an Asia-focused post at home. But that in itself is hardly a coincidence: for much of my career, there were relatively few such posts. Our focus on Asia grew in line with China's burgeoning strength as an economic and then a political power.

In any discussion today on the global context in which Ireland must define itself, there would almost certainly be some reflection on the rise of China, the growing economic and ideological competition between China and the US, and the positioning of the EU in this evolving landscape. (I spoke last year at a panel discussion in the Department of Foreign Affairs which addressed these themes.) The shifting terms of the debate, and the pace at which this is happening, are a measure of how aggressively China is pursuing its global ambitions. But that is a subject matter for future speeches...

Presentation of Lifetime Achievement Award
American Chamber of Commerce Ireland, Dublin
Thanksgiving 2017

This is truly a tremendous honour for me - to accept this award from an organisation that I respect so much, in the warmth and distinction of this gathering.

The day itself also contributes to that special feeling: Thanksgiving. As for so many Americans and those who live there, this is one of my favourite holidays. I have spent the last eight Thanksgivings in America and four more on an earlier posting. I have seen at first hand how people open their homes and their hearts, and have sat around many Thanksgiving tables as people talked about what is meaningful to them and what they give thanks for.

The timing is special in another way too. Yesterday was the 45th anniversary of the date I joined the foreign service. I vividly recall that day, 22 November 1972, walking into Iveagh House for the first time, full of hope and passion. And it did not disappoint! I want to dedicate today's award to all my colleagues in the Irish foreign service: a band of skilled and dedicated men and women, true patriots, unstinting in their devotion and service to our country.

When one is honoured by a lifetimes achievement award, inevitably it triggers quite a range of feelings. Tremendous gratitude of course; a hope that this is not yet the summation of one's life - that more lies ahead. But also - and this in the true Thanksgiving tradition - a reflection on what has shaped one's life, what has given it direction and purpose.

As I consider my own career over the past forty five years, I am conscious of three defining identities and influences: being Irish, being European, and having a strong affinity with America. And so, on this special day, these are the identities and affinities - distinct but intertwined - that I would like to speak briefly about.

Everything begins, of course, with my love for Ireland. This is the community I became part of the day I was born, and of which I am deeply proud. I have always regarded it as an extraordinary privilege - I have often described it as a sacred trust - to represent Ireland abroad.

I hope that this love has always been clear-eyed, acknowledging the flaws and challenges. Last year, our centenary year, provided us with a particular opportunity for introspection. As well as celebrating all the advances and achievements, we measured the ways we had fallen short of the vision of 1916 and especially the Proclamation's pledge to "cherish all the children of the nation equally". For too many, this is a promise that does not correspond to the reality of their daily lives. Indeed, for 50% of the population, the women of Ireland, it is a promise still to be fully redeemed.

But no country is without its challenges, and my pride in Ireland remains undiluted.

Sometimes, we see ourselves more clearly through the eyes of others. Especially during my fourteen years of accreditation to the United Nations, I came to understand what Ireland conjures up for representatives from countries around the world - from Africa, Asia, Latin America. Inspired by our history and by our culture, they see a land of imagination and conscience, spirit and resilience.

Europe, chronologically at least, comes next.

The date of my joining the foreign service coincided almost exactly with the date of our entry to the then EEC.The experience of membership in those early years was heady, liberating, transformative. We were no longer an island behind an island, judging and defining ourselves by the relationship with Britain. The claustrophobic decades were over: the windows opened wide and we breathed a new and fresher air.

Over the intervening years, Irish feelings about Europe have evolved. No longer that "first, fine careless rapture", it has grown into a more mature and complex relationship. Like every other member state, we calibrate and navigate with care and, where necessary, with caution. But in this globalised 21st century, Europe is more than ever our home, the setting within which we as family members find both protection and empowerment.

And then there is that third key relationship: with America. From my childhood I was inspired by the idea of America, and over the years it too has become a true home. The ties are deeply personal. My only child - my daughter Claire, who is here today - was born in Washington during my posting there in the '80s. And my partner Frank, also here today, is a proud New Yorker.

Like generations of Irish people, I have experienced the grace and generosity of America. As Ambassador, I traveled the length and breadth of the country: again and again, in big cities and small towns, in familiar and far-flung settings, I saw the outsize place that our small country occupies in that great beating heart of America. I was humbled by the love and loyalty of Irish America, and grateful for the countless ways in which those sentiments find concrete expression.

Throughout my years there, one of the greatest sources of pride was the evolution of the relationship between our two countries - no longer a lopsided one of benefactor and beneficiary, but one of mutuality of interest and true partnership. Every company represented in the room today bears witness to that. So many times I have heard your American-based CEOs speak with passion of the talent and vibrancy and opportunity which they found in Ireland, just as I have witnessed the confidence and ambition of Irish companies wanting to develop or deepen their footprint in America.

These then are the three interwoven and interlocking relationships that have shaped my past forty-five years: Ireland, Europe, America. And this brings me to my final thought today - perhaps a somewhat sobering one for the occasion, but then I have always experienced Thanksgiving as a day for reflection as well as celebration.

There is a corollary to this deep engagement that Ireland has with both Europe and the US - this dual facing that has always defined us. It means that, among all the European countries, Ireland has perhaps the deepest stake in the relationship between Europe and the US. We thrive when that partnership thrives, and no-one has more grounds for concern when tension, or brittleness, or misunderstanding or neglect enter that relationship.

And yes, I do believe there are some grounds for concern today. All relationships of course have their share of everyday irritants. But of deeper significance, we see the isolationist trends taking hold in America, and hear the drumbeat of sovereignty that is becoming more insistent. Europe, like the rest of the world, is reading these signals and beginning to plan its own future accordingly.

A widening Atlantic is not something to which we should resign ourselves. It is not a historical inevitability, a casualty of shifting world power. On the contrary, a confident and robust trans Atlantic partnership remains as vital in this century as in the last. Never has there been greater need of our joint voice and advocacy in defence of universal human rights, a liberal world order, responsible capitalism, and more equitable globalisation.

Ireland's role and responsibility in all of this may be limited but it is real. Without hubris or self-aggrandisement, I honestly believe that no country is better placed to interpret Europe to America and America to Europe. History, geography, and the current economic relationship all equip us for that role. Alongside our necessary preoccupation with Brexit, and our input to constructing the new Europe that will take shape in Brexit's aftermath, this is a task deserving our attention.

In finishing, let me express my appreciation once again - for this great honour, and for giving me the opportunity to reflect on these relationships that are deeply important to me. May Ireland and America always remain true to their better selves, may our countries remain braided together in friendship, and may Ireland continue to bridge the Atlantic, helping to build and buttress the trans Atlantic partnership that matters so much to our world.

A Union of Values: Issues Confronting the European Union
Louvain University
6th November 2002

I am very honoured to address you this evening.

The theme I have chosen more or less suggested itself. Our setting helped to condition the choice of subject matter: a discussion of values seemed apt given the proud philosophical tradition of Louvain University. There is also my own professional formation: I came to Brussels after six years as Permanent Representative at the United Nations in Geneva, where human rights and humanitarian issues were our daily agenda. And there is the matter of timing: we have just emerged from an Irish referendum which obliged us to assess the values at the heart of our EU membership. That same interrogation of values is central to the whole enlargement process of the Union as well as at the core of the debate in the Convention on the Future of Europe.

The subject is a vast and challenging one and would justify an entire lecture series. I am conscious that I can do no more than scratch the surface tonight. But, speaking on my own behalf and on a personal basis, I intend to pose some questions and offer some reflections.

The values debate is too often seen as a narrow and compartmentalised one: whether or not we should add a declaratory Preamble or new language to a new European Treaty or whether or how we should reinforce the status of the Charter on Fundamental Rights. But the issue goes well beyond this. Institutions, like individuals, define themselves more by actions than words. In seeking to assess what the Union stands for, it is the *lived* values that matter most. As the lecture this evening takes place in the Irish Franciscans' Chapel, I might borrow some biblical language: "By their deeds shall you know them".

I would propose to address two main questions: does the European project imply a value system and, if so, how do we define those values? How do we project our values and ensure they leave an imprint on the world?

Defining our values

The first question is the easier one. As even the most elementary student of the European project knows, the Union was from its post-war origins a political concept given economic expression.

Perhaps not surprisingly at a time when Europe had good reason to distrust rhetoric, the founding Treaty is almost shorn of inspirational language. But the writings and speeches of Monnet and Schumann are a treasure-house of quotations to provide corroborative evidence of their intent. The architecture they put in place tells its own story: the checks and balances that speak to values of equality, dignity and mutual respect among the member states.

With the long sweep of hindsight, it becomes obvious that a project as ambitious and innovative as the European Economic Community could not remain frozen in its original mould. The road map from Rome - through the Single European Act, the Maastricht Treaty, Amsterdam, Nice - could never have been predicted in 1957 but from the beginning there was an inescapable sense of a fluid and evolutionary process.

And it is hardly surprising that this should be so. Economic interdependence will not develop in a values vacuum. A trade and business partnership, if it goes deep enough, also became a values partnership. The critical issue is one of trust: partnership depends on trust and trust is rooted in shared values. The trust which grew within the European Economic Community was the foundation on which the European Union was built.

Although still sparing in what might be called inspirational language, the Treaty on the European Union is more expansive than the Treaty establishing the European Community. Article 6 of the TEU briefly sets out the founding principles of the Union; the Treaty also makes provision on how we might deal with a serious breach of those principles and how our values can be safeguarded and developed through the Common Foreign and Security Policy.

The issue of Treaty language on values is being addressed at the Convention on the Future of Europe. The skeleton text produced by Convention President Giscard d'Estaing last week suggests new language and a link to the Charter of Fundamental Rights, either by reference or incorporation or annexation. The proposed new Article 2 would set out values of human dignity, fundamental rights, democracy, the rule of law, tolerance, respect for obligations and for international law.

The manner in which linkage might be established between a new Treaty and the Charter of Fundamental Rights is sensitive for a number of member states. A key issue is the need for coherence and hierarchy as between different statements of rights. In Ireland, for example, our citizens look to the Irish Constitution as the source and guarantor of their rights. The European Convention on Human Rights is also a known and cherished text. The concern must be to ensure that the Convention work in this area brings genuine added value rather than any increment of confusion. Our delegation has been deeply engaged in the relevant working group and will continue to help shape the outcome.

Whatever decisions are ultimately reached in the IGC regarding linkage to the Charter, reinforced values language along the lines envisaged for Article 2 of the new Treaty is likely to receive broad support. Such headline language serves important functions; it helps to form our self-image and provide a litmus test for our actions, as well as making a statement to the outside world.

However, as I said at the outset, it is more by deed than by word that we define ourselves. In assessing how we *live* our values, I would suggest that the Union deserves to be judged on three criteria: how we do business within the Union; our approach to enlargement; and the terms on which the Union engages internationally.

I mentioned earlier the institutional arrangements designed to guarantee mutual respect between the membership. By and large, these have worked remarkably well to date. In whatever way the Union goes forward, and however we frame the outcome of the Convention and the subsequent IGC, principles of equality and mutual respect must continue to apply. In particular, I think there is widespread recognition that any drawing of battle lines between large and small member states would be corrosive. There would be no winners and the Union as a whole would be the loser.

There is also, of course, the commitment to solidarity that the Union has rightly worn as a badge of honour. It is clear that the Structural and Cohesion funds serve an economic purpose: helping the less well off areas within the Union eventually transforms them into thriving markets for exports from other parts of the Union. But the whole philosophy of solidarity goes way beyond enlightened self interest. It is rooted in a sense of what the stronger owe to the weaker, a sense that sharing is part of what defines a community.

Although Ireland will graduate shortly from being a significant beneficiary of structural funds, it is not in our tradition to forget where we came from. Solidarity is part of the fabric of the Union - as much a value whether one is beneficiary or contributor. And I am confident it is a value we will continue to honour.

The next criterion I have suggested is the Union's approach to enlargement: how we treat the extended family.

A recent New York Times editorial referred to EU enlargement as a "noble" project. I found myself pausing a moment on the word. It is not one which tends to be part of our lexicon in Brussels but it struck me as particularly fitting in this context. Enlargement is about making Europe whole again - a historic act of reconciliation. There is a largeness of vision which inspires the whole project and which has survived the decade long accession negotiations.

This largeness of vision had a real resonance with the Irish people when they went to the voting booths on 19 October. No doubt there will be extensive analysis over the coming months of why people voted as they did in the second Nice Referendum. But it is clear that the desire to extend the hand of friendship was a very significant factor.

As I said, the largeness of vision has survived the tedium and vicissitudes of the decade long accession negotiations. There was a risk that it might be endangered in the final weeks of negotiations - that we would end up with a cheapskate enlargement and an endgame which robbed the accession countries of their dignity. But this has not happened. At the Brussels Council of 24/25 October, vision won through. Of course, realpolitik also played a part: there were calculations as to when and how deals should be struck and what were likely to be the best terms on offer. But there was also a definite sense of rising to the occasion and maintaining the dignity of the process.

Defining the criteria for membership has helped the Union to define itself. The Copenhagen criteria included political requirements: stability of institutions guaranteeing democracy, rule of law, human rights and the respect for and protection of minorities. These criteria amounted to a clear statement about the Union and its values - this is who we are and these are the characteristics you must share if you want to join us. The criteria go to the heart of our identity and, as the Union faces possible further enlargement in the future, it will be essential to avoid any dilution.

The third standard of measurement is the Union's engagement

with the wider world through its development instruments and through the Common Foreign and Security Policy.

The development policies extend the Union's solidarity ethic. Together with its members, the Union provides over 50% of the world's development aid and a substantially higher percentage of its grant aid. Its 'Everything but Arms' initiative provides for duty-free access for almost all products from the least developed countries. The Union has strongly supported the development emphasis of the Doha Round; it was instrumental in ensuring concrete results from this year's Monterrey Conference on Financing for Development, just as it has provided leadership in so many other UN fora on development issues.

In the CFSP area, there is constructive engagement multilaterally and with all parts of the world. The Union is a member of the Quartet on the Middle East, a leading actor in the Balkans, engaged in regular dialogue with all the major countries and regional groupings. In ESDP, our priorities of conflict prevention and the Petersberg tasks - the military dimension and civilian crisis management - have been clearly defined. The Headline Goal - better known as the Rapid Reaction Force - means that as of next year 50-60,000 persons will be available to undertake the full range of Petersberg tasks.

In each of the three areas - internally, the enlargement process, engagement with the outside world - the Union is open to criticism. Who would deny the shortcomings? There is sometimes muddle and powerplay in the way we conduct our internal business. There is less generosity about this enlargement than any previous one. On the development front, we may have insufficiently recognised the darker side of globalisation and critics would argue that we should be taking a more forward position in building an ethical globalisation. There has been incoherence and inconsistency in some of our approaches under the CFSP.

But the picture overall is one in which we are entitled to take considerable pride. Even if we could be doing much better, there is absolutely no reason for breast-beating. The Union's example and contribution is making the world a better place. Across the range of policies and beneath the welter of detail, our core values are clearly discernible.

Projecting our values

This brings me to the second and more difficult question: How do we project our values and can we not do so to greater effect? If the Union is in many respects a giant, why does our footprint often seem so small?

These are unsettling times and the challenges are piling up on the foreign policy front. The shadow of September 11 is a long one. A high stakes debate is being conducted on how to deal with Iraq. The cycle of retribution continues in the Middle East. AIDS is a grim reaper stalking Africa and much of the developing world.

But beyond the challenge of any individual crisis situation, there are more fundamental issues to be grappled with. The context in which the Union is defining and projecting itself has radically changed in the post Cold War period. We are currently experiencing what has been described as "a rethinking of the organising principles of the international order". Some of the familiar doctrines appear on their way to redundancy while other organising principles - sovereignty, deterrence, balance of power - are being reexamined and recast.

Perhaps the most striking feature of the new order is that the United States has become the pre-eminent military power, with a corresponding level of self-confidence. The Strategy Security Statement published on 20th September presents the new terms on which America will engage with the world.

This changing world order poses serious questions for Europe. The superficial reaction may be a shrugging of the shoulders. Given the ties of friendship with the United States, and sharing of fundamental values, there is no need for Europe to feel threatened. Indeed, some might feel a sense of complacency that there is now a global policeman in whom Europe can trust.

But the more thoughtful European reaction obviously goes deeper. No single nation can carry the world on its shoulders and we should neither expect nor allow it to do so. Europe has rights and responsibilities commensurate with its collective weight. It owes it to itself and to the world - including to the US - to exercise those rights and responsibilities. The question is how we can exercise those responsibilities in a way that is value-driven and effective.

The first requirement is to define for ourselves the terms of the debate. A war of words is currently being waged by academics and policy analysts. A recent edition of Policy Review carried a clever and provocative article by Robert Kagan - "Power and Weakness" - which invoked Hobbes and Kant to contrast the world views of the US and Europe. Mr. Kagan is of course entitled to his rather unflattering view of Europe. What is surprising is the hundreds of column inches generated by the article, with much of the European reaction conducted in the terms posed by the article's title.

We do ourselves no favours if we allow the terms of the debate to be defined by the polemicists. This debate is not about power and weakness; it is about ways to exercise leadership. And the measure of military strength is not the measure of leadership.

Europe must have confidence in itself. Our claim to leadership must rest on European values and play to European strengths. Much as we share with the US, our history and geography have shaped us differently. Trying to compete on someone else's terms is bound to leave us in second place.

Multilateralism is a fundamental part of the European worldview. Even on Iraq, where the differences in approach between EU members has been obvious, a strong common thread in the EU position has been the insistence on the United Nations as the source of legitimacy.

Crafting an effective multilateralism is arguably Europe's most important international leadership role.We need to face down the cynics. In his Power and Weakness article, Kagan argues that the European embrace of multilateralism arises - even if subconsciously - from weakness and self interest: "Europeans oppose unilateralism in part because they have no capacity for unilateralism". In other words: multilateralism as a rationalisation for wimpishness.

Multilateralism can indeed seem more anaemic than heroic. "Leadership", according to Michael Mandelbaum in an article in the current edition of Foreign Affairs, "involves not so much marching gloriously at the head of the parade as paying quietly for the parade permit and the clear up afterwards". This description shades into caricature but Mandelbaum has a point. And paying up and cleaning up is something of which the EU has considerable experience!

Multilateralism is unglamorous and often thankless - the hard slog rather than the quick fix. The glory moments are few. The speed can seem glacial. The compromises are real and sometimes painful.

But because in most cases it is the only and necessary route to enduring solutions, we have no choice but to make multilateralism deliver. And deliver on terms that win respect for the process as well as safeguardlng our own self respect. It is not enough to define ourselves as multilateralists: what is key is that we see ourselves as *principled* multilateralists. Multilateralism with a purpose - or to use the current Washington vocabulary, with backbone. If we are prepared to compromise, it is equally important that we have bottom lines, and that when these lines are drawn they do not shift.

Principled multilateralism is much more than a slogan. It means conducting policy in a clear-sighted and tough minded way.

It means consistency, fairness and follow through on UN resolutions. It means a human rights policy that does not bend and sway in response to commercial interests. It means development aid policies that are insistent on recipient governments treating their own people decently.

It means taking commitments seriously. Being selective in lending our support, since the multilateral system is awash with well-intentioned initiatives. But when we do commit, making sure our weight truly counts for something.

In sum, while principled multilateralism might not be easy to define, I think we will recognise it when we see it.

Leadership, as I argued earlier, must be asserted on our own terms. The EU's international leadership will principally rest on its political, economic and moral strength. But we should use the full range of instruments at our disposal, and this includes looking in a wise and mature way at what the ESDP can offer.

I hope the EU will never again have that sense of impotence that we felt in the worst days of the Balkan crisis. In late '92, I was part of an EU team sent to investigate the rape of Muslim women in former Yugoslavia. The whole Balkan tragedy was a horrific reminder of how medieval cruelty can erupt in what appears to be a modern society. Amid all the trauma, I remember being struck by a note sounded by many of those we met: "We are Europeans... how can you have let this happen to us". Their sense of betrayal was all the stronger because they so keenly felt themselves to be part of the European family.

If the ESDP helps us to avoid a repeat of the shaming circumstances of that time, then I think those who care about Union values must surely welcome it.

Conclusion

I have greatly welcomed the opportunity this evening to range a little beyond the day to day issues that preoccupy all of us at the EU coalface.

The question of what Europe stands for is a real and pressing one. I suggested at the outset that the progressive development of the Union to date has been rooted in trust; our citizens' consent to any further development of the European project will equally depend on retaining and reinforcing that trust. If we want people to be proud to be European - as we hoped the Irish voters would express themselves on 19 October - then we have to create a Europe in which people can take pride. And if we want young people to relate to Europe, as they clearly are not doing at present, we need to address the values vacuum that so many of them perceive.

The issues of how Europe is to find a voice and project that voice are under intensive debate in the Convention. Here too, the terms on which the debate is conducted are critically important. Because novelty is always seductive, serious analysis of underlying problems often seems less attractive than the latest ideas about retitling or rebranding the Union, or putting a new figure at the apex without serious consideration of risks and consequences. How to find an authentic and effective European voice is one of the most challenging questions confronting the Convention and an immense amount of work remains to be done.

I conclude by coming back to my original point. This must be an integrated debate. Let us by all means find new values language for whatever new Treaty is to emerge over the next years. But let us not forget that the whole debate about the Future of Europe is in a larger sense a debate about the values by which Europe shall live. Whether we are talking about institutional balance, or Community policies, or a common foreign policy, or the development of justice and home affairs, values questions are intrinsic and inescapable.

Reflections on Irish Foreign Policy
Princess Grace Library, Monaco
February 29th 2008

It is a pleasure to be back in the Princess Grace Irish Library. I came here in January of last year, when I presented my credentials. It is an oasis – a serene and intimate place, where one feels the dignity and intelligence of Princess Grace.

I am honoured to be the first Irish Ambassador to Monaco. The connection is a very special one. Irish people remember the rejoicing and the glamour by association when the beautiful Grace Kelly married Prince Rainier in 1956. The princess' pride in her Irishness made us all walk taller. We are delighted that the connection continues and that Prince Albert too identifies with the country of his mother's ancestry. His presence here tonight is testimony to that.

The topic I have chosen for this evening is "Reflections on Irish Foreign Policy'. It is of course a very broad topic and I cannot hope to be comprehensive. But let me share some thoughts, informed by my personal experience.

I entered the diplomatic service at 20 years of age, immediately on graduation from university. A few months ago, in late November, I looked at the calendar and realised that thirty-five years had passed. In my beautiful Embassy on avenue Foch in Paris, I quietly had a glass of champagne. I felt there was a lot to celebrate. Not simply where I had arrived but the privilege of the journey.

Throughout those thirty-five years, I have engaged with the issues that are at the heart of Irish foreign policy. For the last twenty years, since 1987, I have been dealing in one way or another with what I would consider the three defining issues: Norther Ireland, the United Nations and the European Union. It is on these issues I will focus tonight.

Architecture

Before I move to the policy aspects, let me say a word about the practitioners of foreign policy: the *who* as opposed to the *what*.

We still regard ourselves as a small foreign service – and we are by the standards of most of our EU partners. But we have grown exponentially in recent years. We now have 76 resident diplomatic and consular offices abroad; 450 diplomats, some 750 other Dublin based career grades, 300 locally employed staff and about 120 Honorary Consuls.

In terms of our spread, there is a heavy concentration on Europe and North America. Our EU membership means that we maintain an Embassy in each of the 26 partner countries – including the smallest. We have maintained our strong backbone in the United States: the Embassy in Washington and Consulates in Boston, New York, Chicago, San Francisco. From early on we have had a presence in Australia, Canada, Argentina – countries with a long tradition of Irish immigration. Otherwise we have a fairly thin scattering in Africa, Asia, Latin America, the Middle East.

All of our full time diplomats are career diplomats, without exception. There are no political appointees. Recruitment is by open competition and promotion is also competitive, with a rigorous interview system.

We have a separate identity and separate streaming within the civil service but are subject to the system-wide reform and modernisation that has characterised recent years. In other words, we have strategic plans, business plans, performance related pay at senior levels – the whole gamut of modern management tools.

In any policy area, *the quality of the practitioners determines the quality of performance.* Even if I am an interested party, I believe that the quality of our diplomatic service more than stands comparison with any European service.

There is one point that interests me – and that is the make up of our foreign service. Especially in my early years, when many European diplomatic services were much more hidebound than they now are, most of my British colleagues, for example, had an Oxbridge background. In some continental European services, what I might call the family pedigree of many diplomats was very obvious.

Ireland, by comparison, came to independence with, in class terms, no native elite. Our diplomatic service, like the civil service generally, comprised the sons and daughters of small farmers, teachers and shopkeepers. I and those who came after me were the products of free secondary level education, of university grants, and, later, beneficiaries of free third level education from 1995. Educational standards provided the foundation for a high calibre civil service and diplomatic service, just as it later laid the foundations for our successful attraction of foreign investment to Ireland.

Key Dates
Let me set out four key dates since our independence in 1921.
1923: Entry to the League of Nations
1955: Entry to the United Nations
1973: Entry to the European Union
1998: Good Friday Agreement which finally came fully into effect in May of last year.

Northern Ireland
Of the three major policy areas I have defined, I will start with Northern Ireland. The challenge in talking of Northern Ireland is knowing where to start: the Plantation of Ulster in 1609, the battle of the Boyne in 1690, partition in 1921, the beginning of the 'Troubles' in the late 60s.

Let me start with my personal involvement as of 1987. I had spent four years in Washington from '83 to '87 and returned to spend four years as a Counsellor in our Anglo-Irish Division. It was an exciting time: two years after the breakthrough Anglo-Irish Agreement of 1985 which for the first time set up structures to allow input by Dublin to British decisions on Northern Ireland. Although Unionists rejected the agreement, it was a key milestone on the long road towards the later Good Friday Agreement. Those of us working in the area at the time certainly felt we were on the cusp of something new and challenging.

Tonight, as I am talking to you in a place dedicated to the memory of one of the most famous daughters of Irish America, I want to focus on one aspect in particular of the crisis in Northern Ireland – that is, the American involvement.

The broad outlines of the story are well known. The civil rights movement in Northern Ireland in the late '60s, led by John Hume, was of course inspired by the American civil rights movement. From the early '70s onwards, Irish diplomats and Ministers in Washington lobbied successfully to secure the engagement of the American political establishment.

The purpose was twofold. Firstly, we needed to have the US government on board in trying to discourage support for violence and extremism among elements of Irish America. Secondly, US involvement to some extent supplied a political counterweight in our dealings with Britain. When a small country negotiates with a large country, the scales risk being unbalanced: that is simply realpolitik. US involvement helped to balance the scales somewhat.

The strategy of involving America proved its worth time and time again. A succession of American Presidents committed their time and efforts, none more so than Bill Clinton who made an extraordinary personal contribution.

But aside from this headline effort, the US influence was felt in so many other ways. Just one example from my own experience. I began as I said dealing with Northern Ireland in 1987, fresh from my posting in Washington. I mentioned that, under the 1985 Agreement, we had newly acquired rights to input to British legislation dealing with Norther Ireland.

One of the biggest issues was unemployment. With Catholics two and a half times as likely to be unemployed as Protestants, this was one of the most glaring areas of discrimination. New Fair Employment legislation was being drafted, and I applied myself to developing a series of concrete drafting inputs to strengthen the draft. My approach was conditioned in a very fundamental way by what I had absorbed during my four years in Washington – the rights based approach, benchmarks, and so on. So fighting discrimination in Northern Ireland drew on the tools that had been developed in the United States.

One cannot understand Irish foreign policy since the foundation of the state, and particularly over the last forty years, without understanding the centrality of the Northern Ireland issue. But also, I would argue, one cannot understand our foreign policy without a sense of the key relationship with the United States.

There are differences, often criticism. Great power diplomacy, as I will say later, is not our thing. The war in Iraq has certainly not been popular with Irish people; we have not hesitated to speak out on Guantanamo.

But the ties are deep and enduring. Ireland owes America a great deal, both historically in providing a refuge and currently, with the benefits that continue to flow from American investment in Ireland. But the debt goes in both directions: America too owes Ireland a great deal. Irish blood and sweat helped to build America. And perhaps the most effective way America has repaid this debt is the way it put its shoulder to the wheel on Northern Ireland.

United Nations

Let me move next to Ireland's engagement with the United Nations. I want to touch on a cluster of issues under this heading: development, human rights, disarmament, peacekeeping. In other words: the 'how to be a responsible citizen of the world' issues.

A foreign policy helps to define who we are as people. And for over fifty years, since we joined in 1955, the Irish people have wanted to define themselves by the values of the United Nations. When Dermot Ahern, our Foreign Minister, says that Ireland wants to be "the model member of the United Nations in the 21st Century", people think it not immodest or unrealistic, but a right and appropriate aspiration.

Put bluntly, multilateralism is good for small countries. Any small country wanting to make its mark in international affairs is well advised to look to the multilateral arena. With the right policies and the right personalities, small member states can punch well above their weight.

And Ireland undoubtedly does punch above its weight at the United Nations. It's a combination of a number of factors. We are a developed country but with a history and a folk memory that has much in common with the experience of developing countries. We have networks: the long missionary tradition means that Irish priests and nuns have educated countless young people now in positions of influence in their national administrations. And our present day contribution to the UN is valued.

We are therefore well positioned. One of my happiest memories is when Ireland last stood for election to the UN Security Council. I came from Geneva to New York to join the final campaigning effort. The election was in autumn 2000, for a seat in 2001/2002. We were elected on the first count against stiff competition.

But of course our attachment to the UN is not just about

influence. To put it at its simplest, it's also about morality. This is a loaded word which I rather hesitate to use, but I can't think of better shorthand. Let me be clear: I'm not claiming any superior moral compass for the Irish people – although perhaps our conscience is honed by our history.

I believe that, in most if not all countries, people want to see their better selves reflected in their country's foreign policy. This is not naivety: people recognise there are contradictions and need for compromise. But fundamentally they want to feel that their foreign policy is underpinned by moral imperatives.

In an interesting way, I believe that this attachment to and support for a value driven foreign policy has strengthened in the Celtic Tiger and post Celtic Tiger period. We rejoice in our new found prosperity – the choices, the confidence that come with growth and effective full employment are to be embraced. But there are some valid questions about the kind of society we have become. Has such prosperity, in such a short time, moved us too far from our core values? Are we at risk of becoming a less caring and more materialistic society? There is always an interaction between domestic and foreign policy: with this self questioning on the domestic front, I think the sense may have grown even stronger that our foreign policy should be an area that represents our better selves.

In my six years as Ambassador to the United Nations in Geneva, from 1995 to 2001, I worked on that cluster of issues that interested me most: development and humanitarian work, human rights, disarmament.

It was a period that saw significant rise in Ireland's overseas development aid, although we had not yet made our subsequent commitment to reach the UN target of 0.7% in 2012. Currently, we are at 0.54%, spending over €800m a year on aid. This makes us on a per capita basis, among the most generous countries in the world.

We are big contributors to the range of UN aid agencies. Our bilateral aid is largely concentrated in the poorest countries of sub-Sahara Africa. Our aid is untied, in the form of grants not loans.

The support for meeting the UN aid target is broadly based across the political parties and across the population. There are sometimes questions as to whether this support will hold up as our growth slows, and prioritisation becomes the order of the day. I am reasonably confident that it will.

In maintaining support for this level of aid, there are two key words: identification and accountability. First: identification. People must know what is being done in their name, with their money. Because we have had a limited number of priority countries in our aid programme, and some of these – such as Lesotho – are very small, it has been possible to create a real sense of connection.

As our programmes grows, and we necessarily include more countries, and go into more complex areas such as budget support rather than project support, that becomes more challenging. But unless that sense of identification remains, one risks losing that impulse of generosity on which the programme depends. A recent initiative, which I think is excellent, was to open a drop in centre, a very modern interactive centre on O'Connell Street – the main thoroughfare in Dublin – to let people see what our programme is about.

One of the key lessons that I retain is that generosity will only be sustained if there is accountability. A big challenge for us at the moment, as our aid budget expands so quickly, is to ensure that we have the capacity to administer it in a tight, results oriented way. This applies both to bilateral and multilateral aid. In Geneva, I learned the importance of being an informed interlocutor of the aid agencies, not trying to tie their hands but being clear as to our expectations, asking probing questions.

Only a very brief word about disarmament and peacekeeping. Ireland is a neutral country, and that is unlikely to change anytime in the foreseeable future. But the emphasis has always been on a committed neutrality – a neutrality that counts.

We have a very strong UN Peacekeeping record. This began in Lebanon in 1958; it deepened in the Congo in the '60s and has continued since. Altogether, more than 80 Irish soldiers have died in UN service. Today, Irish service men and women serve in UN mandated missions in Kosovo, Bosnia, Afghanistan, Lebanon and have a leading role in the EU force in Chad.

We have a long disarmament record; there is national pride that Ireland, in 1961, was the first to propose what subsequently became the Non-Proliferation Treaty. During my time in Geneva, I negotiated Ireland's entry to the Conference on Disarmament and tried to seize various opportunities to push the work forward. Currently, one of Dublin's big initiatives for later this year is the organisation of a conference on Cluster Munitions.

I want to spend a few minutes on Human Rights, since I invested so such time in this area throughout the Geneva years. My posting there coincided with our former President Mary Robinson's period as High Commissioner for Human Rights. I also chaired the UN Commission on Human Rights for one of its most fraught years, 1999-2000. This was one of the biggest challenges – if not *the* most daunting – of my diplomatic career.

It was a rewarding but a frustrating year. Eleanor Roosevelt had been the first chair of the Commission on Human Rights. It was humbling to be in a direct line of descent – standing on the shoulders of giants. But it was even more humbling as human rights activists from all over the world came to Geneva, looking for a hearing, looking for justice. You could not but contrast the cocoon of comfort in which we were meeting – stolid, correct, Geneva with the UN building looking over the lake to the majestic Alps – with the nightmare situations to which some of them were bearing witness.

For all of us, human rights is one of the ultimate tests of our foreign policy. In the short term at least, it can pit values against interests, principle against pragmatism. We all struggle with the same issues. It is easy to denounce human rights violations in far-away countries that are poor and powerless. It is more difficult to stand up to Vladimir Putin as he erodes democratic rights in Russia. Or to stand up to China as there are indications of stifling dissent in the run-up to the Olympic Games. Or to speak forthrightly to countries such as Saudi Arabia about violations of women's rights.

The UN Commission on Human Rights has been reformed in the past few years and the new Council on Human Rights has emerged. But there is a risk that much the same fault lines are emerging – the same selectivity, the same reflex of regional solidarity, the same tendency to dismiss universal human rights standards as an imposition of western values.

How does Ireland stack up in all of this? Reasonably well, I think. We tend to be reasonably robust and at times have had considerable backbone in speaking up. Within the EU Common Foreign and Security Policy, we have to be vigilant that our voice does not become a little blurred. In most cases now, there is an attempt – usually successful – to agree a joint statement by the 27 member states. Of course, such a joint statement – if it's a good one – has a real weight and resonance and is much more effective than anything we might say nationally. But there can also be a lowest common denominator element, with a final statement involving so many compromises that is more fudge rather than substance.

I am conscious that I haven't been comprehensive. I have not, for example, mentioned climate change. It is an issue to which we came relatively late and where we are now becoming much more engaged, with binding EU targets for emission reduction likely to be set before the end of the year. I am conscious that Monaco is very much to the fore in this area, and I congratulate you on it.

European Union

I arrived in Brussels in summer 2001 and spent four years there until summer 2005. Ireland's Presidency of the Union was in the first half of 2004 and it dominated my time there from the outset.

Perhaps I can take a step back and look at Ireland's membership of the Union: what is has meant to us and how the relationship is likely to develop for the future.

It is difficult, I think, to exaggerate what EU membership has meant for Ireland. Of course there have been significant net financial transfers over the more than thirty years of EU membership through the Common Agricultural Policy, the Structural Funds and regional Funds. But for me the biggest gain we made in becoming a member of the Union was *psychological* – it transformed the way we saw ourselves.

There was a new increment of confidence. We were no longer seeing our history only or mainly through the prism of 800 years of British colonisation. We re-found our European identity; suddenly, we were participating around a table of then fifteen EU members, dealing on equal terms with our British neighbours as well as the thirteen others. Our perspective widened; it was a real liberation.

EU membership also meant a transformation in our social legislation. Gender equality was one example. We were required to introduce equal pay for men and women. The legislation that had required women in the public service – including the diplomatic service – to resign on marriage had to be abandoned.

The transformation was not achieved overnight. No magic wand was waved in Brussels that turned Ireland from a European backwater to the Celtic Tiger. Our public finances were in a mess for well over a decade after we joined the Union. We had to learn belt-tightening and self-discipline to get a grip on our own future. But I firmly believed that the new and wider horizons which Europe offered, the new confidence, the redefinition of our identity, was fundamental in creating the conditions which saw our economy take off so dramatically.

Ireland has changed and so has the Union of which we are a part. We are now, after Luxembourg, on a GNP basis the second wealthiest country in the Union. We will shortly become a net contributor to the EU budget, rather than a net beneficiary. A new generation in Ireland takes for granted the benefits which EU membership has brought. The confident, outward looking young Irish people today, highly travelled, used to full employment, have no sense – and don't want to be reminded of – what we were in the decades before we joined the Union. "The past is another country". The pre-EU Ireland truly is another country.

For its part, the Union has grown, become more diffuse, more complicated, and arguably more distant from its citizens. Further enlargement, perhaps to include Turkey, is a confusing – almost a dizzying – prospect for citizens in many member states. With endless discussions about whether to enlarge or deepen or both, many of our citizens feel they've had enough: they don't want to either deepen or enlarge.

Any relationship can grow a little tired after 35 years. It is not easy today to recreate the romance of the earlier years of our EU membership. One has to work at it. There is no doubt the Irish people are still fundamentally very positive about Europe. But we need reminding just how much, and in how many ways, Europe matters. How EU membership has been a profoundly positive and liberating experience for us. How, in foreign policy terms, it amplifies rather than muffles our voice in the world.

We face a major challenge in a few months time when Ireland will be the only EU member state to have a referendum on the Lisbon Treaty. We are optimistic about the outcome but can take nothing for granted. Our biggest potential enemy is apathy on the side of these who are well disposed towards Europe. If we fail to engage these voters, they will stay at home and the result may be determined by a small but zealous minority of 'no' campaigners.

For the Irish diplomatic service, there is no doubt that EU membership has been a great challenge and a great opportunity. We have had to raise our game at all levels.

At my post in Brussels, and particularly during our Presidency, I experienced very directly what it meant to be at the heart of Europe. We piloted the Union through a fascinating time – we reached agreement on the terms of the Constitutional Treaty, even if it was later rejected in France and the Netherlands. We negotiated the agreement on having President Barroso as President of the EU Commission. We organised all the celebrations for the big enlargement of 1 May 2004. And the unglamorous but essential backroom work: we chaired literally hundreds of working groups, as well as all the Council formations – the machinery on which the EU turns. Our EU Presidency was universally seen as a huge success.

During those Brussels years, I became more conscious of what we are good at and where we need to try harder. We are good at building relationships. I think the way we worked with the new member states before, during and after accession in 2004 was in many ways a model of its kind. We provided a huge amount of technical assistance: advice about how Ireland had benefited from membership. We built personal relationships that have already stood to us in good stead, and will into the future. And of course the decision to open our borders to workers from the new member states was warmly welcomed.

We need to be better at seeing around corners. Small diplomatic services tend to have very little spare capacity. Our diplomats are fully occupied with 'doing' and we don't have the luxury of sections devoted to strategic analysis. We need to make a conscious effort to try to see beyond tomorrow and the day after tomorrow and see what's coming down the track five and ten years hence. On the Common Agricultural policy, for example, we are major beneficiaries of the existing system – it is going to change, perhaps radically, post 2013 and we need to be in there at the design stage, being pro-active rather than reactive.

The Lisbon treaty currently being ratified is going to throw up some new challenges for Irish diplomacy. I am sure you are aware that there will be new posts – a new President of the European Council, and a strengthened post of High Representative, something close to an EU Foreign Minister. The High Representative will be assisted by a new External Action Service, which will include diplomats from member states as well as from the Council and Commission. The role of the External Action Service, how it meshes with national foreign services, what role we can carve out for Ireland – all will be up for discussion in the months ahead.

Bilateral Diplomacy
Before finishing, let me say a brief word about the particular challenges of a bilateral post.

My job in France is to help advance the bilateral relationship in all its aspects – politically, economically, and culturally. In some ways, it's an easy job; the French Irish relationship is centuries old (we had a common enemy for much of that time) and we have a relationship of great warmth; you just have to see the positive buzz around the French/Irish rugby match.

But, at the same time, I'm under no illusion. I represent a small country to a large country. Paris is a very competitive environment; it requires effort, energy and creativity to ensure that Ireland is on the map, that we are respected and listened to. In sending me to Paris, the Taoiseach specifically instructed me to strengthen the working relationship with France on EU issues – in the areas where we share interests, such as agriculture and where we differ, such as on tax harmonisation.

The other aspect in which I invest most time is promoting our economic interests. For some time past, there has been an increasingly strong emphasis on this aspect of Embassy work. The leisurely days of the diplomat taking his or her time to craft finely honed political reports are over. Obviously, there is always a place for focused political reporting that brings new insights and added value. But, in the internet age, there is no market for diplomats regurgitating what is readily available at headquarters.

With the Celtic Tiger years behind us, the economy is slowing down to a likely growth rate of around 2.5% this year. Our competitiveness has eroded, our export performance needs significant improvement. We are going to have to run very fast to match the kind of inward investment that we attracted over the last couple of decades. In a global economy that is looking shaky, there is no immunity for any of us. In these circumstances, we need to rein in public spending and see clear returns that ensure value for money. Our performance increasingly, and rightly, is being judged on concrete foreign earnings criteria.

So how to conclude? Perhaps with just a few sentences. Oscar Wilde said 'The truth is never pure and rarely simple'. Foreign policy is rarely 100% pure and almost never simple. But, despite the complexities, I profoundly believe – and this is perhaps my main point this evening – that our people want a value-driven foreign policy and will rally to support such a policy.

The EU and UN will continue to provide the essential context for our foreign policy formulation. EU membership increasingly conditions both our domestic and foreign policy. One might have imagined that the United Nations would become less relevant as our identity within the EU strengthens. Far from it. The UN is still a rallying point, a custodian of values, the indispensable organisation.

I will give the last word – almost – to President Mary McAleese who gave a major address in Berlin this week. Summing up our foreign policy, she said: "As a small country with baleful experience of colonisation, Ireland has traditionally had grave reservations about Great Power politics. We seek patient diplomacy, persistent, respectful dialogue and dogged persuasion as the best instruments of creating a better world".

Creating a better world. I started on a personal note and perhaps will finish on one. I can think of no career more satisfying than being a diplomat in the service of my country. Through the years, there has been endless variety, interest, and from time to time the great privilege of evenings like this one. But at the core of it all is the challenge for diplomats – as for princes – to help create a better world. It is that which gives shape and purpose to it all.

Ireland and the World
Symposium at Fairfield University, Connecticut
20th November 2010

The news from Ireland this week has not been happy news. Most of you will have read of the visit by European and IMF experts to assess the situation of our banks, and to see whether loans may be necessary to continue recapitalisation of the banks and to restore stability to the bond markets. As well as the immediate Irish interests, there are wider issues of Euro Zone stability and confidence in the Euro that are playing out in this drama.

As you might imagine, this series of events is causing immense trauma in Ireland. The people of Ireland, who have already accepted significant income and social welfare cuts, are bracing for further measures of austerity. There is deep distaste for any measure that may suggest any loss of control over our own decision making. It could not be otherwise in a country whose people fought so long for our independence and who so cherish our sovereignty.

And yet the headlines of crisis do not begin to tell the full story. The banking crisis is real and urgent and the contagion effect on the rest of our economy is obvious. But the fundamental strengths which underpinned the Celtic Tiger years remain intact. Our high-end exports are booming. The picture as regards foreign investment remains a very upbeat one, with continuing expansions and new investment by top international corporations, particularly from the US. We continue to have a young workforce that is among the most highly educated and dynamic worldwide. In terms of our cost base, the competitiveness that was eroded during the boom is being restored in these recessionary times.

So yes, the news from Ireland these days is difficult and

unpalatable. But it is important to restate the message that the underlying strengths of our economy remain, and the basis for a recovery is there. Times are tough, but we are a tough and resilient people. It is not for nothing that we have been labelled the "indomitable Irishry".

It is also worth noting that, beyond the immediate fire-fighting as we cope with this crisis, there are some important re-evaluations taking place in Ireland. During the boom years, it sometimes felt as if the sound of cash registers was drowning out everything else. I have been struck by the depth of reflection triggered by the recession – reflection as to what are our fundamental values as a people and how we project these values as we define Ireland's place in the world.

The cultural community in Ireland has been helping to lead this reflection. In Ireland last week, for example, Colm Toibin made an eloquent address whose theme was that, although Ireland's economic crisis may be making headlines, the more serious and influential image of our country emanates from the culture we send out into the world. This is a theme that is resurfacing in many of our discussions with our diaspora, as we explore with them how Ireland needs to confront the current range of challenges.

Next year, in the US, there will be a very ambitious project 'Imagine Ireland' which will present a range of Irish culture – theatre, literature, the visual arts – in a way which will remind this country of the richness and diversity of cultural life in contemporary Ireland. It has been planned over an extended period, but it could hardly be timelier to invite America to look beyond the headlines to all that is so rich and deep and varied in our Irish culture.

In my own outreach, as I speak from time to time to audiences here in the US about Ireland's role in the UN, I feel myself to be conveying a somewhat similar message. Our cultural contribution allows us to hold our head very high in the world; equally, I see our multilateral contribution as a source of tremendous pride. We have a track record and an ongoing contribution that is entirely disproportionate to our size, and that reflects great credit on the principles and the generosity of the Irish people.

So, let me turn to the subject of Ireland at the United Nations, which is of course the arena in which I carry out my daily work.

One of the favourite quotations of many Irish diplomats is from a leading article in *The Economist* fifty years ago, in the Autumn of 1960. Referring to the United Nations as the "Afro-Irish Assembly", the article began "Ireland bestrides the UN like a colossus". It was of course an exaggeration even at the time, but gives some sense of the legacy that Irish diplomats at the UN have inherited.

The bare bones of our story will be familiar to many of you. Ireland joined the UN in 1955, having applied nine years earlier. There have been many highlights in the fifty five years of our membership and I will sketch in some of them. But maybe a remark at the outset as to how we are perceived by the membership generally.

On my arrival in New York last year, I was reminded of how warmly regarded Ireland is at the UN. It is the tradition for a new Ambassador to pay courtesy calls on his or her colleagues. It allows an opportunity for some initial feel for the bilateral relationship – a taking of the temperature. The calls of course are always courteous – that is the diplomatic tradition – but time and again in my calls I received a reception that went way beyond the usual niceties.

I think it is explained by a number of factors. Firstly, there is our past as a country that was colonised for 800 years and the empathy this create with so many UN members that bear a similar imprint of history. Secondly, there is the extraordinary legacy of Irish missionaries around the world. Time and again in my meetings with Ambassadors from developing countries, I am told of their education by Irish priests and nuns which proved a key stepping stone to their subsequent entry to the civil or diplomatic service. Thirdly, there is the fact that Ireland has generally been on the right side of the big issues of conscience – on apartheid, for example, we are remembered for being among the early and most committed opponents.

The resonance, therefore, is positive. But there is also the track record of effort and achievement. I want to touch on some concrete examples in four areas: peacekeeping, disarmament, human rights and development.

Peacekeeping: Our first major engagement with UN peacekeeping was in 1960 when a contingent of Irish soldiers joined UN peacekeepers in the Congo. A high price was paid for our involvement, with the death of nine Irish soldiers in an ambush in the Kivu in eastern Congo. In this 50th anniversary year, it is poignant to read some of the accounts of that first foray. There was such pride in service, and idealism, and – following the deaths of our soldiers – a determination to continue the commitment so as to give meaning to their sacrifice.

This proud tradition of peacekeeping has continued. In the fifty years since the Congo involvement, Irish defence forces have participated in 75 peacekeeping missions worldwide, contributing 60,000 individual tours of duty. Earlier this year, 400 of our troops returned from a particularly complicated mission in Chad. We are now beginning a discussion about a possible return to UNIFIL next year. The professionalism and commitment of Irish peacekeepers is a byword in the UN.

Disarmament: As a neutral country, outside any military alliance, Ireland has long had a very active involvement in UN disarmament issues. In the 1960s we were the lead country in the initial steps towards the Nuclear Non-Proliferation Treaty, which was finally agreed in 1968. The Treaty subsequently became informally know as 'The Irish Treaty', given our role. The interest and engagement has been maintained over the years, and indeed in May of this year Ireland was a key player at the NPT Review Conference, brokering an important breakthrough on sensitive Middle-East related issues.

As well as the NPT, we engage in a range of other disarmament activities. A recent highlight was the Cluster Munitions Treaty, finalised at negotiations in Dublin two years ago. In the past couple of weeks, we were very active in the first review conference under the Treaty held in the Lao DPR.

Human Rights: Our best known engagement in human rights has been Mary Robinson's role as a strong and energetic High Commissioner for Human Rights between 1997 and 2002. During one of those years, 1999, I was elected Chair of the Commission on Human Rights in Geneva, and there were two Irish women on the podium! It was a tough and challenging year, and I look back on it as one of the defining periods in my career.

Beyond that engagement, Ireland continues to maintain a strong and rigorous approach on human rights issues. There are independent Irish experts on important Human Rights Treaty bodies and we will be seeking election to the Human Rights Council for the period 2013-2015. We are active within the HRC on a range of thematic and country resolutions, including human rights defenders, gender equality, freedom of religion and belief, issues relating to sexual orientation and gender identity, and addressing situations of violations of human rights in particular countries. Most recently we helped with outreach to secure passage this week of Resolutions on DPRK, Myanmar and Iran.

Development: During recent years, Ireland has made major progress in reaching the UN goal of devoting 0.7% of our GNP to development. We made huge strides during the Celtic Tiger years and, despite the very critical economic situation, we remain on target to reach the 0.7% figure in 2015. Currently, the figure stands at 0.52%. I should also say that the quality or our aid programme is very highly regarded, with the OECD DAC giving it a very high rating in terms of its effectiveness.

Our aid programme is highly focused on a relatively small number of countries, mostly in sub-Saharan Africa, but also on a priority list of themes. In terms of our own past, and the Irish folk memory of the Famine, it is not surprising that hunger and food security are areas of particular attention; our intention is to devote around 20% of our aid expenditure to that area.

A recent bilateral initiative with the US deserves particular mention. On 21 September, in the margins of the Millennium Summit at the UN General Assembly, Ireland and the US jointly launched a Special Project on Child Hunger: 1000 Days to Save a Life. This was a very high-profile event, co-hosted by Foreign Minister Martin and Secretary of State Hillary Clinton, which brought together a range of key actors, including Secretary-General Ban Ki-moon.

Beyond the financial contribution, we have a strong policy input across a range of UN bodies. This year, for example, we are on the Executive Board of UNICEF, and next year we will be on the Board of UNDP. Also next year, we will take over chairing of the Humanitarian Liaison working Group, so as to buttress the work of OCHA.

Before leaving the discussion of the UN, I might add a word about our availability to assist as co-facilitators in various reform processes. Ireland is frequently turned to when there are discussions involving the review of particular bodies or looking at UN working methods. For example, my predecessor, Ambassador Paul Kavanagh, was deeply involved in the improvement of System-wide Coherence. For my own part, I was asked last December to be a co-facilitator of a Review of UN Peacebuilding, and I invested a great deal of time in the earlier part of the year in holding consultations and in preparing a detailed report. It was gratifying when our report was welcomed in resolutions simultaneously adopted in the General Assembly and the Security Council last month.

In summary, in relation to the UN, the message I want to leave you with is that Ireland is an active, committed member, that we take the responsibilities of membership very seriously, and that we are always prepared to put our shoulders to the wheel when it comes to reform and improvement of the Organisation.

Before concluding, I would like to speak briefly about our role in the European Union, as any discussion of "Ireland in the World" would be incomplete without a comment on our EU membership. In a sense, my diplomatic career has developed alongside our deepening EU membership; I first took up duty in the Department of Foreign Affairs in late November 1972 and some five weeks later – on 1 January 1973 – Ireland joined the Union.

Membership of the Union over almost 38 years has transformed how Ireland engages with the world. The implications for the conduct of our foreign policy have been enormous, both in policy terms and in practical ways. EU membership has meant that our diplomatic service has had to up its game and extend the spread of our expertise. If we were to engage in a meaningful way in foreign policy discussion in Brussels, we had to be knowledgeable about situations beyond our traditional areas of interest and involvement. If there were going to be EU pronouncements on an almost daily basis on crisis situations around the world, we had to help in drafting them and be ready to stand over statements being issued in our name. All of this involved a growth in personnel at HQ and in the spread of our Embassy network abroad.

As co-operation at EU level has deepened, we have had to take account of new arrangements as they developed. Now, with the

Liston Treaty in effect, we are seeing the construction of a European External Action Service, and we will have to see precisely how this will mesh with our national diplomatic services.

Indeed, in my current posting as Permanent Representative in New York, I am experiencing the need to accommodate two identifies: firstly, given Ireland's extremely strong national 'brand' at the UN, I am determined to do everything to maintain and strengthen it. At the same time, as a loyal and supportive EU member, I am committed to ensuring a strong EU voice and input. The ideal is that the two identities should work in a complementary and reinforcing way – and mostly they do. Sometimes, however, it can be something of a balancing act in practice.

Even if the title suggested by your organisers for today's address "Ireland and the World", is so broad as to be very liberating, I obviously could not begin to do justice to it in the time allotted. There is, for example, the unique resource of our diaspora, which I have barely touched on, which greatly magnifies Ireland's influence in the world. There is our role in international bodies beyond those I have described – for example, for the first time in 2012 we will take on chairmanship of the OSCE which comprises 56 member States, with a geographical spread from North America to Central Asia.

We are a small island on the periphery of Europe. But our tradition of emigration, our extraordinary cultural contribution and our missionary history, have ensured a vibrant relationship with the wider world. A strong sense of our place in the world has always helped to define us as a people. It gives us a sense of perspective, a sense of responsibility and – even in these difficult times – a real sense of pride.

The Role of the European Union in Global Affairs
United Nations Association of New York: Panel Discussion
28th March 2012

The European Union is emerging from what is probably the roughest period since signature of the Treaty of Rome fifty five years ago.

The storm has been concentrated in the Eurozone. In retrospect, we are all clearer about the original sin of the Eurozone: we created a common currency based more on optimism than realism, bringing a new currency into being without putting in place the strong foundations that would safeguard it through the inevitable future stresses and strains.

The Eurozone storm hit us at a time when the Union was facing a range of other challenges. We were – and still are – bedding down the Lisbon Treaty, which reconfigured some of the Union's basic architecture. Meanwhile our citizens, while still believing in the necessity and benefits of the Union, have been growing progressively less starry-eyed about the European project. And, as we struggle with internal challenges, a new geopolitical balance is being established. Strategic alliances are changing: the emerging – and emerged – powers have moved from the wings to centre stage; the Arab world is reinventing itself.

All told, this has come close to being the perfect storm.

Nevertheless, many of us in Europe would feel that the picture as presented in the media – particularly in what our Continental friends describe as the Anglo-Saxon media – has been too apocalyptic. There has been a drumbeat of negativity. We are told that Europe is adrift: short on solidarity, lacking in leadership, retreating into nationalism. Indeed, a regular subject of speculation has been whether the Union itself is not doomed by design flaws, at risk of collapsing under its own contradictions.

The narrative has scarcely got much better when Europe is situated in the wider world. By some media accounts, it would seem that the sun is rising just about everywhere as it sets over Europe. As the BRICS sprint ahead, Europe will hardly be seen for the dust. The exceptional growth rates of Asia and Africa are leaving Europe behind. The basic message: Europe is beginning a slide into irrelevance; the future belongs to others.

Here in the United States, views about Europe are more nuanced: along a spectrum from sophisticated analysis and genuine embrace of partnership to simplistic and reductionist views. We Europeans undoubtedly have to be pretty thick-skinned at times. For example, the image of Europe as it emerges from the Republican primaries is pretty depressing. The contenders may disagree on just about everything else, but seem united in a view of Europe as a spoiled and sclerotic continent, overtaxed and under-performing – certainly the last place in the world that America should emulate.

This then is the rather sober backdrop against which to situate any discussion of our standing at the United Nations.

Thankfully, perceptions of the EU at the UN are a great deal more balanced and sophisticated than some of those I have outlined. Overall, it is fair to say that the UN offers a relatively benign atmosphere for the EU. There is widespread recognition that the EU is among the most staunch supporters of the Organisation; that we have a deep and carefully considered policy input across every major area of UN activity; and that we back our policy input with serious financial heft.

But even in this relatively benign atmosphere, not all is plain sailing. For EU member states, it is an ongoing challenge to reconcile a continued projection of our traditional national identity at the UN with support for a fully fledged EU role. And one cannot ignore some structural issues: the fact that France and the UK retain permanent seats on the Security Council is widely seen as anachronistic, and many believe that a reformed Security Council will need to take some account of how the European identity and European foreign policy making has evolved.

In terms of our image among the wider membership, the Union experienced a wake-up call in the past couple of years as we sought to be represented in a new way at the UN in implementation of the new arrangements in the Lisbon Treaty. What we sought seemed to us relatively modest. But we encountered prolonged difficulty, sometimes in unexpected quarters, and the final outcome fell short of what we hoped.

In summary I would say: a generally positive experience for the EU at the UN but some questions as to whether we truly have a presence and influence that is proportionate to our weight in the world.

At this point, let me look forward and try to project – in very broad-brush terms – how the EU standing might develop over the period ahead.

In the short term, there is reason to hope that the worst of the Eurozone crisis is now behind us. A succession of European Councils have inched us forward towards solutions. A new Fiscal Treaty has been signed by 25 of the 27 member states; we are in the final stages of agreeing a financial 'firewall' of hundreds of billions of euro to buttress the common currency.

It would be foolish to be in any way complacent about the road ahead. The financial markets are a beast of voracious and unpredictable appetite, and we could easily find ourselves in their sights again. The austerity that is being required in a number of EU countries is taking a heavy toll. But there is a sense that a corner has been turned: prospects are slowly improving and the predictions are of a return to modest growth for the EU as a whole in the second half of 2012.

My main point however is not about the immediate future but a wider and longer term one about Europe's place in the world; our continued relevance and the 'fit' between our values and 21st century realities. And here I might link with the phrase 'Modern Evolution' that you have used in the title of this evening's discussion, because I would particularly like to emphasise the 'modernity' of the EU.

One argument, perhaps slightly provocative, I might make is this: The 21st century, more than any previous century, will be the century of 'soft power', and the European Union – in a more developed way than any comparable entity – is a body that is defined by 'soft power'. In that sense, this can be 'our' century.

Let me pause for a moment on this question of "soft power". Most of us would accept that there are limited and exceptional situations where there is no realistic alternative to use of military power – for example, it was military intervention that finally toppled Ghadaffi from power in Libya.

But, in this second decade of the 21st century, the lessons we have known all along are becoming more blindingly obvious. Military intervention has rarely been a quick fix – in most cases, neither 'quick' nor a 'fix' – and the cost in human suffering has always been high. Particularly in our world of instant images – where mobile phones potentially turn every citizen into a frontline war reporter – that cost is more visible and can seem intolerably high.

In the large majority of situations, it is the slow and unglamorous work of addressing the root causes of conflict, helping to build resilient societies, sticking with the incremental work of peacebuilding, that will yield dividends.

These are the areas of strength for the European Union. They are the areas where we have established capacity and have invested resources. For decades, the Union has espoused a comprehensive, holistic, approach to international security. Our civilian missions have outnumbered military missions; we have deployed diplomats and development workers, judges and police, patiently helping to build rule of law institutions in fragile states.

I would make just three points in support of the Union's 'modernity'.

Firstly, our very growth as a Union has relied on a continual process of internal dialogue and compromise. Consensus building is in our DNA. This continual search for accommodation can at times frustrate others, and indeed ourselves. But it equips us to understand and deal with the kind of compromise and accommodation that is the only viable way to respond to most of the problems of the 21st century.

The European way from the outset was seen as a modern way. Jean Monnet, a founding father of the Union, insisted that European cooperation "was not an end in itself, but only a stage on the way to the organised world of tomorrow". Despite recent setbacks, Europe can still lead by example – indeed the progressive enlargement of the Union, and the steady queue of applicants for membership, demonstrates the continuing appeal and attractiveness of our model.

Secondly, development remains unquestionably the greatest challenge of our modern world. And this is an area of strong performance for the Union. We are not a military superpower, but we may fairly be called a developmental superpower.

The EU and its member states collectively account for more than 50% of global Overseas Development Assistance. We stand up well to any statistical comparison. If we look at the latest OECD DAC figures, for example, the EU members of the DAC average .46% of Gross National income in development aid, compared to .21% for the United States. And we were among the earliest to accept the need to move beyond aid transfers: more than ten years ago, the 'Everything but Arms' initiative allowed duty free access for almost all exports from least developed countries.

Thirdly, the Union is undeniably in the vanguard when it comes to early identification and seeking to grapple with some of the defining challenges of the 21st century: issues such as women's empowerment or climate change. For decades, the Union has been at the cutting edge in advancing women's rights, both in terms of the internal EU legislation and international advocacy. On climate change, the critical negotiations in Durban last December were particularly interesting in terms of the new alliances created. Those countries most vulnerable to climate change – mostly small island states in the developing world – came together with the EU to pressure countries such as China, India, and the U.S. into taking more progressive positions.

My purpose is not to present Europe through rose-coloured spectacles. As I have said, the challenges are very real. Beyond the immediate Eurozone crisis, we have to make our economies more flexible, more entrepreneurial. In the foreign policy area, we have to increase our clout and sharpen our message. On the Middle East, for example, we are a necessary voice – and it is regrettable that our internal disunity has not allowed that voice to be heard more clearly. And we need to continue to ensure that our Security and Defence Policy is fit for purpose.

The challenges will also extend to the United Nations. As well as equipping ourselves with robust and coherent policies, we will need to project those policies in a way that makes sense to the rest of the membership. We will have to continue to work on outreach and alliance building. And EU member states will need to reconcile a continued strong national imprint with a clear and authoritative voice for the Union.

To conclude with a final point.

It has been recognised for some time that we have entered a

multi polar world. As Europe has looked inward over the past couple of years, and as the media has feasted on our woes, it seemed as if the European pole of that new world was pretty unsteady. But the critics have underestimated our underlying strength and resilience – they have underestimated our essential modernity.

Despite the slogans, the 21st century will not easily be labelled the Asian century, or the African century or any other geographical denomination. We have entered a period of qualitative change, where the conditions and instruments of exercising power are changing, where technological progress will be transformative, and where people power – fuelled by social media – will become ever more assertive.

The history of this century remains to be written, but, in so far as its defining characteristics are beginning to emerge, it is likely to be a century that allows Europe to play to its strengths. As our modern multipolar world takes shape, we can be confident that Europe will continue to provide an important part of the ballast.

"Future of Europe" Panel Discussion
Columbia University, New York
25th February 2013

Let me nail my colours to the mast at the outset. I am a committed European, intellectually and emotionally. Ireland's membership of the European Union has shaped my whole adult life, and in a very positive way. At the same time, I do not consider myself a cheerleader for the European project. I see the mistakes and shortcomings, and the potential pitfalls. My optimism, I hope, is of the sober and vigilant variety, rather than anything more starry-eyed.

In my remarks today, I want to make two points (i) my belief that, despite current difficulties, Europe will continue to have a forward momentum and (ii) my confidence that my own country, Ireland, will contribute to this momentum.

The dictionary defines momentum as 'strength or force gained by motion or by a series of events'.

If we look at the series of events that created the European momentum, there is one inescapable fact: the political and economic are inextricably interwoven.

At its very origins, the EU was an economic answer to a political question. In the early 1950s, the question could hardly have been more profoundly political: how do we prevent a relapse into the savagery of war? The answer could hardly have been more unglamorously economic: the creation of the European Coal and Steel Community.

This same intertwining of the political and economic has marked each of the successive leaps forward. In their initial dream for the euro, Kohl and Mitterrand were grappling with the changes flowing from the collapse of the Berlin Wall and the re-unification of Germany. And as we celebrated the historic enlargement of 2004, we sang and danced not because of the enlargement of the Single Market, but because we felt we were 'making Europe whole again'.

Many commentators – and perhaps some of my co-panellists – will argue that the past is not prologue to the future: that there has been a rupture, and that Europe today is mired not just in a euro crisis but also in a deeper and even existential crisis.

I don't accept that view. While I don't for a moment discount the problems, I would argue that there is a continuing political imperative that will carry us forward.

If we look at the big picture today, there is one big story. And that is that world power is shifting. For all their problems and setbacks Asia, Latin America and Africa are on the rise. The choice for Europe is innovate, integrate or decline.

And, in Europe, *we get it*. From the outside, it may look at times as if we have lost sight of the wood and are lost in the trees. But we do have a strategic sense: we can see the shape of things to come.

Of course there are huge challenges ahead:

• We need to continue to retool institutionally so that we are fit for purpose – the Lisbon Treaty still needs to be fully worked through and further steps may be needed.

• We need to connect much better with our citizens: there are very real issues of democratic legitimacy and democratic accountability.

• We need to face up to the challenges posed by enlargement, and more honestly address the debate on widening versus deepening.

• We need to work on our external relationships – and that, for example, is what the Transatlantic Free Trade Agreement is all about.

And of course most urgently, we need to continue to try to correct the original design flaws of the euro. There have been some false starts and perhaps some misdiagnoses. But there is now clearly a determination to tackle the problems comprehensively. The ECB has fully stepped up to the plate. The European Stability Mechanism is the biggest financial firewall in the world. And the work underway towards the Banking Union is a huge step forward.

On the economic front more generally, some of the most recent data from around Europe is a further call to action. We clearly must become more competitive: we need to fully work through the Europe 2020 agenda, rather than pay lip service.

All of this is a huge challenge, but I believe it is doable.

Ireland

Most of you will be familiar with the Irish narrative – our Celtic Tiger years of phenomenal growth, the property bubble, the banking crisis which metamorphosed in a sovereign debt crisis, the bail out, the austerity measures, and now the glimmer of recovery.

I do not want in any way to underplay the hurt and difficulty in Ireland. But the underlying trend is positive. We are now much more competitive than we were. Our exports and foreign investments are doing exceptionally well. We are back in modest growth and expect to be back to the bond markets in a sustainable way by the end of this year.

You may have heard us called the 'poster-child for European recovery' or 'Europe's model pupil'. Even if they capture the positive trend, we don't especially like those terms – they underestimate the hurt, and they are patronising. Europe is a club of grown-ups, and ours is a grown-up story of mistakes and recovery.

In looking at grown-up solutions, we have to balance two realities:

Firstly, we in Ireland have to shoulder our own responsibilities. We are doing this through very painful austerity measures from which nobody is spared.

Secondly, everyone in Europe has to understand that we are all in this together. Solidarity is what the Union is all about. But there are additional factors at play here: if Irish banks borrowed heedlessly, those who loaned to them were just as heedless. If the Irish government had not behaved so responsibly in dealing with bank debts, the repercussions would have been felt all over Europe. We took one for the team.

So we are owed solidarity. And we believe that this solidarity is beginning to come through for us. I mentioned earlier some of the steps that have been taken at European level. And many of you will have read about the deal secured a couple of weeks ago on the Anglo-Irish promissory notes.

It is that balance and accommodation between national responsibility and Union solidarity that will provide the key to the future – we won't shirk doing our own bit, but are certainly not shy about seeking solidarity.

In Ireland's case also, let me return to the big picture: whatever our current difficulties, we are incomparably better off than if we were outside the Union, or than we were in the '80s for example.

And I will finish on that note: if you want to map where Europe is going, you have to keep your eyes on the big picture.

We in Ireland are a proud and resilient people. Europe is an old and resilient continent. We are pulling through. And we will re-find our momentum.

Ireland, Europe and the US: A Road to Recovery and Renewed Partnership,
Atlanta Council on International Relations
29th May 2014

I am honoured to be here with this distinguished group.

It is organisations like yours - promoting dialogue, debate and deeper understanding - which provide the backbone to our diplomatic work and the impetus to make our international partnerships stronger and more meaningful.

I have chosen a rather ambitious title for my remarks today: "Ireland, Europe and the US: A Road to Recovery and Renewed Partnership". As you might have noticed over the years, diplomats love topics like roads to recovery, just as we enjoy pathways to prosperity and anything which manages to be both alliterative and upbeat!

And my story today is indeed a positive one, with a lot of good news to impart. At the same time, 1 promise not to be relentlessly upbeat. 1 have too much respect for this audience to avoid the questions and the complexities.

As 1 begin to tell the story, I should perhaps underline the experience and perspective which informs my own approach.

When I discuss Ireland, Europe and the US, I regard myself as having a firm footing in all three camps. Ireland of course is my beloved country, which I have served as a career diplomat for over forty years. I was just twenty years old when Ireland entered the European Union in January 1973. Thirty years later, I was privileged to serve as Ireland's Permanent Representative, or Ambassador, to the European Union from 2001 to 2005.

And this is my ninth year to live in the U.S., having been here as as a young diplomat from 1983 to 1987 and then as Ambassador to the United Nation in New York from 2009 to 2013, before moving to my current job as Ambassador to Washington last summer.

I count myself very fortunate that my time as Ambassador in Washington has been a time of such good news from Ireland. After the difficulties we experienced in the aftermath of 2008, our economy is back on its feet again - with buoyant foreign investment, rising exports, very healthy tourism, and reducing (even if still much too high) unemployment. The mix we provide - highly skilled workforce, very competitive corporate tax rate of 12.5%, an English speaking gateway to the European Union — continues to demonstrate its attractiveness. I have been so glad to be able to talk to American audiences of our resilience, as well as so much else in the Irish story in which we can take legitimate pride.

Alongside this strong pride in Ireland, I also count myself a loyal and committed European. I am conscious of a deep personal debt. My generation in Ireland, and particularly women of my generation, were quite simply liberated by membership of the Union. Equal pay, equal rights and all manner of progressive social legislation, got a huge push forward from our Union membership. Our small country had to open its windows on the wider world.

The economic and financial benefits of membership were hugely significant. But the psychological effect was equally transformative. We were finally free to claim our European identity: to play our part on the wider European stage. That increment of confidence proved extraordinarily powerful.

Decades later, as I played my role in Europe at the time of EU enlargement, when Ireland held the EU Presidency in 2004, I saw and experienced the sheer joy when the European Union enlarged from 15 to 25 member states. We celebrated "Europe, whole and free". For once we were all focused on the big picture - Europe writ large - rather than the interminable squabbling over the small print that consumes so much of our time.

And then there is the attachment to America. I hope I am not overclaiming if I say I sometimes think of the United States as my alternative home. When I was invited a few weeks back to address the Democratic Caucus in Congress on the theme "America the Beautiful", I was more than happy to do. The energy and optimism of America, the generosity and open-heartedness of its people, have always profoundly appealed to me. In the years of my postings to the United Nations — six years as Ambassador to the UN in Geneva and four years as Ambassador to the UN in New York - I saw the humanitarian and human rights efforts of   American foreign policy: the day-in, day-out dedication to making the world a better place.

Let me say at this point how much it is in Ireland's interest that there should be a rich, vibrant, positive relationship between Europe and the US. Some years back, there was a headline debate in Ireland about what was perceived as a certain schizophrenia in our identity. The shorthand title of the debate was: "Boston or Berlin?". Of course the answer isn't either/or, it's both. Our EU membership is deeply imprinted on us in every way; we have a true sense of belonging within the European family. But situated on the geographical edge of Europe, we also look west. We will never forget that America embraced our people at our time of greatest need, as the ravages of famine devastated our country in the mid 19th century.

Today, America is home to over 35 million people who count themselves of Irish descent. Our two countries are joined by blood, by language, by an empathy that is hard to define but impossible to underestimate.

It is very important to underline that the Irish/US relationship is by no means confined to history or sentiment. The contemporary economic ties are extraordinarily strong. Over 70% of our FDI comes from the US. It is our largest market for export of goods, our second largest tourism market. And the economic relationship is truly two-way, with investment and trade flowing both ways. Right here in Atlanta, the success of Irish building materials company, Old Castle, is a striking illustration — headquartered here, the company now employs some 37,000 workers across every State in the Union.

Having set out my own perspective and where we are coming from in Ireland, I now come to some of the harder questions. Why is it that the US-Europe relationship seemed to have became somewhat jaded over recent years - to the point where it became commonplace to speak of the need for renewal? Even if the relationship never deteriorated to the point of needing a "reset", there has been regular talk of renewal and renaissance. Implicit in that terminology is a sense that things have not been quite as they should be.

Following the fracturing around the Iraq war, and the apparent disinterest in or downgrading of multilateralism during the Bush administration, hopes and expectations ran high - maybe impossibly high - in the aftermath of President Obama's election in 2008. Inevitably, the reality as it played out wasn't quite so simple.

In the foreign policy area, some of the underlying discontents rumbled away. There was still no settled transatlantic view of the relative roles of soft power/hard power. The Europeans, as before, were prone to feeling taken for granted. it was Chris Patten whom I first heard say, many years ago when he was Commissioner for External Relations, that the "Americans get to cook dinner, and the Europeans do the washing up." In other words, the Europeans have consistently felt undervalued for their slow and steady diplomacy around the world, underpinned as it is by deep financial contributions to development assistance.

For their part, the Americans have long been frustrated by the complexity of European decision making, the slowness to react, and what they perceive as unwillingness to step up to the plate when it comes to defence spending.

These underlying frustrations were being played out in a changing international landscape. As with any long and essentially stable relationship, attention can easily be distracted. President Obama's "pivot to Asia" was not intended as a pivot *away* from Europe, but it was hardly surprising that the Europeans felt it in this way. And indeed in both Europe and the US there was a certain excitement about the new. Our business people were intrigued by the opportunities opening up in China, the growing middle-class in India, the growth rates in Africa. The BRICs were increasingly claiming our attention, both economically and politically. Hardly surprising if Europe and America perhaps began taking each other for granted.

Another key factor over the past few years was the degree to which both the EU and the US were obliged to look inward and focus on domestic issues. After the collapse of Lehman Bros in 2008, the contagion spread like wildfire. The banking crisis took hold in a number of European countries, including Ireland. We rather belatedly woke up to some of the design flaws in the euro, which risked destabilising the Eurozone and by extension the Union itself. In parallel, President Obama was dealing with the 'great recession' here, and nation - building at home became a priority.

Today things have very definitely moved on, and much of this somewhat jaded feeling in the US - Europe relationship is now firmly behind us. A range of both domestic and foreign policy factors have brought our relationship back into foreground focus.

Firstly, there is the fact that Europe has come a considerable distance in dealing with the internal crisis it faced over the past few years. We have a Eurozone with new fiscal rules. We have a definitive European commitment to formally break the link between banking debt and sovereign debt. We have a European

Central Bank stating unequivocally that it will do "whatever it takes" to ensure stability. And we are well on the way to developing a single banking regulatory system for the common currency area. That is real progress.

The US too is back on its feet again, with the economy growing, and employment levels recovering.

In parallel, the wider political landscape also has evolved. Asia and the BRICs continue to offer important opportunities to strengthen partnership, but the views have become more nuanced, less simplistic. There is a careful appraisal of election results in India, the fluctuating relationship between China and Japan, demands for social change in Brazil. In brief, the rest of the world is looking like the complicated and challenging place it always was.

What has happened in Ukraine has been a major jolt. President Putin's annexation of the Crimea, and the posturing in Eastern Ukraine, have powerfully reminded us of the need for the US and Europe to stand together — protecting not just our shared values, but the values which are enshrined in international law. The work of devising and calibrating sanctions, both punitive and dissuasive, has brought us back into the closest of working relationships.

In parallel, the US and Europe are working very closely together on the hugely important issue of dealing with Iran's nuclear threat. There is no question but that EU sanctions played a very important part in bringing Iran to the negotiating table, and the US side is fully conscious of this.

Further, the profoundly disappointing playing out of the Arab Spring — and the continuing unconscionable suffering of the people of Syria — also forcibly reminds Europe and the US of joint challenges and responsibilities. This region is on Europe's southern border, but what happens there has direct and major implications for American foreign policy.

And apart from our joint work on the political front, we have put our shoulders to the wheel on the economic front.

As you know, Europe and the US are engaged in the hugely ambitious task of negotiating TTIP - the Transatlantic Trade and Investment Partnership. The stakes are high; the potential benefits are huge. Just in this state of Georgia alone, where 88,000 people are already employed directly by European companies, TTIP could be worth more than 24,000 new jobs and lead to a more than 30% increase in Georgia's exports to the EU.

The fifth round of negotiations took place in DC in the past week or so. The EU teams comprised 100 negotiators - this gives some sense of the scope and complexity of what is under negotiation.

It was clear from the outset of the TTIP negotiation that the economic stakes and interests were high. But I think over recent months there has been a readiness to look beyond the basic arithmetic to the wider picture - a growing sense that, with multilateralism under increasing pressure, a strong TTIP outcome would be an important restatement of free trade values, properly regulated to ensure fair and balanced outcomes.

All of this, as I said, points to a renewed focus on the EU/US relationship, a renewed recognition that we are indispensable partners on both the political and economic fronts. When President Obama visits Europe at the beginning of June, 1 have no doubt that this will offer the opportunity for a strong restatement of the strength and centrality of the relationship.

I promised at the outset of my remarks that I would try not to shy away from the complexities or airbrush the problems.

Undoubtedly we face issues on both sides of the Atlantic. The European Parliament elections this past weekend were a sharp reminder of some of the challenges ahead for Europe. And there are also major issues to be faced in the United States.

All of you will have read of the outcome of the European

Parliament elections. Caveats are required in interpreting the results. Participation levels were relatively low, and there is no question but that, across each of the 28 member states, national issues weighed heavily in the voting. People were sending messages to their own governments as least as much as they were transmitting messages to Brussels.

It is still very early days in the analysis of the results, and a whole separate address - or indeed series of addresses - would be merited. But some very basic things are clear. Across the EU, significant sectors of the population are feeling unsettled and alienated. They feel buffeted by globalisation, distanced from what is happening at European level, threatened by change that they cannot control. There are communication issues, and underlying policy issues.

European leaders are trying to come to terms with the election outcome, and we saw the beginning of that process as they gathered on Tuesday night in Brussels. As the dust settles, important decisions will have to be taken - leadership choices, but also policy choices.

There has been no comparable jolt in the US. We await the mid-term elections in November to see what message the voters will send. But I am not being disrespectful if I acknowledge what every commentator here points to: the gridlock in Congress which is causing so much concern about dysfunction and paralysis.

Of course, one should not equate the situations in the European Union and the US. Our history is different; our constitutional make-up is vastly different; our mindset is in many ways different. But what I am saying is that each of us has challenges in ensuring our policy-making apparatus is fit for purpose and responsive to what our citizens expect and require.

And in this highly unsettled world, it is more than ever imperative that the US and Europe have a close and functioning relationship. We certainly need to try to deal with irritants such as the NSA spying allegations. But beyond that, we need a deep understanding of how we assert and defend shared values, how we protect multilateralism, how we effectively exercise and project soft power — or smart power, as it is perhaps better described - and how we see each other's roles and responsibilities when it comes to defence spending and exercise of hard power.

As this debate develops, both on recovery and renewal in Europe, and continued renewal in the transatlantic relationship, Ireland will be a very engaged contributor to the discussion.

REGARDING THE UNITED NATIONS

I spent about a third of my diplomatic career - fourteen years out of forty-five - accredited to the UN in various capacities. My first posting abroad, from 1976 to 1980, was as a First Secretary at our Mission to the United Nations in Geneva. Later I returned to Geneva for a six-year spell as Permanent Representative ('95-2001) and my second-to-last posting was as Permanent Representative at UN Headquarter in New York from 2009 to 2013.

Over these fourteen years, I made countless interventions at various UN fora. This section contains only five speeches - why not more? A variety of reasons: many I don't have copies of; others are too particular in their focus to be of wider interest; many draw on drafting inputs from Mission colleagues and so will contravene my rule of including only speeches that were wholly my own.

The first speech here dates from twenty years ago but the occasion - the atmosphere and feel of it - is still seared on my brain. It was 20 March 2000, the final day of my year-long stint as Chair of the UN Commission on Human Rights. There was relief and a measure of satisfaction. But I was physically exhausted and emotionally drained.

Chairing the Commission on Human Rights was one of the most gruelling roles of my entire career. The Commission had a venerable history: founded in the aftermath of the Second World War, it held its first session in 1947 and Eleanor Roosevelt was its first Chair (I was only the fourth woman to chair). By 1999, it had become a sprawling annual exercise: a six-week session with over three thousand participants representing nearly four hundred delegations - almost one hundred and fifty of them Member or

Observer governments and the rest mostly non-governmental organisations from around the world.

I knew in advance the chairing role would be tough but I hadn't anticipated quite the degree of pressure and how alone I would feel. The Commission did important and necessary work but its structure was skewed - the fifty three member governments, nominated by the various regional groups, included a number whose own human rights records were deeply flawed and who lacked any moral authority to criticise others. Its proceedings were subject to constant criticism, much of it justified, for bias, selectivity, lack of objectivity (its successor body, the UN Human Rights Council, is exposed to the same criticisms). I fought every step of the way to try to ensure fairness, transparency and rigour - with almost every decision vigorously contested by one regional group or another. While I had stalwart support from my own Mission there was insufficient backup from a UN Secretariat that often seemed cowed by its responsibilities.

The challenges kept piling up. In addition to the six-week Spring session, I presided over a very fraught special session in September, responding to the violence that had erupted in East Timor in the aftermath of its vote for independence. Over the strident objections of Indonesia and its supporters, we adopted a resolution requesting the UN Secretary General to establish an international Commission of Inquiry to investigate the human rights violations that had occurred.

And throughout the year, I had the additional responsibility of chairing a working group on "Enhancing the Effectiveness of the Mechanisms" - code for certain delegations (who had a numerical majority of the membership) to try to further weaken the Commission. I saw my job as staving off these efforts, trying to protect the Commission and its mechanisms without having my even-handedness called into question. I vividly recall writing up the final draft report of the working group at my kitchen table one long wet evening - entirely by myself so as to be able to defend myself against the charges of being in the pocket of any regional group.

In the fog of tiredness at the end of that year, I tried to put some care into my wrap-up speech, with some short reflections on the relevance and credibility of the Commission. The issues that I grappled with throughout the year, and touched on in that speech, are as sorely relevant now as then.

As well as all that internal grappling, part of my role as Chair was to be an outward face of the Commission, and in order to fulfil that responsibility I had accepted a wide range of speaking invitations in the course of the year. One of these brought me to São Paolo in Brazil, to address a conference on the "new multilateralism", and I am including the speech I made on that occasion. I talked with some frankness about the strengths and weaknesses of the international human rights regime; my trip was also intended to encourage the Latin American countries to take a more forward position at the Commission.

The three other speeches date from my New York years. Coincidentally, two were made within a few days of each other during the last week of October 2010. The first of these two was a keynote address at a United Nations Day lunch in Boston; the audience was by definition supportive of the United Nations (something never to be taken for granted in the US) and this gave me permission to "take the clear-eyed look that is possible among friends". The subject I chose was "Our Collective Challenge: Restoring the Authority of the United Nations". That challenge was already a considerable one during the Obama years; it has grown depressingly more so with the reflexive and pervasive hostility to multilateralism that characterises the current US administration.

Three days later, I was presenting the first five-year Review of the United Nations Peacebuilding Architecture at the United Nations General Assembly. I was one of the three Co-facilitators for this Review; while the draft of the speech was mine, it was cleared in advance with my fellow Co-facilitators: the Ambassadors of South Africa and of Mexico.

I am making an exception in including this speech - the only one in the collection in which I am speaking for others besides myself - because it has a particular resonance for me. The preparation of the report was quite arduous (although nothing like as fraught or as lonely as chairing the Human Rights Commission, and I had excellent support from Mission colleagues throughout) and we tried to find a style that was direct and frank, avoiding the turgid prose that too often characterises UN reports. The work of that period also laid the basis for a continuing involvement with UN Peacebuilding. Following my retirement, I was appointed by the UN Secretary General to be a member of his Advisory Group on the Peacebuilding Fund. I served for an initial period from 2018 to 2020; my tenure has now been renewed and I have agreed to chair the group for the next two years.

In April 2013, during my final months in New York, I was invited to give the annual Gannon Lecture in Fordham University. This was an opportunity for an extensive speech, and I knew exactly what I wanted to talk about. Just a few months earlier, we had come to a successful conclusion of a hard-fought campaign to secure Ireland's election to the Human Rights Council. There were lessons from that campaign that I wanted to share, and the speech took shape under the title "UN Elections: Power, Influence, Reputation". I was subsequently asked to allow the speech to be included in a major academic publication on the UN, and it felt good to see it sitting alongside speeches and essays by Kofi Annan and other luminaries. (I am greatly looking forward to a future telling by one of me Departmental colleagues of the story of Ireland's triumphant campaign for election to the Security Council this year.)

I like the symmetry that this section begins and ends with a human rights focus: starting with that searing experience of chairing the Commission, and finishing with a reflection on the major effort to secure Ireland a seat on its successor body, the Human Rights Council. The human rights lens is one through which I would like to view much of my life's work, including the preoccupation with gender issues. And it is one that I hope will not fail me in the years ahead.

**United Nations Commission on Human Rights 56ᵗʰ Session
Statement by Outgoing Chairperson
Geneva
20ᵗʰ March 2000**

This morning, the chairing of the Commission on Human Rights passes to my my   successor. As I step down, I would like to do two things. Firstly, to give you an account of my stewardship during the inter-sessional period and secondly, to share a few valedictory reflections.

The Inter-Sessional Period

At the outset, I would like to express my thanks to the High Commissioner and her team. I saw close up during the year the High Commissioner's tremendous courage and commitment. I also benefited greatly from the advice and assistance of the Deputy High Commissioner, the Commission secretary, and many other members of the Office staff.

I knew by the end of the last session that I was fortunate in my Bureau. The experience of the inter-sessional period has amply confirmed that. I am deeply grateful to the Bureau members and to the colleagues in their missions who assisted them.

As a Bureau, we tried to be engaged, active and at all times transparent. We met fifteen times inter-sessionally; minutes of our discussions were made available on all occasions. We debated all the issues that came to our attention during the 55th session and left a legacy in the form of a Reflections document which we have passed to our successors.

We sought to strengthen the links within the ECOSOC family - in meetings with the Bureau of ECOSOC and in contacts with other Bureaus, notably the Commission on the Status of Women.

Our biggest challenge came on the issue of a special session on

East Timor. As I said at the time, none of us - irrespective of our views on the substance - would have wished for the procedural complications that arose. Within the Bureau, we sought to deal with the issues fairly, as a team who fully trusted each other even when our views diverged.

I tried to bring the same attitudes of openness and fairness in discharging the responsibilities that fell specifically to me as Chair. I appointed five Rapporteurs in the course of the year, all to important posts and some to extremely sensitive ones. I believe all five are individuals of integrity and substance. They come from countries belonging to different regional groups: two from GRULAC and one each from Africa, Asia and Europe. There are three men and two women.

I tried also to be available to everyone who wished to have contact with the Chair. Among others, I had discussions with the Rapporteurs at their annual meeting, the Chairs of the Treaty Bodies, the Sub-Commission, and the NGO consultative forum. More formal contacts were supplemented by a range of informal contacts with individual rapporteurs and individual or small groups of NGOs.

I learned a great deal in all my contacts. My respect has grown further for human rights defenders around the world who have such strength and courage but also - as the year has shown - are often so vulnerable. I hope it will prove possible to take concrete steps during this session to strengthen their protection.

The chairing of the Working Group on Enhancing the Effectiveness of the Mechanisms was a separate but related task. I will have the opportunity at a later stage to comment in more detail. But I would refer back to my closing remarks at the end of the session last year. I said then: "All of us have a huge interest in seeing that the working group we established succeeds. It can become a meeting ground or a battle ground; the choice is ours".

We made our choice on 11 February when the Working Group agreed its report by consensus. Inevitably it is a compromise document, leaving some hopes unfulfilled. There is more work to be done in the future. But acknowledging the need for future work should not lead us to undervalue what has been achieved. The choice we have made - to meet each other on common ground - will I hope begin a new chapter in the Commission, enabling us to leave behind some of the tensions over working methods which have characterised recent sessions.

In looking back at the inter-sessional period, I also want to mention the important progress made in relation to children's rights - the subject of our special dialogue last year. Work on the Optional Protocol on Children in Armed Conflict has been brought to fruition, and a successful outcome seems within reach on the Optional Protocol on Sale of Children. These will be landmark achievements, owing a great deal to the skill and determination of the Chairs of the two Working Groups.

Relevance and credibility of the Commission

The question that continues to challenge all of us, and in a particular way every Chairperson, is how to assure the relevance and credibility of this Commission. That is the issue on which I would like to address a few valedictory remarks.

The theme I suggested at the outset of the 55th session was "taking responsibility". The past year has reminded us - if we needed reminding - that defining and meeting those responsibilities is sometimes neither easy nor comfortable. Shifting the burden elsewhere will always be a seductive option. But the United Nations is truly the indispensable organisation. As custodian of universal values, ours is a unique responsibility.

The minimum credibility of this body requires that we acknowledge the problems where they exist, that the victims of human rights violations know that we are not blind and deaf to their suffering, and that as a global body we do whatever is possible to reinforce the mechanisms that may be available at national and regional level.

We need to find a better marriage between deep solidarity with those who are suffering and a rigorous objectivity in analysis and in framing solutions. It is a sad comment on our culture that the term "bleeding heart" should have become a pejorative one. It ought not to be so - there are acts of cruelty and inhumanity which should make every heart bleed. I believe the NGOs have much to teach us in the vocabulary of empathy.

But empathy is only the starting point. The credibility and effectiveness of this body requires the most exacting professionalism. The output of the session must be built on reliable and accurate information. The responses we offer must be adapted to the requirements of specific situations. The special mechanisms must work to the highest standards, and must be resourced to do so.

And the selectivity question is one we cannot ignore. At the end of the last session, I said "I still feel without a convincing answer to charges of selectivity on the part of this Commission. I also believe we need to challenge ourselves to ensure that the moral outrage rightly provoked by the Kosovo crisis does not become blunted when we confront conflict situations in other parts of the world."

I would make the same point as strongly today, as the 56th session opens under the shadow of another conflict in Europe.

There may be genuine reasons to differentiate between situations in terms of analysis and response. We should recognise such reasons where they exist. But we need to be clear as to the ground on which we stand. If a discomfort about criticising the powerful nations of the world is sufficient to blunt our conscience, then that is bound to be corrosive of the authority of this Commission.

There is also another type of selectivity I had in mind in speaking last year - the selectivity that is so easily induced by the arbitrariness of media coverage of situations of human rights abuse. If suffering seems to matter less to us when it is far away, when it is borne by the poorest and those with least access to power and publicity, then what claim do we have to cherish human life equally? Being forgotten by the media must not mean being forgotten by the Commission on Human Rights.

Despite the setbacks, I profoundly believe that history is on the side of human rights. Women and men in every part of the world are asserting more strongly than ever before the sense of human worth and the claim to human dignity. The communications revolution, and the slow but steady development of international law, are among the most powerful agents of change. The challenge to our Commission is to help shape rather than follow the process. It is perhaps salutary to remind ourselves that being on the wrong side of our conscience may also mean being on the wrong side of history.

In the end, the responsibilities go beyond the professional to the personal. Many of you will remember that last year, to mark the 50th anniversary of the Geneva Conventions, the ICRC mounted an exhibition on humanitarian law in the hallway outside this room. Each morning, on my way to the Chair's office behind the podium, I passed a particular display. One photograph with an accompanying quotation kept catching my eye. It was a photograph of a conflict survivor and the quotation was "During the war, each man has to act as a human being for himself, because he must live with himself after the war".

The Commission of course is not a war and we should not treat it as such. But the imperative is the same - to be true to human values so that we can live with ourselves into the future, when our professional responsibilities have come to an end.

I would like to thank all of you for the honour to my country and the trust you placed in me. Chairing the Commission on Human Rights has been the greatest privilege of my diplomatic career.

"The Rio Summit and the New Multilateralism": The Fight for Human Rights and the Importance of the International Criminal Court
São Paolo, 25th June 1999

I am very honoured to participate in this meeting. Although I am speaking in a personal capacity, the rationale for inviting me is the fact that I am currently Chairperson of the United Nations Commission on Human Rights. It is therefore largely through a United Nations prism that I propose to comment on some of the issues confronting us in this discussion.

The "new multilateralism" in human rights

It is absolutely right to acknowledge that there is a sense of reinvigoration and renewal in the human rights debate. The end of the Cold War meant that human rights could begin to recover their proper place in international relations. The Cold War was a long distortion, with priorities skewed and geo-political strategies obscuring human realities. The past decade has seen landmark developments such as the establishment of the post of UN High Commissioner for Human Rights in 1994 and the adoption last year of a Statute providing for the establishment of the International Criminal Court.

There are encouraging trends worldwide. The tide of democracy, even if it advances at different rhythms, begins to seem almost inexorable: in quick succession already this year, we have seen the ending of fourteen years of military rule in Nigeria and forty four years of military rule in Indonesia. Non-governmental organisations are growing in confidence in very many countries; the Internet is prising open closed societies. It is reassuring - perhaps even realistic - to believe that history is on the side of human rights, that the auguries are positive ones as we cross the threshold to the next century.

But we all know the other side of the coin. The internal conflicts that have replaced the Cold War; the grim litany of names - Rwanda, Cambodia, Sierra Leone, Kosovo - that are testimony to the evil forces that can tear a people apart. The repeated failure of the international community to take effective preventive action. The terrible statistics of world poverty, hunger, illiteracy, avoidable disease, that shame us all. The fall in development aid that shows the conscience of the developed world remains relatively untroubled by these statistics.

It will take some time to absorb the lessons of Kosovo. We would all wish to believe that a resounding message has been delivered to dictators everywhere. The Security Council debate on 10 June, at which the resolution on Kosovo was adopted, was noteworthy for the way in which delegations discussed the balance to be struck between state sovereignty on the one hand and respect for human rights on the other. Many delegations noted a decisive shift in that balance and saw the Kosovo crisis as marking an important step towards a broader definition of security - a definition that ensures that human rights and humanitarian concerns are given new weight in the Security Council's approach and its calculation as to when and how the Council should engage.

But while it was reassuring to see the Security Council role re-asserted towards the conclusion of the Kosovo crisis - and we know that the UN will take a lead in building the peace - who could say that the whole episode has been a vindication of a new multilateralism? The sidelining of the United Nations at the outset and at the height of the crisis - or as some would see it, the sidelining of itself by the United Nations - shows just how far we are from a world where the international community can collectively define what constitutes a just cause and act promptly and effectively to defend that cause.

Fragile foundations

And when one probes beneath the surface, the foundations of the new multilateralism seem fragile indeed. Yes, we have a High Commissioner for Human Rights who is committed and courageous and backed by a UN Secretary General who has vowed that human rights will be at the centre of every aspect of UN work... "at the core of the sacred bond with the people of the United Nations". But the Office of the High Commissioner remains seriously under-funded and receives only lukewarm support in political and moral terms from the majority of UN members. Yes, we have the breakthrough for the International Criminal Court but it was profoundly disappointing that, despite all the concessions made to ensure a more palatable text, the Rome Conference ended with the US, China, India and Israel registering their opposition.

And when I look at the Commission on Human Rights, I am struck by the extent to which the battle for hearts and minds remains to be fought and won. Immensely useful work is done in the Commission - we are an irreplaceable meeting ground for the international human rights community: we have a network of mechanisms who prepare high quality reports; we adopt resolutions which say important thing. But so often it seems as much a battle ground as a meeting ground. The monitoring mechanisms of the Commission attract considerable resentment; they are refused access by some countries; their recommendations are too often ignored. Suggestions for improving the efficiency of the mechanisms are bitterly disputed. There are recurring debates about co-operation versus "confrontation", with the clear implication that engagement must imply an end to public criticism and vice versa.

And so we witness these contradictory trends: on the one hand a sense that we are moving decisively forward to a new multilateralism and, on the other hand, a sense of retrenchment and increased sensitivity on the part of national governments. Perhaps it is not such a puzzle. Globalism in all its manifestations is refashioning the entire international landscape but is perceived by many governments and societies as more threat than opportunity. The loss of control at local and national level creates a sense of vulnerability and powerlessness. It is hardly surprising that in the most sensitives area of human rights, there is a reaction, an attempt to ring-fence against criticism and "outside interference" and to contest the legitimacy of international expressions of concern.

Shoring up the foundations

How can we shore up these fragile foundations? In the limited time available I would like to make four points.

First: Building national institutions

We need to recognise that multilateralism must be built on and buttressed by strong foundations at national level. The first and most important layer of human rights protection is at national level. The international spotlight is a necessary and powerful one but its light tends to be intermittent rather than constant. It will never illuminate all the darker corners in our societies. Building genuinely independent and resilient national human rights institutions is rarely comfortable for national governments. But such institutions - coupled with a flourishing civil society - offer the best protection for our citizens.

The next layer of protection is at the regional level. Regional institutions form the bridge between the national and multilateral levels and can combine "insider" knowledge with "outsider" detachment. They too are a key part of the structure. However, even strong regional institutions cannot lead to any complacency or lack of focus on the multilateral level. Otherwise we have a kind of "variable geometry" where some are left very far behind.

Second: An integrated approach

The Vienna Declaration and Programme of Action, adopted by the World Conference on Human Rights exactly six years ago today, affirms that all human rights are universal, indivisible and interdependent and interrelated. Over the past six years, genuine efforts have been made to ensure that economic and social rights move up the agenda in the discussion of human rights. But there is still a great deal of compartmentalisation in analysis and in policy-making.

Those who concern themselves with political and civil rights too often pay too little attention to the economic and social context in which these rights are being exercised. And the economic policy makers, at national or international level, have too easily absolved themselves of responsibility for an ethical dimension to their work.

Integration obviously needs to occur at national as well as international level. In preparing for this, my first trip to Brazil, I read the Communiqué of the National Conference of Brazilian Bishops, in July of last year, entitled "The Challenges Facing Brazil". It sets out the problems of the 100 million or so citizens that are described as "excluded" or "invisible" in this society. Serious discourse about human rights in Brazil clearly must take full account of these economic realities. And the same holds true for all our societies.

At international level, the need for a greater level of consistency and coherence is even more apparent. In Geneva, for example, the WTO and the Office of the High Commissioner for Human Rights are located practically beside each other but their approaches can often seem a world apart. The Bretton Woods Institutions - the IMF and the World Bank - at times scarcely seem like twin institutions and their relationship with the UN system needs to be further strengthened. In short, the "new multilateralism" must find a better way of integrating economic and social with civic and political rights.

Third: Ownership and Leadership

We need to work harder in creating a sense of shared ownership and shared leadership in the human rights area. At the Commission on Human Rights, for example, a disproportionate number of the resolutions are tabled by members of the Western European and Others Group. This lends an edge to the complaints of those who would have us believe that the multilateral approach to human rights is a thinly disguised attempt to impose Western standards on the world community.

This argument is becoming increasingly threadbare. The Vienna Declaration, as I have said, ringingly proclaimed the universality of standards. The UN Secretary General has passionately and eloquently repeated the point that human rights are not the property of any one region. As is pointed out in the article before us, developed and developing countries worked seamlessly together in the lead-up to the creation of the International Criminal Court.

But it is nevertheless an argument which continues to have a resonance in some quarters. It is therefore important to see Latin American countries take initiatives at the Commission on Human Rights - as Brazil does, for example, on assistance to states in strengthening the rule of law; as Chile does on compensation for victims of grave violations of human rights; as El Salvador does on building a culture of peace - and I believe there is more scope for this.

Fourth: Addressing selectivity

Alexandra Barahone de Brito, in her introductory article for our conference, makes the point: "Not all dictators can be judged, not every just war fought. But this does not mean that no effort should be made to judge when the opportunity arises. Justice is always selective but, as long as it is done according to the rule of law, it should be welcomed...".

I agree with this up to a point. To argue that the international community cannot address any human rights problem unless and until it addresses all of them amounts to a rationale for inaction, indeed paralysis. Some kinds of selectivity are justified. If there is a hierarchy of human rights violations, we are right to act first on the most grievous ones. If there are situations where constructive engagement is likely to achieve tangible results, and other situations where public pressure is likely to be more effective, then we should choose our approach accordingly. But if the targets of our public criticisms are the soft ones - the countries that can be offended without paying too high a political price - then we leave ourselves open to charges of cynicism and undermine the moral foundations which give legitimacy to our actions.

Finally, let me emphasise how much Latin America has to offer to the human rights discourse. The recent history of so much of this continent is scarred by human rights abuse and trying to fully come to terms with that past continues to challenge you. But your past and present experience, and the regional mechanism you have developed, have given you a great deal to share. Your role in building the new multilateralism in the human rights area will be a critical one. There is no more worthy task for the twenty-first century, but hardly a more difficult one - and it has only just begun.

"Our Collective Challenge: Restoring the Authority of the UN" UN Association of Greater Boston: United Nations Day Luncheon 26th October 2010

It is a genuine pleasure to address you today. An Irish person is always at home in Boston - and with our Consul-General here and many Irish names on the guest list, I feel myself to be among family.

I am among family in another sense also. By personal conviction and professional background, I will always be at home in a gathering of UN supporters. Ireland is among the most loyal and committed UN members. For myself, I spent a total of ten years accredited to the United Nations in Geneva, first as a young diplomat and later as Ambassador. For the past year, I have had the great privilege to represent Ireland at the United Nations in New York.

It is obvious from today's attendance that there is a strong and flourishing United Nations Association in Boston - fittingly so, as the great traditions of this city make it a natural champion of principled multilateralism.

It is because this room resonates with belief in, and support for, the United Nations that we can take the clear - eyed look that is possible among friends. We know how much we need and value this Organisation. We know the good it does, too often unsung or insufficiently appreciated. But we know too the erosion that has taken place: the role and relevance of the United Nations is not what it was, what it could be, and what it should be.

The canvas, of course, is a vast one and only a broad-brush approach is possible within the time limits of my address. But as part of the wider and deeper conversation around these issues, I think it useful to exchange some views today.

The title l have chosen refers to the collective challenge we face in seeking to restore the authority of the United Nations. I shall return to the word 'collective' - I mean it in multiple senses, collective as between large and small UN members, collective as between member States and civil society which you represent.

For the moment, let me focus on the word 'authority'. It is a firm word, and I chose it deliberately. For it is that sense of a purposeful and respected organisation - one whose will and opinion truly count - that we need to reclaim.

The UN's authority is legal, political and moral. The Charter is the foundation stone. It is the document which enshrines the legal powers of the UN but, in its reach and rhetoric, it also speaks to the aspirations and ideals which surrounded the birth of the Organisation.

A clear-eyed look means eschewing sentimentality or nostalgia. There never were halcyon days for the UN. Any serious examination of those early decades shows the frustrations and setbacks as well as the achievements. But the UN truly mattered: for our governments, it was at the heart of their foreign policy-making; for our citizens, it held their attention and was a repository of their hopes.

The past will not be summoned back: the years since the foundation of the UN have arguably been more transformative than any equivalent period in world history. The stage on which the UN was the lead actor has been greatly changed. It is now thronged with other actors jostling for space. New arrivals, like the G20, are flexing their muscles. Others that have been with us all along, are increasing their visibility - the IMF, for example, inevitably commands the headlines in the current financial crisis.
Even the analogy of a theatre, implying actors and audience, hardly fits any longer. Ours is a fractured and urgent world, whose most influential conversations are conducted not through grand discourses but on the internet and Twitter.

And yet, in this fractured, damaged and cacophonous world,

one can argue that a unifying narrative is more than ever necessary. Individually and collectively, we struggle to make sense of multiple and interrelated challenges. The ravages of the financial crisis are everywhere. Climate change threatens not just polar bears, but almost every aspect of our way of life. And as extremism and fanaticism incubate in poor and far-flung places, the terrorist threat arrives on our doorsteps.

Individual organisations can and must tackle specific issues or sets of issues but the joined-up vision of the UN, backed by the unique legitimacy conferred by its universal membership, is irreplaceable.

I need not, in this room, defend the UN's core mission of caring for our fellow human beings and exercising our custodianship of this fragile planet. It is a vocation which should be worn as a badge of honour. But multilateralism is also, as it has always been, a vehicle for our enlightened self-interest. To adapt the Bette Davis quote about old age, the UN is no place for sissies. It is a place for determination and cool heads, for leadership and joint action to deliver defined common objectives.

How does the Organisation face up to the challenges?

I think that we would all agree that the score sheet is an uneven one. In the humanitarian and developmental area, the UN continues to show real leadership and achieve meaningful results. Across so many of the Programmes and Agencies, extraordinary work is being done by dedicated staff. When humanitarian disasters strike, of the scale we have seen in Haiti and Pakistan earlier this year, the UN is irreplaceable in assembling a global response. In 18 missions around the world, UN peacekeepers are damping down the fires of conflict that could otherwise flare out of control.

None of these areas is without challenge. Budgets in all our capitals are under recessionary pressures, and governments are asking searching questions about the comparative benefits of multilateral and bilateral aid. There is increasing insistence on value for money and results-based budgeting.

We know we have to do better in our responses to large-scale emergencies. And, in the peacekeeping area, the UN is grappling with issues of overstretch, qualified consent by some host governments, and an increasing awareness of the limitations of classical models of peacekeeping.

However, without understating them, one might consider these the normal challenges of improving performance and delivery. In the political arena, the challenges can seem more existential, with more fundamental questions arising about the UN's role and relevance.

The controversy over Iraq — and what was seen by some as the use and abuse of the Security Council in the run-up to the war — casts a long shadow. Two of the major crises of our time, the Middle East and Iran, are in large part being dealt with outside the UN framework. The Security Council devotes by far the greatest percentage of its time to Africa, yet - as the ugliness of the conflict in DRC becomes ever more apparent, and the situation in Sudan seems increasingly fraught with risk - the quality and effectiveness of engagement leaves much to be desired.

What is to be done? In this complex, grown-up world, there are no simple answers to the challenges, no likelihood of securing the necessary support for a single, radical blueprint for reform that could transform the Organisation. What is required is dedicated, painstaking work - guided by a big vision but with the will and staying-power to translate that vision into a series of concrete actions.

We must strengthen our resolve to advance the reform of UN bodies. The Security Council is clearly anachronistic in its composition. As for the General Assembly, the challenge is to try to break out of a vicious circle where frustration as to its impotence can lead to self-indulgence as to its conduct of business. And the current five-year review of the Human Rights Council offers an opportunity for some serious stock- taking.

As we cope with so many challenges, it would be over-optimistic and hardly plausible to suggest to you that the UN is on the threshold of re-invention. But, without allowing ourselves to be distracted from the reform agenda, we need also to see around and beyond it. Speaking as someone at the coalface, I want to give you some reasons why I feel we are at a moment of opportunity. Let me focus on three specific developments over recent weeks.

Firstly, the Millennium Development Summit, which brought world leaders to the UN at the end of September to assess where we stand ten years after the establishment of the Millennium Development Goals and five years from the target date for their achievement. There was inevitably some jaded media reaction to the Summit, as well as genuine and well-founded concern as to how far we are falling short in relation to many of the Goals.

But I am resolutely in the glass half-full camp. Over the decade since the Goals were adopted, there have been some remarkable gains: for example, in reducing the rate of extreme poverty, in boosting primary school enrolment, in combating HIV and malaria.

The Summit had a galvanising effect: commitments were made amounting to close to 70 billion dollars - much of it genuinely new money. If that galvanising effect can be sustained in the period ahead, the UN's capacity to make a difference will be dramatically illustrated. Tens of millions of people worldwide will benefit, and the leadership role and moral authority of the UN will have been vindicated.

Secondly, the establishment of UN Women, with the Secretary-General's appointment last month of Michelle Bachelet, former President of Chile, as head of the new body.

UN Women brings together the disparate parts of the UN structure dealing with women's issues. This is far more than organisational reform. The creation of UN Women reflects a wider movement to ensure that women's perspectives and priorities are imprinted across the full range of UN issues — security, development, human rights, peacekeeping and peacebuilding. The creation of UN Women was a hard - won achievement; it has tremendous potential to amplify women's voices.

When I visited Africa earlier this year, and attended a conference in Durban which brought together a cross-section of African participants, 1 was struck in particular by the clarity and determination of women's inputs. It was hard to escape the thought that the future of that continent is female.

I believe there is a tide slowly gathering pace around the world — at a different speed in different parts — which will inexorably bring women to a more central place. UN Women can catch that tide, helping to channel and reinforce it. If the UN succeeds in becoming a more forthright and compelling voice on women's issues worldwide, it will have found a new kind of relevance and authority.

Thirdly I would like to focus on the elections to the Security Council which took place two weeks ago today on 12 October. The need for Security Council reform is self - evident: as 1 have said, the current composition is anachronistic, and re-configuration is well overdue. The arguments of principle have dragged on for far too long; a new pattern of practice over the next couple of years might do something to break the log-jam.

The General Assembly each year elects five new members of the Security Council to take their seats for the following two years. This year's elections will result in a Security Council of unusual strength. Taking together the new and existing members, the Council next year will comprise all of the BRIC members — Brazil, Russia, India and China — as well as the African power-houses of South Africa and Nigeria; Germany's election means that three of the G4 aspirants to permanent seats will also be there.

Given the unique composition, expectations for this Security Council are high. There is of course no guarantee it will deliver on those expectations. But there is an unparalleled opportunity to demonstrate what a strong, cohesive Council can achieve. If that challenge is grasped, it could constitute an important step towards restoring the frayed political authority of the UN.

I am conscious that these three examples are selective and that there are other rendez-vous points in the weeks ahead. On climate change, for example, where last year's Copenhagen meeting showed the UN at its most dysfunctional, there is considerable apprehension about the prospects for the forthcoming Cancun meeting. Nevertheless, I believe the larger point is justified - recent developments create a moment of opportunity for the UN; there is movement on various fronts; and important new vistas are opening up.

For the final section of my address, I would like to focus on the collective nature of our challenge, and our collective responsibility. This means a responsibility for States, large and small, and also for civil society. Before I speak about how we in Ireland shoulder our responsibilities, I might say a word about the US.

The US approach is absolutely critical. Yours is the indispensable nation, in the indispensable Organisation. The Obama Administration is instinctively multilateralist, understanding that building international support is not just desirable in itself but critical to the delivery of key foreign policy objectives. That multilateralism has been eloquently articulated and followed through with a new level of engagement across a range of UN Work.

This commitment to multilateralism is no doubt being tested and will be further tested. The UN is a slow and deliberative body, whose compromises come at a price and whose processes can often seem too accommodating of spoilers. Keeping faith with the UN requires patience and determination. And it must also, of course, be a two-way street, with a genuine US effort reciprocated by a genuine effort on the part of others. Continued strong engagement by the US Administration, as well as a readiness by the wider UN membership to recognise and build on the opportunities which that engagement offers, are critical to any effort to rebuild UN authority.

In Ireland's case, there has always been an emotional charge to our connection to the UN. On that day in 1955, when we joined the UN, the dream of generations of Irish patriots - that a free and independent Ireland would take its place among the nations of the world - was finally fulfilled. Five years later, in 1960, we felt an extraordinary sense of pride and service as our soldiers joined UN peacekeepers in the Congo. And there was another milestone before the end of that decade: the Nuclear Non-Proliferation Treaty, agreed in 1968, became informally known as 'the Irish Treaty' because of our initiating role.

The drama of those early days is hard to recapture. But the UN remains central to our foreign policy, and we are in the first ranks of those seeking to restore its authority.

Our commitment to UN peacekeeping has not wavered over the past 50 years. During those years, Irish defence forces have participated in 75 peacekeeping missions worldwide, contributing 60,000 individual tours of duty. Equally, we have maintained our leadership role on disarmament issues: a further significant milestone was the meeting in Dublin two years ago which finalised negotiations on the Cluster Munitions Treaty.

The Irish voice has remained among the strongest and clearest in human rights advocacy. Our former President Mary Robinson was an outstanding High Commissioner for Human Rights. In my own career, one of the defining periods was a year-long chairing of the UN Commission on Human Rights in 1999. As only the fourth woman in that role, I took special pride in serving in direct line of succession to the incomparable Eleanor Roosevelt.

Despite the very difficult economic times in Ireland, we are maintaining our goal of reaching the UN target of devoting 0.7% of our GNP to development by 2015. We remain on track to reach that goal, with 0.52% currently being allocated. In the midst of so many domestic cutbacks, it is heartening that public support for the development effort has been sustained.

Beyond these broad outlines, let me try to give you a flavour of the kind of contributions we make on a day to day basis. I will limit myself to a few examples over recent months:

●   In May of this year, Ireland was a key player in the NPT Review Conference, brokering an important breakthrough on very sensitive Middle East-related issues.

●   In July, we handed over a detailed report which reviewed UN activities in the area of peacebuilding and made recommendations for their improvement. Together with the Permanent Representatives of Mexico and South Africa, I had been asked last December to take on this co- facilitation role, which involved intensive work throughout the first half of the year.

●   On 21 September, in the margins of the Millennium Summit, Ireland and the US jointly launched a Special Project on Child Hunger: "1000 Days to Save a Life". This was a very high profile event, co-hosted by Foreign Minister Martin and Secretary of State Clinton, which brought together a range of key actors including Secretary-General Ban Ki-moon. Ireland has long been a leader in addressing world hunger - reflecting the imprint on the national consciousness of our own Great Famine - and it was a source of tremendous satisfaction to be able to take this important new step in partnership with the US.

● Just yesterday in our Mission in New York, in the presence of Michelle Bachelet and many others, we launched the report on a novel cross-learning initiative which Ireland has sponsored over the past couple of years. This initiative brought together women from Ireland, North and South, with counterparts from Liberia and Timor-Leste to exchange views and draw lessons from their experience of conflict. The exercise has been an inspiring one, and the report makes a worthwhile contribution to the commemoration of the 10th anniversary of Resolution 1325 — the landmark UN resolution on Women, Peace and Security.

I mention these examples to illustrate the range of work Ireland does, much of it undramatic and out of the headlines. The Irish 'brand' at the UN is a very strong one and we are determined to keep it so. The experience may be less heady than in the early years, but our pride in serving the UN remains undiminished.

And now to the role of representatives of civil society. I need hardly underline that the support of civil society is more than ever important for the UN. There is a particular challenge in the US, where the distrust of multilateralism is sometimes expressed in terms that distort the UN beyond recognition. The supporters of multilateralism need to demonstrate a conviction equal to the passionate intensity of the opponents.

More generally, however, in a world transformed by new methods of communication, the influence of civil society continues to grow. The UN is no longer the place of the past, where men in grey suits deliberated the great questions of the day as their citizens maintained a reverential distance. Civil society is engaged and influential, and has its own dedicated UN fora. With its access to the airwaves and the internet, it has multiple and highly effective pressure points on governments. The potential is enormous, and I encourage you to use it to the full.

As I conclude, let me repeat that now more than ever, the world needs a strong and authoritative UN. With the frankness to which friendship entitles us, it is important that we recognise and work through the challenges. But we must not underestimate the strengths, nor fail to recognise opportunities when they present themselves. And right now, I believe there is a combination of circumstances which could allow the UN to make real strides forward, and to reclaim some of the authority which has been eroded.

The sceptics and the naysayers are out in force; those of us - in governments and civil society - who believe in the UN must ensure that our voices are heard. True friends are neither uncritical nor complacent. Our Organisation needs us, not as cheerleaders, but as loyal supporters who understand the challenges and are ready to put our shoulders to the wheel.

Review of the United Nations Peacebuilding Architecture
UN General Assembly, New York
29th October 2010

Mr. President,

The co-facilitators - Ambassador Baso Sangqu of South Africa, Ambassador Claude Heller of Mexico, and myself - warmly welcome today's debate and we hope that the draft Resolution as circulated will be adopted at the conclusion of our discussion. We trust that member States will have had the opportunity over the past three months or so to reflect on the contents of our Report, and we look forward to hearing views today. On behalf of the Co-facilitators, I would like to present some brief comments on process, content and the way forward.

Firstly, process. It seems to us that the way in which the membership engaged on this exercise represents the UN at its most constructive. We felt throughout a true sense of common purpose. There was extensive participation at each of the open-ended consultative meetings. Inputs from 332 other stakeholders, in our various seminars and in our engagement with the Geneva community, were also impressive. Throughout, interventions were thoughtful and detailed, with views cogently set out and opposing viewpoints listened to with respect.

The co-facilitators tried both to encourage this approach and to reflect it in our work. In framing our Analysis and Recommendations, we sought to distil the experience and good sense of the full range of interlocutors. As we have made clear, our purpose was to define approaches which could keep the membership together while meeting the essential test of strengthening the peacebuilding architecture.

Finding a consensual approach, without sacrifice of honesty or clarity, is not easy. Even if we fell short, we hope that member States will accept that this was the spirit which inspired our work.

As regards content, we would highlight just a few brief points in relation to the four principal chapters of the Report.

Following identification of key issues, we begin our Analysis in the field. We cannot over-emphasise the importance of the field perspective. In our consultations, we found it sobering to see the insufficient understanding on the ground of what is being attempted in New York. The New York/field connection simply has to work better. And we also felt it essential to underline again the imperative of national ownership. This works both ways: the international community must understand the limits of its role as midwife to a national birthing process, and the national authorities in turn must recognise the responsibilities which ownership confers.

Our second major focus is on the role and performance of the Peacebuilding Commission at Headquarters. In this Chapter, we try to work systematically through the issues arising, including in particular the relationship between the Organisational Committee and the Country-Specific Configurations. We define the challenge in this relationship as the need to combine innovation and vibrancy with weight and solidity.

Amid the generally very positive reactions to the content of this Chapter, some delegations have expressed disappointment not to see a fuller embrace of their positions on certain specific aspects. Such a reaction is always understandable. But we would say to those delegations that, if their views were not fully embraced, it was because there were countervailing views which also had validity and which deserved to be taken into account. That was in the nature of the exercise.

Our third major area of focus is on Key Relationships: both within the UN - with the Security Council, the General Assembly and ECOSOC - and other partnerships.

As we make clear, the PBC relationship with the Security Council is critical in shaping the PBC Agenda and in determining its relevance within the United Nations architecture. We are conscious of the view of some that the Report shows insufficient circumspection in treading on this sensitive ground. In all honesty, we do not think we could have said less. There has already been an opportunity for discussion in the Security Council; today, we would want only to emphasise that the emergence of the new dynamic we envisage - between a more forthcoming Security Council and a better-performing Peacebuilding Commission — is essential if peacebuilding is to assume its proper place in UN priorities.

Together with the Security Council, the General Assembly is also of course a co-parent of the PBC. The Assembly's co-parenting responsibilities have not been exercised as fully as they could have been, and our Report tries to suggest possible ways to achieve a more structured and interactive relationship. Already in this session, and under our current President, we hope that these avenues will begin to be explored.

Our fourth area of focus is the Peacebuilding Support Office and the Peacebuilding Fund. We look at changes necessary within the PBSO, including staffing issues, but also at the role and weight of the PBSO across the Secretariat as a whole. In this regard, we particularly underline the importance of a clear and unequivocal message from the Secretary-General that Peacebuilding is central to UN priorities, and the need for his support for organisational arrangements that reflect this.

Finally, a word about the path from here on in. The Co-facilitators extend our thanks to the President of the General Assembly and to the President of the Security Council and their respective teams for their work in framing a Resolution that could command consensus in both bodies. It is consistent with the way this exercise has been conducted from the outset that there should be a consensual text; any other outcome would fracture the sense of common purpose that is so important to safeguard. Even if the draft before us does not in every word reflect the preferences of everyone, we trust and believe it has sufficient strength and clarity to ensure that the Recommendations in the Report are appropriately taken forward and implemented.

Our Report concludes with a sense of urgency, and a hope that the Review will have served as a wake-up call. It would be very easy to lose that sense of urgency, to feel - now that we have a Report, and a Resolution, and with a new country, Liberia, on the PBC Agenda - that all is basically well, and that we can revisit the subject in five years' time.

There is no room for any such complacency. The World Development Report - to be issued shortly - will set out again the grim realities, and remind us of how corrosively conflict eats away at developmental gains. The needs remain very great; our Report will have value in so far as it leads us to respond to them more effectively.

UN Elections: Power, Influence, Reputation
Gannon Lecture, Fordham University, New York
18th April 2013

I am honoured to be invited to deliver the Gannon Lecture, celebrating one of the most distinguished past Presidents of this great university. The ties between Fordham and Ireland are deep and longstanding, guaranteeing that an Irish Ambassador will always feel at home here.

As the title of my lecture indicates, I propose this evening to take a look at the United Nations through the prism of elections. I will avail of the freedom which this platform offers to speak in a personal capacity.

It hardly comes as a surprise that I should focus on the United Nations.

This is my fourteenth year representing Ireland at the UN. At the outset of my career I spent four years at our Permanent Mission in Geneva; a couple of decades later, I returned to Geneva as Ambassador from '95 to 2001, and I am now completing my fourth and final year as Ambassador to the UN in New York.

So it has been a long-term relationship with the UN. And, while of course the relationship will change when I take up a new assignment this summer as Ireland's Ambassador to the United States, there will be no divorce. Even if one moves on from this Organisation, one never quite leaves it behind. Despite the undoubted blemishes, the United Nations will always continue to speak to what is best in all of us.

But why the focus on internal UN elections? One could choose multiple lenses to look at this sprawling, complex organisation. But elections for me exert a particular fascination.

Just as in political life more generally, elections in international Organisations provide a snapshot - a moment that illuminates much about the Organisation at a particular time. Of course snapshots never capture the whole truth, and sometimes may even mislead. But we can see the bones and sinews, and judge what we find attractive and unattractive.

And, as everywhere, elections bring a special intensity. The campaigns are long drawn out and passionate; on the day, the outcomes come quickly and with clinical exactitude. In the UN world, where movement is necessarily incremental and sometimes glacially slow, the drama of an election is particularly keenly felt.

My fascination with UN elections has been reinforced by personal experience. The first time I entered the UN building in New York was in the early days of October 2000. Although I had already been working on UN matters for nearly ten years, I had not previously had occasion to come to the NY Headquarters. I arrived to play a modest part in the final push for Ireland's election to the Security Council, which took place on 10 October 2000.

This was a classic Security Council campaign, which had been brilliantly masterminded by colleagues in Dublin and New York. It culminated in a triumph for Ireland when we topped the poll ahead of Norway and Italy. None of us in the Irish seats that day will ever forget our shared euphoria.

Twelve years later, in November of last year, I was back biting my nails in the General Assembly Hall as I waited for the results of the Human Rights Council election. Once again, there had been a tremendous Irish team input. Our political leaders, particularly Tánaiste (Deputy Prime Minister) Eamon Gilmore, and my Departmental and Mission colleagues had spared no effort. But, given the key role of the Permanent Representative in New York, I felt the weight of responsibility heavily on my own shoulders.

It was a highly contested HRC election with a very uncertain outcome. Ireland was one of five candidates for three seats. Our competitors were the US, Germany, Sweden and Greece. The results came through quickly and decisively: US 131, Germany 127, Ireland 124, Greece 78, Sweden 75. Hearing the numbers read out, I felt that same dizzying sense of pride and relief that I had experienced twelve years earlier.

My lecture this evening is not about the history of last year's HRC election campaign - that would be too limiting and, in any event, a veil of diplomatic discretion must be drawn over certain aspects. But I will invoke the campaign experience to illuminate some points I want to make.

The Non-Elections

In looking at what elections tell us about the United Nations, I must enter a couple of caveats to this story There is an equally compelling narrative about the elections we do *not* have, or do not have in any meaningful sense.

The Security Council is the most powerful organ of the United Nations, charged with "primary responsibility for international peace and security". But, as we know, one-third of the membership is unelected. Five states - US, Russia, China, UK and France - constitute the group known as the P5. Not alone do the P5 have permanent membership; they also have a higher status of membership: equipped with veto powers, and constituting an inner circle that effectively runs this elite club.

The composition of the Security Council reflects the post war world in which the UN was conceived. It is a world long gone, and the intervening seventy years have seen a radical redistribution of global power and influence. We are left with a Security Council that is anachronistic, unrepresentative, and in urgent need of reform. Yet decades of effort have brought us no closer to an agreed blueprint for change. And so we stagger on, burdened by the distortions and resentment engendered by the current composition.

With hindsight, it might have been preferable that there should not have been a category of permanent members in the first place.

And the power of veto - at least in its current form - should probably never have been conferred. But these were the political imperatives of the time, and this is the Charter we have inherited.

Since the P5 must acquiesce in any change of arrangements, it may safely be predicted that there will be no reform which divests them of any of their current status or privileges. This creates a dilemma. On the one hand, there is a legitimate concern that, if we do not create further permanent members in an enlarged Council, existing imbalances will be perpetuated and the privileges of the current P5 even further entrenched. But there is an alternative view: that permanency has inherent drawbacks; that, no matter the size or economic weight of a country, the need to present periodically for election ensures accountability and helps safeguard against an arrogant or complacent use of power.

I am personally sympathetic to the latter view. Whatever the original design flaws, we should surely not feel compelled to repeat them in whatever extension we bolt on to the existing structure.

A second point relates to the selection process for the Secretary-General. The Charter states that: "the Secretary General shall be appointed by the General Assembly upon the recommendation of the Security Council". In practice, however, the General Assembly does little more than rubber stamp the choice of the Security Council — in effect the choice of the P5. Various reform proposals have sought to reinforce the General Assembly role through initial hearings, or some kind of interview system.

I believe we should be open to any reasonable moves - within the Charter - to enhance the General Assembly role. Well beyond being the Chief Executive or the public face of the Organisation, the Secretary-General is the custodian of its values. As well as having the trust of the P5, he or she could only benefit from the enhanced legitimacy that would come with a meaningful GA role in the selection process.

Hierarchy of Elections

Another important ground-clearing point is about the hierarchy of UN elections. Elections take place constantly across the UN system and one could train a lens on any of them. Governments compete, for example, for membership of the Economic and Social Council and its range of functional Commissions, or for the Executive Boards of various Programmes and Funds - such as the UN Development Programme or UN Women. There is also a range of advisory or expert bodies, for which individual candidates campaign based on their personal and professional qualities.

But not all elections are equal; there is a distinct hierarchy, and the value of winning depends on the regard in which the prize is held. My focus this evening is on the biggest prizes, those elections where most passion is invested: the Security Council and to a lesser but increasing degree, the Human Rights Council.

During my years here as Permanent Representative, I have witnessed four Security Council elections, each autumn from 2009 to 2012. There have been some epic contests, particularly in the Western group (or the Western European and other Group, WEOG, to give its full title). In 2010 Germany, Canada, and Portugal battled for two seats, with Canada losing out. In 2012, Australia, Luxembourg and Finland fought it out for the two WEOG seats, with Finland the loser. The Eastern European Group in 2011 also saw an impassioned contest, this time with Azerbaijan taking the single seat ahead of Slovenia and Hungary.

During the intense campaign for last November's Human Rights Council election, a number of colleague Ambassadors commented to me that "this is more like a Security Council election". At times it felt so, given the intensity of lobbying both in capitals and in New York. One of the candidates, Sweden, appointed a roving Special Envoy for a year in advance of the election - a standard practice in Security Council elections but not heretofore a feature of Human Rights Council elections.

Given the role of the Security Council, and its place at the apex of the system, it is not surprising that there should be such competition for membership. More intriguing is why the Human Rights Council should have moved up the hierarchy in the way it has. I would suggest both a positive and negative reason.

On the positive side, we are witnessing a reformed and reinvigorated Human Rights Council. The 2006 transformation from Human Rights Commission to Human Rights Council has seen the emergence of a stronger and a more prestigious body, generating - certainly as far as WEOG is concerned - more intensive competition for a more limited number of spaces.

The negative reason relates to the current fractured state of the Security Council. After a relatively brief post-Cold War period, when it seemed that the Council might regain a unity of purpose and enter a new era of activism, the Security Council is once again dogged by a malfunctioning relationship between its permanent members, particularly between the US and Russia. Although no other body can fill the vacuum created by Security Council inaction, the Human Rights Council is possessing some of the territory. In the face of Security Council paralysis on Syria, the HRC has gone out front with a series of special sessions and resolutions, including the establishment of an Independent International Commission of Inquiry. It was similarly proactive on Libya in 2011, taking steps which led to Libya's suspension from HRC membership.

Mechanisms & Resources

Before considering the power play of elections, it is important to understand the nuts and bolts of how the system operates.

The general practice in UN elections is that votes are cast by the full membership - all 193 governments - although for some subsidiary bodies voting is confined to those who are members of the parent body, and in the case of Treaty bodies to those who are States Parties to the relevant treaty. Usually, but not always, a fixed number of seats will be allocated to each regional group. Thresholds for election vary, with the highest being a two-third requirement for election to the Security Council. Voting is by secret ballot, so as to protect the privacy of the vote and thus shield members from undue pressure.

Although it is generally accepted that the rationale for secret ballots remains persuasive, there is nevertheless a vein of questioning and criticism. It is true that the pressure on countries to commit their votes in advance does not sit easily with the principle of secret balloting. And the degree to which these advance commitments are reneged on has led to calls for open voting as a guarantee of honesty.

Whatever the problems, I do not anticipate - nor would I advocate - any move away from the principle of secret ballots. The membership in general, and small states in particular, would find it extremely difficult to withstand the ratcheting up of pressure that would accompany open voting.

A further point relates to what has become known as "short voting". It is generally expected that a country will make full use of its ballot: for example, if there are three vacancies, that votes will be cast for three candidates. This is seen as responsible voting, trying to shape the best possible overall composition and performance of UN bodies. Unhappily, a practice of short voting - voting, say, for one or two candidates when there are three vacancies - has begun to creep in.

It may occasionally happen that an electoral slate is such that filling all vacancies would involve voting for a country that we would regard as a pariah, whose election would undermine the body on which it seeks to serve. Far more often, however, short voting is manipulative rather than principled, designed to further increase the weight of a vote for a single candidate.

Short voting was a significant factor in the 2010 Security Council election and it was disappointing to see it re-emerge in the HRC election last November. From our analysis of the HRC election results, it was clear that there were forty "missing" votes on the WEOG slate — meaning that 20 countries voted for only one candidate or 40 countries for two candidates, or something in between. The pariah state argument clearly could not have been applicable in this case. Instead, what we saw was one or more of the candidates pressurising their friends not to exercise all of their votes or, possibly, countries of their own accord feeling they owed this to their friends. Either way, we found it regrettable and very much hope the practice will not develop.

Resources

Anyone exposed to election financing, particularly here in the US, knows what a crucial role resources play. From my exposure to Ireland's Security Council election in 2000, I knew how tough the contest was, involving a significant commitment of financial and personnel resources. But the intervening years had certainly seen the stakes mount higher.

One example: in both 2010 and 2012, each of the WEOG contestants hosted large numbers of New York - based Permanent Representatives on visits to their respective capitals. This was not tourism: each visit involved seminars on relevant topics, as well as giving the PRs a deeper sense of the priorities and perspectives of the various candidates. But the fact that such visits were becoming *de rigueur* for contestants was bound to drive up campaign costs.

Ireland's budget for our Security Council campaign in 2000 was around €1.5 million to cover all salary, travel, and entertainment costs. Last year, the Australian authorities publicly stated that the Australian budget was $25 million. While this was undoubtedly at the upper end of the scale, reflecting - at least in part - the higher travel costs to Australia, it gives an indication of the upward trend of expenditure.

In the Eastern European contest for a Security Council seat in 2011, Azerbaijan prevailed over its two rivals, Slovenia and Hungary, in a contest where Slovenia was widely considered to be the frontrunner. While of course no single factor can explain an election outcome, most analysts would accept that Azerbaijan's ability to devote significant financial resources to the campaign was a key ingredient.

Campaign costs for the HRC are also inexorably creeping upwards. But in truth, there is still a long way to go before HRC campaigns reach the level of Security Council campaigns. In our case at least, there was an additional budget of only €10,000 which covered logo design, printing of pamphlets and such like. Although some additional travel was undertaken, which allowed us to avail of lobbying opportunities at international meetings, this was multipurpose travel rather than justified exclusively in lobbying terms.

Given the effort that is now needed to prevail in a contested Security Council election, one might well ask: At what point does the effort required to secure election outweigh perceived benefits? The calculation will obviously differ depending on a country's resources and foreign policy priorities. In broad terms, however, it certainly does not seem that the tipping point has yet been reached. Elected members of the Security Council may voice - in private at least - their disappointment with the experience of membership, and complain about the narrow space which the P5 leave to them. Yet this does not seem to blunt the appetite of other aspirants, nor indeed deter countries from seeking to return to the famous horseshoe table.

And I would suspect that, as far as the Human Rights Council is concerned, given the steadily increasing relevance of that body, the potential is probably there for further intensification of campaign efforts over the coming years.

Even if we baulk at what is now required by way of electoral effort, what is the alternative?

The "clean slate" approach — arrangements among regional groups to put forward the exact number of candidates to match the number of vacancies — is the only practical alternative to competition. Proponents of clean slates point to their efficiency, and would claim that they offer more predictability and perhaps (although this is debatable) a greater degree of fairness in distributing opportunities among members of a regional group. Clean slates can also look more attractive in the aftermath of trauma, as happened in GRULAC following an extraordinarily difficult Security Council election in 2007, when Venezuela and Guatemala were locked in arm to arm combat through 48 rounds of voting before both withdrew in favour of Panama.

Although most of the regional groups use clean slates for some elections, there is considerable controversy surrounding their use when it comes to the most high profile bodies. Clean slates can allow countries of questionable credentials to have a smooth path to membership of key UN bodies. Of course we all value diversity of membership. Neither the Security Council nor the HRC can be a club of saints: if so we would all be debarred. But it is damaging to the Security Council if its members include those who are manifestly not upholders of peace, just as it damages the HRC if egregious violators of human rights are among its elected members. And the reputational cost goes beyond the individual organs, to tarnish the image of the UN as a whole.

There is a further consideration: having to undergo the rigours of a campaign arguably makes us perform better as members. Having to "sell" our candidacies means thinking through our pledges and priorities, engaging our whole system in crafting a campaign platform.

Clean slates therefore are not the answer. But neither can it be desirable that campaign costs are allowed to rise exponentially. If extravagant spending becomes the norm, it follows that those with deep pockets will be advantaged and those with limited resources will be edged out. Within WEOG at least, there has been some debate — so far inconclusive — about developing codes of conduct in order to regulate campaign expenditure. We need to get serious about that discussion.

In trying to assess what dictates a campaign outcome, my title suggests: power, influence, reputation. These of course shade into each other and compartmentalisation is to a degree artificial. And neither do they tell the full story — as in all good stories, the human factor is always present: relationships, trust, even betrayal.

Power

Power and influence are indeed bedfellows — power involves a capacity to wield influence. But there is a difference. Power implies a demonstration of strength, a flexing of muscle — the creation of a belief that there will be consequences if support is withheld. Influence relies more on a capacity to persuade. Power speaks with a loud voice; influence adopts a softer tone.

I am a practitioner rather than a theoretician and am generally reticent about quoting scholars. But I make an exception for the great political scientist Joseph Nye. I find his distinction between hard power and soft power particularly apt. He writes: "this soft power — getting others to want the outcomes that you want — co-opts people rather than coerces them. Soft power rests on the ability to shape the preferences of others." A good distinction, in my view, between what I have termed power and influence.

Assessing power at the UN brings us squarely to a discussion of the respective roles of large and small states. The tension or balance between large and small — between the sovereign equality of all countries in the General Assembley and the pragmatic recognition of a hierarchy based on size and economic weight — has always played out in the UN.

"The rich are different", as Scott Fitzgerald is supposed to have said. Well, large countries have always been different. And they seem to be becoming more different.

Over recent years, one detects an increasingly pronounced sense of entitlement on the part of large states. This is manifest in various ways: they tend to present their candidacies more frequently across a range of bodies, and to seek re-election after relatively short absences. In Security Council elections, for example, small countries typically announce their candidacies very many years in advance; there is an emerging pattern - evident across regional groups - of large countries "crashing" slates at late dates. In the Human Rights Council too, a habit is taking hold of large states seeking two consecutive terms, followed by the minimum prescribed one year absence before campaigning to return.

When it comes to seeking votes, large countries have more instruments at their disposal than small states. They have a more extensive Embassy network, a weightier economic and political presence. It makes sense, therefore, for large countries to do most of their campaigning in capitals, where Foreign Ministries will be keenly conscious of the cost-benefit analysis of saying yes or no to a powerful country.

Small states, by contrast, are somewhat more New York focused - not that the power calculus does not apply in NY, but its effects are mediated and softened by the professional and personal relationships that govern interactions here.

During the Human Rights Council campaign, Ireland lobbied extensively and effectively in capitals. Throughout, however, we were very conscious that our Embassy network is far smaller than any of our four rivals. There is clearly no contest when it comes to a comparison with the US or Germany, but both Sweden and Greece are also well ahead of us in the Embassy count.

At a rather fraught moment in the campaign, I vividly recall the Ambassador of an African country telling me of a large competitor: "they are squeezing the hell out of us in capital." One had the sense of a juggernaut beating down... we had to hope that the degree of pressure being exerted would not overturn the firm prior commitment we had received from the country in question.

Squeezing is not, generally speaking, an option for small countries. But, even if we lack the squeezing muscles, we do have a degree of power that comes through our collective strength. Small countries account for the majority of UN members. The Forum of Small States, whose criterion for membership is a population of less than 10 million, has 105 members. If we came anywhere close to voting as a bloc, we could certainly change outcomes. And small state solidarity does work sometimes. It was undoubtedly a factor in helping Portugal onto the Security Council in 2010 and Luxembourg in 2012.

But for Ireland, as for others, there is no automatic reflex of support for small states. We recognise that small states, like large ones, inhabit different places along the policy spectrum and their suitability for election to particular bodies needs to be assessed on a case by case basis.

Nevertheless, what we do hold to strongly is a view that small states have a right to an equitable share of places on key bodies. It was an argument we made forcefully during our Security Council campaign in 2000 and again in our Human Rights Council campaign last year. And it is always a consideration we bring to bear ourselves in weighing how to allocate our own votes.

In so far as the electoral ambitions of large states grow, the space for small states risks being eroded. Partly in reaction to this, a heightened "small state consciousness" is beginning to emerge.

Last year was the 20th anniversary of the Forum of Small States, and it was marked by a major conference at which the Tánaiste, Eamon Gilmore, was among those who played a prominent role. A study on small state potential, initiated by New Zealand, is currently under way. It will be interesting to see where it leads us, and Ireland will certainly be a very engaged participant.

Before leaving the subject of large and small states, let me open a parenthesis.

As we consider large and powerful states, the US is *sui generis*. Even in our multipolar world, the US still occupies a special place. It is hardly surprising, therefore, that it has special issues and sensitivities when standing for election. If a country's identity and self-image is that of the "indispensable nation" then the idea of electoral defeat - carrying as it does other countries' verdict as to your dispensability - is particularly difficult to countenance.

As a P5 member, the US of course is spared the exposure to Security Council elections. It has approached Human Rights Council elections with a degree of caution - over a decade later, the shock defeat of the US in the 2001 elections to the predecessor body, the Human Rights Commission, has still not entirely faded.

The distinctiveness of the US position is apparent not just in how it campaigns but in the electoral arguments it employs. In last year's HRC campaign, it was notable that the rationale put forward by the US for election was different from all other candidates. Its essential claim was that the HRC without the US would be a very much weaker body: that US membership is required to assure the weight and relevance of key UN bodies. Many of us who were genuinely sympathetic to this point would be happy to see the same logic applied elsewhere — for example, to help persuade the US to accept the jurisdiction of the International Criminal Court.

Influence

Influence, as I suggested earlier, means ensuring that countries are sufficiently attracted to your candidacy to choose to vote for you: making other countries want what you want for yourself.

Attraction can have quite a complex chemistry, but it is essentially built on liking and respect. Neither of these sentiments can be switched on in the course of a campaign; both are normally built up over time.

Respect and liking are closely linked to reputation, which I will consider in a moment. But reputation is more the backdrop against which the contest plays out. Respect and liking are foreground factors, built on the contemporary day to day engagement with fellow member states.

Respect has to be won and sustained every day at the UN. It comes from policy engagement and visibility across the range of UN work. This is neither abstract nor hard to measure: all of us have a keen sense of which delegations bring greater or lesser added value. Ireland works hard to be positively rated in this regard. Week in and week out, we seek to ensure that our voice is heard and our input made in debates, in committee work, as co-facilitators or chairs of various processes.

And how can we define 'liking'? Each of our countries, in all sorts of ways, projects a personality at the UN. What helps to define that personality is how we articulate policy, how we connect to others. Much of that projection is done by our political leaders, as they engage with their counterparts at high level UN meetings (particularly in the series of bilateral encounters - what we colloquially refer to as "speed dating" sessions - that occur in the margins of the UN Ministerial week in September) and in other bilateral engagements. And the Permanent Representatives, in their daily interactions within the UN "village", also play an important part.

Human beings are no different at the UN than elsewhere. We are all attracted to people who can listen as well as talk. We respect, indeed require, principle and backbone, but we do not want to be patronised or preached at. We are better disposed and more receptive towards colleagues who have built a relationship with us over time, than to those who seek us out when they want something from us.

And so at the UN personal relationships, built on social interaction, really matter. One can be somewhat cynical about it. The late Richard Holbrooke, a former US Ambassador to the UN, commented that the UN runs on food "Boy, do these guys know how to eat!" But, at a dinner with fellow Ambassadors a few weeks back, I was struck when a departing PR colleague spoke of the "treasures of the heart" she would take with her. I know I will feel the same when I leave New York in a few months' time.

For us diplomats, even more so than in most other walks of life, the personal and the professional are intertwined. We are itinerants who build our lives afresh every few years, and we find connection and friendship with colleagues who are living a similar experience. These relationships can indeed have a read across to voting: where there is discretion or leeway allowed by capitals, which is the case for some Missions and for some votes, colleagues will naturally tend to remember their friends. But, I re-emphasise, our relationships are not just transactional; most of us will develop truly meaningful ties that, in some cases, will endure well beyond a posting.

In measuring the impact of attraction, there is of course the complicating factor of reciprocals: the trade which says "I will vote for you at this election in exchange for your vote for me at an earlier or later election." The theory and practice of reciprocals probably deserve a whole lecture by themselves.The US is large and powerful enough to do without them. For the rest of us, reciprocals are a necessary fact of electoral life.

At their best, reciprocals can still fit within the "attraction" model - arrangements based on friendship between countries and a recognition of respective merits, rather than a crude exchange of votes. Certainly for Ireland, as I believe for most other countries, we apply qualitative criteria before entering any reciprocal arrangements.

And whatever one's view of reciprocals, there is a critically important point: no matter how many reciprocals are stacked up, advance commitments will never guarantee outcomes.

Here I come to this difficult matter of "betrayal" that I alluded to earlier. I was referring to the gap between promises and delivery: between voting commitments and actual outturn on the day. "Betrayal" is an ugly word. There is quite a lexicon that has developed to describe this delivery gap: it is politely referred to as "slippage" or the "discount factor", less politely as the "lie factor". However one chooses to describe it, this gap is becoming progressively wider. It used to be that a discount factor of 10/15% was standard; now it can be well over double that.

Far too often over the past few years, I have seen Permanent Representatives and their delegations in shock as election results were read out - it goes beyond the disappointment of defeat; it is the difficulty in human terms of seeing commitments you count on, from colleagues you believe in, simply fail to materialise on the day. Especially given the kind of relationships among colleagues that I described earlier, the letdown is bound to feel personal as well as professional.

Apart from decrying what is happening, we need to try to understand it. Countries can renege on earlier commitments for a whole range of reasons. It may be attributable to poor administrative arrangements, with earlier voting commitments lost sight of, or poor transmission between capitals and New York. There can also be cultural inhibitions about saying "no", leading to a negative being so courteously phrased that it may be misinterpreted as a positive. At its most cynical, a vote can be treated as a bargaining commodity to be maximised in as many quarters as possible.

Fortunately for Ireland, the discount factor in our case has always been well down at the lower end of the scale. This was true in the Security Council election of 2000 and it was certainly a decisive factor in the Human Rights Council election in November. As we heard subsequently of the slippage experienced by some of our competitors in that election, we had reason to be grateful for the level of loyalty shown to us.

But even if nationally we have been spared disappointment, the phenomenon clearly is highly regrettable, especially in an organisation such as the UN which should be a touchstone of integrity. Whatever the cause, it is corrosive of relationships between delegations. It will be almost impossible to eliminate entirely as long as there is secret balloting. But we need to work to try to change the culture - to develop a greater collective recognition of how our Organisation is being devalued.

Before leaving this heading of 'influence', I would like to touch briefly on two further points.

Firstly, it is worth noting that the attraction factor can be affected positively or negatively by group membership. After some recent electoral setbacks, the Nordic Group for example, has been analysing its collective "brand". The EU also has some soul searching to do. Because, even if it might seem counterintuitive, it would appear that EU membership is on the way to becoming more of a hindrance than a help in a difficult campaign. Despite the Union's immense financial and policy contribution at the UN, its messages can often encounter resistance and its operating mechanisms are not a natural fit in the intergovernmental structure.

Ireland is in a particularly interesting position in this regard. Time and again, across the UN membership, our distinct identity is acknowledged. When a diplomat colleague described us recently as "EU, but with an Irish voice", it was clear that it was the Irishness that he was drawn to. I think there is a lesson for us here: consistent with being a loyal and fully committed EU member, we need to retain our distinctively Irish voice which has such a resonance.

A second point relates to the interaction between power and influence. We can point to instances where one of the other seemed more effective, but there is no doubt that, when they operate in tandem, the combination is fairly unbeatable.

Many observers were surprised that the US - which, after all, carries considerable baggage at the UN - should have topped the poll in the HRC election. What accounted for this? Muscle exercised in capital may have got the commitments, but could not be guaranteed to bring out the vote.

There was clearly an element of attraction. It must be recalled that the election took place in the immediate aftermath of President Obama's re-election; this is a President whose belief in multilateralism has always won him friends at the UN. And Secretary of State Clinton - known and popular in capitals worldwide, having indeed visited very many of them - made a number of telephone calls in the crucial final days. I would suggest that what we saw in this poll-topping performance was a demonstration of both power and influence, reinforcing each other.

Reputation

As for an individual, a state's most precious asset is its reputation. Many of us will remember the quote from Shakespeare: "I have lost my reputation! I have lost the immortal part of myself". Reputation is a country's brand or currency — the set of values and images that come to mind when a country's name is invoked.

And of course reputation counts electorally. In national politics, we as voters will very often not study the detail of the policy manifesto. We vote because someone's name speaks to us in a certain way, conjures up something for us. We gravitate towards a candidate based on a general sense of track record and trustworthiness. Even among a sophisticated and well-informed international electorate, the same phenomenon applies.

Today's world is not compartmentalised and the same events and headlines help to shape all our thinking. But to some degree, reputation can still be context-specific. Viewed through an EU prism for example, Germany and Greece conjure up very different images and weightings. But, going into the Human Rights Council election, it was by no means evident that this would be reflected in the outcome. And, while there was likely some impact, I do not believe that the results were shaped in a direct or decisive way by the drama being played out on the EU stage.

In Ireland's case, the headline stories internationally over the past few years have been of our economic difficulties, the bank crisis, and now the beginning of our comeback. If, like Icarus, we fell to earth, we are now — more prudently this time — getting ready to take to the air again.

And yet, even during the worst of these times, our reputation at the UN was not dented. This of course is a matter of satisfaction and pride to me as Irish Ambassador. But, from a more detached analytical viewpoint, I find it interesting to consider what it is that has so sustained our reputation and proofed it against setback. We undoubtedly continue to benefit from the towering achievements of earlier generations of Irish political leaders and diplomats at the UN. But it goes beyond that.

The empathy factor is very important. Throughout all my years at the UN, I have been struck by how Ireland's history still resonates. The Irish story influenced and inspired so many countries emerging from colonisation decades in our wake. Our history - of suffering, of resilience, of determination - chimes with that of so many others. And, when we speak of Ireland's empathy with the developing world, it is not a fuzzy concept invoking a distant past; it is buttressed by today's reality.

The sustained commitment of the Irish Government and people to development aid certainly does not go unnoticed. Throughout the current period of austerity, despite all the domestic cutbacks, our levels of Official Development Assistance have remained largely intact. The aid statistics speak for themselves: compared, for example, with our two largest rivals in the HRC election campaign, Ireland allocates 0.51% of GNP to ODA; Germany 0.39%, and the US 0.2%.

There is another factor I should mention, especially in this Fordham setting. Irish diplomats are the legatees and beneficiaries of the work done by Irish missionaries in so many countries of the world. Time and again, I have met Ambassadors — from Africa, Asia, Latin America — who recalled with affection and gratitude how Irish educators had set them on their way.

Indeed, in the course of the HRC campaign, after we had encountered a decision-maker from a small African country who fondly recalled the Irish nun who had taken him in hand in his kindergarten years, we began to refer in shorthand to the "Sister Scholastica vote".

Conclusion

As I conclude, let me emphasise that I have not tried to define any iron laws of election - I do not believe that they exist; we operate in a shifting environment where different factors will combine in different ways at different times. Nor have I been in any way exhaustive: that I leave for more academic study. My purpose has been to offer some reflections based on personal experience at the coal face.

And if I have described electoral contests in gladiatorial terms at times this evening, it is certainly not to take away from their underlying seriousness. Elections matter because the UN matters.

Those who sit on key UN bodies shape the decisions of those bodies. Members of the Security Council deliberate war and peace; members of the Human Rights Council will shine a light into the world's darkest corners.

And of course elections matter for candidates. Any country with a serious foreign policy wants to be a player rather than a spectator, to leave a policy imprint, to help realise objectives we hold dear.

For us in Ireland, so deeply marked by our history, elections have a special resonance. There is scarcely an Irish woman or Irish man who at some level has not absorbed Robert Emmett's dream of Ireland "taking its place among the nations of the earth." The UN is the world's theatre: the Parliament of Man. An election validates our position there. It is the recognition by our peers of what we contribute. It is an affirmation that Ireland continues to earn its place among the nations of the world.

And that is why, when an Irish victory is announced in an important UN election, it is a moment of such joy. The hall is thronged with the unseen presence of those who have gone before. We feel the pride and the privilege, and renew our determination to be worthy of the trust placed in us.

WRESTLING WITH THE CELTIC TIGER

This is the most ruthlessly culled section in the collection. Initially, I had envisaged a rather different chapter, one that would focus on projecting the Irish economy abroad. Like all Irish diplomats, this was an aspect of my role that I took very seriously and it occupied a high proportion of my time. There is a sizeable stack of speeches that I delivered in French and US settings - speeches that presented the strength of our economy, extolled the benefits of Ireland as a location for Foreign Direct Investment (FDI), and underlined the mutuality of economic interest that linked our respective countries.

Particularly during the Washington years, I travelled extensively: opening Irish-owned ventures, visiting the headquarters of US-based companies with a presence in Ireland, addressing a range of business bodies around the country. I looked through a range of speeches I delivered on these occasions, and recalled the considerable input of time and effort by myself and often by Embassy and Consulate colleagues. I like to think the speeches were effective; I tried consistently to go beyond a simple selling job, and to inject context and analysis that would engage the particular audience. Nevertheless, as I re-read them, they felt very much of their time and place and I doubted they would be of much interest at this remove.

I am including, however, one speech that was a little out of the ordinary run - an address I delivered in Paris in June 2009 where I stood back a little to look at the economic collapse of 2008 and some of its reverberations. The occasion was a colloquium on "Unethical Business Practices", a joint venture between University College Cork and business schools in Paris and Bucharest. The speech came almost at the end of my Paris posting and provided an opportunity to reflect on French views of the "Anglo-Saxon" model, the crisis of capitalism and issues of individual responsibility. The question I asked then - "how did we allow a deviant and dumbed-down version of capitalism to take such hold?" - is now, eleven years later, more urgent than ever.

Just one other speech survived my cull for this chapter. It was 2014, and the Irish economy was firmly back on its feet after the grim experience of 2008-2013. I was invited to be a panelist at a conference in the Wilson Center, a leading think-tank in Washington DC, and was asked to speak to the title: "Ireland: the Celtic Tiger Reborn". This is a less reflective speech than the Paris one - partly because I had time constraints as a panelist but also because I was more in "selling" mode. We were all pitching hard the "Ireland is Back" message and there wasn't much scope for self-doubt or pondering the bigger philosophical questions. But at least I did include some acknowledgment of the challenges and declare a definitive end to the hubris of the Celtic Tiger years!

Conference on Unethical Business Practices
ISC Business School, Paris
18th June 2009

It is a privilege to address this Conference jointly organised by the ISC Business School Paris together with University College Cork and the Bucharest Academy of Economic Studies.

I am interested to participate for three reasons. Firstly, I believe deeply in these initiatives which gather student groups from different EU member states and bring to bear their varying perspectives on themes of common interest. Secondly, the three countries represented here all have a particular resonance for me. Ireland of course is my own country and France my country of accreditation. My interest in Romania dates from my time as Permanent Representative in Brussels: it was during the Irish Presidency of the EU in 2004 that decisive steps were taken towards the accession of Romania and Bulgaria. Thirdly, the theme you have chosen for today's conference could hardly be more relevant, in the midst of the current global economic crisis which is largely rooted in the erosion of ethics in the business world.

I propose to divide my address into three parts. To begin, some comments about the Irish economy. Then a word about the French and Irish economic models - leaving it to our Romanian friends to adjudicate between the two! And finally some comments about the current ethical crisis.

Irish Economy

In the midst of the global crisis which has left no European country untouched, the Irish economy appears to have attracted a disproportionate amount of attention. This is no doubt because our reversal of fortunes has been so dramatic. The Celtic Tiger years had made us the envy of Europe, with double digit growth figures annually at the height of the boom. This year, the predictions are for a slowdown by as much as 8% in our GDP. The turn around is obvious.

The Irish storyline can be made to seem a simple one: Icarus, who flew too near the sun, has fallen to earth. In other words, we are paying the price of excessive self-belief and excessive risk-taking. As always, the real story is more complicated. It is indeed obvious with hindsight that there were some mistaken domestic policy decisions; in particular, the economy was allowed to become too dependent on house building and property prices escalated dramatically. With wage and other cost increases, our competitiveness was eroded.

But perhaps our biggest problem is that as a small, open economy, we are particularly vulnerable in a time of global downturn. We were agile enough to ride the wave of a booming international economy, and it is hardly surprising we are suffering when the tide recedes. It is an inescapable fact that small countries have small domestic markets. Our population base is 4 million compared to France's 64 million or Romania's 22 million. Exports are our lifeblood; when our key markets are in difficulty, the effects are felt upstream. I am conscious that both Romania and France are also facing a serious export challenge, and would in no way minimise your problems, but the relative size of your domestic markets may offer a somewhat greater degree of protection.

Although the Irish economy faces significant challenges across a range of fronts, it is important to point out the strengths that remain and that hopefully will provide the basis for recovery. I might identify a few of these strengths.

As all Eurozone members have discovered - and as some of those outside the Eurozone have discovered to their cost - membership of a common currency provides invaluable support and stability. Crucially, flows of foreign investment, which have underpinned our economy for decades past, continue to hold up. And, less easy to quantify but absolutely real in its economic significance, the optimism and ambition of the younger generation of Irish people - as measured by recent polls - remains largely intact.

I do not make this latter point because I am speaking to a student body; I am absolutely convinced of it. It is our young and well-educated population, and the confidence and "can do" attitude of the young Irish, that hold the key to our recovery.

With the government taking determined action to restore competitiveness, and to get our banks back on a solid footing, there are grounds to hope that recovery may begin as early as 2011. This is not merely wishful thinking, but projections shared by respected independent bodies such as the Economic and Social Research Institute, and articulated by the Governor of the Central Bank in recent days. A leaner, more competitive, Irish economy is expected to emerge from this crisis. We will have learned lessons, and paid a high price in human terms. But I hope the resilience that we have so often demonstrated in the past will stand to us again.

Different Economic Models

At this point, I would offer a reflection as I near the end of my four year term in France. Throughout these four years, I have found myself regularly in discussion with French policy makers and members of the French public about different economic models. As a Celtic country, with our distinctive history, we are never comfortable about having the "Anglo-Saxon" label attached. But, as a kind of shorthand, that has become a widely used label for a low-tax, flexible, fairly lightly regulated economy.

There have been two phases during my time here. In the earlier years of my posting, my interlocutors tended to be either strong admirers of the Anglo-Saxon model as they understood it, and impatient for France to shake off its more strait-jacketing, statist approach, or - in the other camp - critics who felt that the Anglo-Saxon model was the apotheosis of an unregulated, free-wheeling, soulless capitalism that had little to offer France. In recent months, not surprisingly, sentiment here has shifted towards the latter view: the predominant feeling has been relief that the higher degree of regulation in the French system has left this country somewhat less exposed in the global storm.

In each phase, I have found myself seeking to qualify somewhat the views of my interlocutors. In the first phase, both to admirers and detractors, I tried to offer some corrective to their understanding of Anglo-Saxon capitalism, at least as practised in Ireland. More flexible, less bureaucratic, more lightly taxed, yes; but it never was the kind of free-wheeling jungle capitalism that some have seemed to imagine. Social partnership, for example, was key to the successes of the Celtic Tiger years. And trade union membership in Ireland is significantly higher in percentage terms than it is in France.

In recent months, I have listened carefully to those who feel vindicated in their criticisms of the Anglo-Saxon model. They were of course to some degree right, and were prescient in their warnings about the risks of lighter regulation and the generally more facilitative and enabling climate of Anglo-Saxon type economies. We have learned from this crisis, and I would note that Ireland is now broadly supportive of the De La Rosière report and its recommendations for action at EU level in a way that we probably would not have been previously.

At the same time, I have suggested to some of my interlocutors that they should not draw the wrong lesson. When the recovery comes, as it will, the entrepreneurial economies - sobered and disciplined as they will have been by the crisis, but still recognisably entrepreneurial - will be best positioned to benefit. To imagine that we are now seeing a justification for a large-scale and long-term return of the State would seem to me to be misreading the direction of history.

The Ethical Crisis

As is obvious to everyone on the planet, the global financial system is in crisis. As we look around us at the wreckage, the question being asked over and over again is how we allowed the system become so dysfunctional. With hindsight, the warning signs seem so obvious: the dizzying growth in the scale and profitability of the financial sector, emergence of a shadow banking system, frenetic financial innovation to the point where hardly anyone seems to have understood the extraordinarily complicated new products emerging, ballooning household debt, growing global macroeconomic unbalances, bubbles in asset prices.

Among so many who have lost so much, there is real anger that those who were seen as the custodians of the system - bankers, regulators, and to some degree governments - failed in their responsibilities. Particular wrath is directed against the reward system in the financial sector, where vast bonuses were paid for what was portrayed as exceptional performance but in retrospect looks like short-termism, excessive risk-taking, and arrogant disregard for true shareholder interest.

Amid calls for a new capitalism, it is salutary to remind ourselves of what really happened: that capitalism as originally conceived lost its way. I recently read an interesting article by the Nobel Prize-winning economist Amartya Sen: "Adam Smith's Market Never Stood Alone". Sen's basic argument is that the market economy we allowed to develop in no way did justice to its founding father. He draws attention to Adam Smith's first book *The Theory of Moral Sentiments,* published exactly 250 years ago, where Smith extensively investigated the powerful role of non-profit values. While stating that "prudence" was "of all virtues that which is most helpful to the individual", Smith maintained that "humanity, justice, generosity, and public spirit, are the qualities most helpful to others".

As we contemplate the wreckage of the global financial system, we need to ask ourselves how the values of prudence, humanity and justice lost out to a belief that "greed is good". How did we allow a deviant and dumbed-down version of capitalism take such hold?

Much ink is being and will be spilled on this question and I am certainly not qualified to give anything like a comprehensive answer. But I would like to focus for a moment on what seems to me one element of the problem: the phenomenon of "group think" that has operated at so many levels in our societies. I think it especially worthwhile to highlight this issue in a seminar that brings together three educational institutions because, in my view, the answer and the antidote must come fundamentally from within the educational system.

Moral Compass

When we look at the more unsavoury side of human behaviour, there is a spectrum from the less-than-admirable to the actively corrupt. Bracketing out for a moment that corrupt element, we might look at what is less than ethical shading into what is borderline illegal. Gordon Brown spoke some days ago, in the context of the UK political scandal about Parliamentary expenses, of "behaviour that offends my Presbyterian conscience". Quite apart from any view one may have about Prime Minister Brown, or about the expenses controversy in Britain, I think his phrase is quite a good way of categorising behaviour that is questionable if not illegal.

I have little doubt that the vast majority of those in the business world whose behaviour would "offend a Presbyterian conscience" are not bad people. Indeed, many of them were icons in the financial world of yesterday. Their actions didn't strike them as wrong: they were simply doing what their peers were doing. Their individual moral compasses just weren't working any more. "If everyone is doing it, I would be a fool not to join the party."

And indeed the same "group think" affected consumers. In many cases, people who engaged in perfectly responsible financial behaviour were simply let down by those who should have been safeguarding their interests. But it is not always the explanation. In accumulating unsustainable household debt, in gambling on property prices only ever going up, in excessive risk taking, people often seemed to be doing it out of herd instinct: "everyone's doing it and I wouldn't want to miss out".

As I said, it is the business of our educational systems to try to proof us, at least to some degree, against such herd instinct and group think. Of course, we need laws and codes and penalties to regulate the business and financial world. But there will always be grey areas along that spectrum between what is less than admirable and what is actually illegal. There will always be ingenuity in devising new schemes to enhance individual and company profit.

I strongly believe that our educational system in general, and our business schools in particular, must actively try to build a sense of individual responsibility, an individual moral compass that does not become dysfunctional as readily as seems to have been the case over the past years. Financiers, entrepreneurs, consumers: all of us need a robust ability to ask the right questions, make informed judgements, and resist the herd mentality.

Outside Scrutiny

My final point moves from the level of the individual to a much wider canvas. When it comes to unethical practices and particularly to issues of corruption, I believe that all our societies benefit from receiving rigorous scrutiny from independent outside bodies and from being held to international standards. This is certainly not to substitute for vigilance and action at domestic level, but to recognise that the outside mirror will often show up a more honest if less flattering picture.

This kind of scrutiny tends not to be very comfortable. In the case of Ireland, for example we were jolted somewhat by a quite critical OECD review in 2007 of our implementation of the organisation's Anti-Bribery Convention, which outlaws the bribery of foreign public officials, and which we had enacted into Irish law in 2001. But the jolt prompted reform of anti-corruption law in Ireland and the launch of the Government's anti-corruption website.

To take another example, I am sure that the EU's scrutiny of the measures in place in Romania to counteract corruption must sometimes seem onerous. I understand that Romania has been given various benchmarks, particularly in the area of judicial reform, and that the next Cooperation and Verification Report is due out next month. But onerous as it may seem, the reality is that this kind of active surveillance, and putting in place the supports for improved performance, is not only important from an EU viewpoint but can only be good for Romania.

Organisations like Transparency International also do an excellent job and I am sure that all of us take careful note of their periodic reports and rankings. In their last report, the Corruption Perception Index 2008, out of 180 countries surveyed, Ireland ranked alongside the UK as the 16th least corrupt country, France was joint 23rd, and Romania joint 70th. However one may quibble with the detail, or question some of the yardsticks, a report like this shows that none of us has grounds for complacency. It is worth noting that the three Nordic members of the Union scored extremely well - with Denmark and Sweden joint first and Finland fifth. I have no doubt that concerned citizens in each of our countries would want us to emulate the Nordics in this regard.

My main point, however, is not to focus on the individual ratings but to underline the importance of the outside eye. As EU members, we look first and foremost to Brussels. But whether it be the EU, the OECD, the UN, or NGOs, the scrutiny is necessary and valuable. Apart from anything more venal, there are always forces of inertia at work within our societies. We need the monitoring, the health check, from outside to see how we are measuring up and to monitor progress made.

Conclusion

In concluding, let me say that I will be very interested to hear the results of your discussions over the next couple of days. The range of topics you are addressing is impressive, and sufficiently precise to yield quite concrete results. I hope you will be rigorous in your analysis and robust in your conclusions. Society in all our countries can benefit from your deliberations.

Ireland: The Celtic Tiger Reborn?
Panel Discussion, Wilson Center, Washington DC
16th December 2014

Let me get one point out of the way at the beginning. None of us in Ireland retains the slightest nostalgia for the term "Celtic Tiger". The tiger, I might remind you, is not an animal that is native to Ireland. "Celtic Tiger" was a catchy term to describe how the Asian economic miracle seemed to be replicated in Ireland. But it turns out that, in the long term, animals don't flourish so well out of their natural habitat.

So yes, we're once again seeing tremendous strength and energy and vitality in the Irish economy. If we must name it after some animal, we might run a competition to find the most appropriate one. But let the Celtic tiger rest in peace - or perhaps, in the Buddhist tradition, it can be reborn as another animal. Maybe, given our equine tradition, it can return as an Irish thoroughbred or something along those lines!

But let's not get bogged down in semantics. The real question for our panel discussion is this: is the recovery underway in Ireland genuine and sustainable?

Our belief is yes; it is both genuine and sustainable - assuming we continue to take the right policy decisions and avoid the risks that are undoubtedly there.

I know this is an economically literate audience. And so I don't want to rely on assertion of belief, or expressions of optimism. I'd like to take you through some of the statistics and the factual elements that underpin that belief.

Snapshot of the Economy
First, let me rehearse the growth forecasts for our GDP this year. There is broad convergence among the various forecasts. Our

Department of Finance is predicting 4.7% growth; the EU Commission 4.6%; and the OECD 4.3%. The IMF prediction from October is lagging slightly behind at 3.6%. But you get the general, very upbeat, picture. And let me put this figure in a wider European context. The latest OECD forecasts are 0.8% growth for the Euro area as a whole, 1.5% for Germany, 3% for the UK. So, by a considerable margin, we are expected to be the fastest growing economy in Europe.

Projecting forward over the next couple of years, the growth predictions remain very reassuring - again there is a convergence: our own Department of Finance, the EU Commission, and the OECD are all predicting that Ireland's GDP growth will be in excess of 3% both in 2015 and 2016.

A couple of other statistics related to our public finances. We remain on course to bring our deficit below 4% this year and below 3% in 2015, as required by EU rules. And while our debt to GDP ratio is still too high, the trajectory is certainly in the right direction - debt peaked at 123% of GDP in 2013; we expect it to decline to 110% of GDP this year and to continue to decline over the period ahead.

One other statistic that I particularly want to highlight is the unemployment figure. This is perhaps the figure that is being most intensively monitored in Ireland, because it is critical to assessing how broad-based the recovery is, and how it is being experienced by the women and men in the street. The current unemployment rate stands at 10.7% - still much too high, but down by 4.4 percentage points since it peak at just over 15% in February 2012. Good quality jobs are being created in significant numbers: over 31,000 new jobs in the year to the second quarter of 2014.

Drivers of Recovery

Assessing the sustainability of our recovery, the obvious question is this: what's driving the recovery: what are the key factors involved and will they continue to act as drivers into the future?

As I am sure you all know, Ireland is a small and very open economy - one of the most globalised economies in the world. So it should come as no surprise that growth in exports and growth in FDI have been hugely important in driving the recovery.

Let's first look at exports. It's no exaggeration to say that Ireland lives by its export performance. With such a small domestic market, we export 80% of everything we produce. That means we have to keep on challenging ourselves: growing our established markets and finding new ones. And we're succeeding in this: total exports from Ireland are currently at an all time high, well ahead of the pre-crisis peak in 2007.

The same is true of FDI: investment in Ireland is powering ahead: 2013 was the best year in a decade and 2014 is looking to be at least as good.

While exports and FDI performance are critical, of course it also matters greatly what's happening at the domestic level. Here too, I'm happy to report good news. There has been a strong surge in investment from domestic sources, and a growth in personal consumption expenditure is supporting a recovery in domestic demand.

Good as it is, what gives us confidence that all this is sustainable? I would adduce three reasons. Firstly, the underlying conditions are conducive to growth. I'm not going to take your time here to recite all the accolades we have won internationally for our pro-business, pro-investment environment. Check out the list on our Embassy website: it speaks for itself. And reinforcing those underlying conditions, I would add that the structural reforms we have made over the past few years should stand us in good stead as we go forward.

Secondly, there is the increase in our competitiveness over the past few years. At the height of the boom, there was a fear we might be pricing ourselves out of the international market. Our labour and other business costs have come down fairly dramatically - at the end of this year, our competitiveness is forecast to have improved 23% since 2008 compared to the Euro area average.

Thirdly, as we approach the end of the year, we have a very good sense of the pipelines and prospects for 2015. The IDA, our inward investment agency, is feeling very upbeat about the 2015 outlook. We offer a very strong package, and investors continue to respond to that.

The same is true of Enterprise Ireland in relation to our export forecasts; they are predicting further increases on this year's record performance.

As a grace note, let me add that our food and drink exports, which have been growing rapidly over the past few years, are set to take another big step forward next year. EU-imposed milk quotas - which have been in place for over 30 years - will finally be lifted, and we can again play to our natural strengths in this area.

On the domestic front, the fall in unemployment, and the recovery in employment, as well as the steps taken by the Government in the budget, should mean a further boost to domestic demand.

For all these reasons, we believe that our confidence in a sustained recovery is very well founded.

And looking to the macro climate for exports in the few years ahead, it is worth flagging to this audience that, if TTIP comes through, Ireland will be a major beneficiary.

Challenges

Of course, I'm not going to airbrush the problems and the challenges. They are undoubtedly there.

Firstly, there are what might be called political and psychological issues. Many of you will have heard of - and perhaps been somewhat surprised by - the marches in the streets of our towns and cities over recent weeks on the subject of water charges. Apart from the specifics of the water charges issue, I think most commentators would say that the level of protest we witnessed tapped into something wider and deeper.

It was our great national poet WB Yeats who said: "Too long a sacrifice can make a stone of the heart." I might adapt that and say that "Too long a sacrifice can test the patience of even the most forbearing". There is no question but that huge sacrifices have been demanded of the Irish people over the past few years. Through a combination of expenditure cuts and additional charges and taxation, there has been a budgetary adjustment of almost $40bn since mid-2008, about 18% of GDP. Of course this has been painful - how could it not be?

At the worst of times, there was a sense that we simply had to get through it and get out the other side. Now that the worst is behind us, the pent-up frustration is being expressed. And the government will want to ensure that this is heard, and channelled, and responded to.

Apart from these political challenges, the economic issues are there. Perhaps the biggest point of vulnerability is the debt overhang. As I said, the debt level is coming down but it's still very high, especially in a very low inflation context. As the economy gets back on its feet again, the government will continue to face tough choices on how to allocate the fruits of the recovery: how to prioritise between on the one hand bringing a measure of relief from the most painful effects of austerity, and on the other hand, paying down our debt.

Thirdly, since these are the drivers of growth, we will need to keep growing our exports and also keep our foreign direct investment levels as healthy as they are. There are both internal and external factors involved here.

We obviously need to stay competitive - we can't afford to give up the competitiveness gains we made over the past few years. There are other factors we can't easily control. The current weakness in the Eurozone is worrying for us all. Because the Irish economy has such deep connections to both the US and the UK markets, and both of these economies are doing pretty well, we are relatively shielded. But of course, we are in no way inured to Eurozone difficulties - we are members of a shared currency and also, as we deliberately diversified over the years, Eurozone countries account for an increasing share of our exports.

We also know that the climate for attracting FDI is becoming increasingly competitive. The moment we become complacent, we're going to fall behind. So we have to ensure that every element of our FDI package remains "best in class". Our talent has to stay great; our tax offer has to remain compelling. In this regard, our Minister for Finance has repeatedly said: "We play fair but we play to win." This means that our corporate tax rate of 12.5% will remain unchanged, while at the same time we will continue to involve ourselves fully in the OECD BEPS work to ensure fairness and transparency in international rules.

So: to sum up. The Irish economy has shown its resilience. We are back on our feet again. We have sound, evidence-based, reasons for our optimism regarding the period ahead.

No more of the hubris of the Celtic Tiger. We should perhaps allow ourselves a degree of legitimate pride in our resilience - we have prevailed, come through, and shown our strengths. But there is not the slightest reason for complacency. We need to be focused, purposeful, tempered by our experience. We can't let the hard-earned lessons of the last few years go to waste.

CREDITING CULTURE

To be an Irish diplomat is to have a career-long engagement with culture. Early in diplomatic life, you discover that culture is one of our most valuable assets and you find yourself drawing on that asset over and over again. You grow accustomed to, and eventually grow into, a variety of roles: impresario, front-of-house presenter, party giver.

There is the hard-headed professional case for showcasing our culture. But alongside and beyond that, there is the private exhilaration that many of us feel - the privilege of meeting and spending time with cultural figures we have always lionised. Introducing Irish cultural icons to foreign audiences requires re-immersion in their work; that re-immersion greatly enriches our own lives and reconnects us to the truth and beauty that is at the heart of the work.

The engagement with Irish culture is a feature of every post, including the multilateral ones. I recall some wonderful Bloomsday evenings at the residence in Geneva, with Latin American colleagues in particular demonstrating their fluency across the range of Joyce's work. In Brussels, we kicked off our 2004 EU Presidency with a superb concert, and Irish singers and musicians held a huge theatre spellbound. Years later in New York, as we sought a seat for Ireland on the Human Rights Council, events to showcase Irish culture were woven into our campaign.

But it is in the bilateral posts - in my case in France and in the US - that the partnership with the cultural community really blossoms. My first public engagement as Ambassador in Paris was at the Irish Cultural College, and that began an immensely fruitful four-year relationship. My time in Washington coincided with the centenary of the 1916 Rising; the centrepiece of our celebrations was a three-week-long cultural festival at the Kennedy Center.

I have chosen for inclusion in this section a small selection of the speeches from the Paris and Washington years; a few are particularly vivid in my recollection because of the circumstances in which they were given or whom they celebrate.

The first from the Paris years is a tribute to Brian Friel on the occasion of the festivities organised by the Irish College to coincide with his 80th birthday celebrations. Brian travelled to Paris for the festival and, the day after the opening, I hosted a lunch in his honour for about twenty guests at the Residence. It was one of the happiest occasions I recall in that beautiful, wood-panelled dining room. The sunlight slanted in; Brian - although physically fairly frail - was in fine form, and the conversation flowed like a ribbon of light around the table. Brian wrote a lovely letter of thanks afterwards, with a characteristic blend of modesty and charm.

The circumstances and atmospherics of the Oscar Wilde tribute could hardly have been more evocative. Oscar is buried in that renowned Paris resting-place, the Père Lachaise Cemetery. The sprawling cemetery is invariably full of tourists, snapping pictures of each other posing in front of the tombs. Wilde's tomb is a place of particular pilgrimage, with lipsticked kisses constantly being left and erased.

Merlin Holland, Oscar's grandson, is a serious and likeable person. He is protective of his grandfather being claimed in death by institutions that despised him in life, and averse to hypocritical displays at the graveside. In 2009, to commemorate the hundredth anniversary of Oscar being interred in Père Lachaise (the death took place in 1900 but the remains were moved to Père Lachaise nine years later) he wanted something small and private. So early on a bright July morning, before the cemetery opened to the public, a group of eight or ten of us accompanied Merlin and his wife to the graveside.

In that usually thronged place, we paid our tribute surrounded by silence and birdsong. There was no ban on photos, but we all instinctively kept to an unspoken agreement and our mobile phones stayed in our pockets; the occasion seemed more meaningful and sacred for not being recorded. Merlin spoke first, and I tried to find words to honour Oscar's greatness without making his life less complex than it was.

Afterwards, the group came back to the residence for breakfast. We sat at a small round table in the elegant library, with green carnations as a centrepiece. It was a day or two before I left Paris definitively, bound for my next posting in New York, and I was in a state of heightened emotions. But I know we all felt that quiet graveside experience had been an extraordinary one, and that Oscar's spirit had brushed us.

Four years later I was newly arrived in Washington when the news of Seamus Heaney's death shocked us all. It was astonishing how many people felt bereft, with a real sense of personal loss. I shared that sense, although I had known Seamus only a little, and only over the previous few years.

The circumstances of our introduction stayed with me. For perhaps the only time in my life, I had written out of the blue to someone whom I greatly admired but had never met. It was Spring 2009; I was posted in Paris and on the TGV speeding to the south of France. I had brought along a Saturday edition of the *Irish Times,* and two unrelated articles caught my eye. The first was a major piece on human rights and it carried at the bottom of the page Seamus's poem, "The Republic of Conscience". The second, a couple of pages later, was a review of *Chasing the Flame,* Samantha Power's book on the life and career of Sergio Viera de Mello, the UN High Commissioner for Human Rights who tragically died in

August 2003 when terrorists bombed the UN Headquarters in Iraq.

I was struck by the juxtaposition of these two articles, entirely coincidental. They took me back to my days as Permanent Representative in Geneva. I had come to know Sergio quite well, who then worked in a senior position at the UN Refugee Agency. When he relocated to New York in 1998, I had given him a copy of "Republic of Conscience" (much less well-known than it now is). In his note of thanks, Sergio vowed that in his new role he would live by the principles of the poem.

Reading the two articles these years later, I felt an impulse to get in touch with Seamus and tell him about the coincidence. And so I wrote to him, not really expecting or needing a reply. But he wrote immediately and graciously, describing my letter as "one of the most fortifying" he had ever received. (He also sent an inscribed copy of his Nobel Lecture: "Crediting Poetry", and it is his word - "crediting" - that I have borrowed for the title of this section.)

I subsequently met Seamus a handful of times during the New York years, and encountered that exquisite intelligence and uncommon courtesy. In the weeks after his death, those of us at the Embassy found our own way to pay tribute. Years earlier, Seamus had been invited to plant a tree in the grounds of the Residence, and there was a small plaque at its base. I invited a range of people who would have known or interacted with him to a commemorative ceremony. On a damp October day, with bagpipes in the background, we read from his works and gathered over lunch to tell stories.

The event in the Folger Library came some months later, in April 2014; enough time had passed to focus on Seamus's immense capacity for joy, and to claim that joy as part of his legacy.

Some brief remarks about other speeches in this section. Each year during my Washington posting, I was invited to open the annual Irish evening at HoCoPolitSo (the Howard County Political and Literary Society); their tradition of an Irish evening stretches back over forty years and speaks to the energy and dedication with which local and regional organisations all over America promote Irish culture. The honouree in 2015 was Emma Donoghue and my words for Emma are included here.

I wanted to include some testimony to the many ways we celebrated Bloomsday in successive years, always a challenge to our creativity. In 2014, we marked the 110th anniversary of Bloomsday and the 100th anniversary of the publication of *Dubliners*. I tried to weave in themes of emigration, given how much immigration reform was a priority for us at the Embassy.

The following year, 2015, our celebration could not have been more poignant. We had organised something special - an elaborate event in the prestigious Cosmos Club, combining a celebration of Bloomsday and of the 150th anniversary of the birth of WB Yeats. The day before the event, we were all shaken to the core by the tragedy that occurred in Berkeley, California, when a group of Irish J1 students fell from a collapsed balcony (I write about this in later chapters). After much agonising, we decided to go ahead with our Bloomsday event and included a moment of silence. But the night stays in my memory for its undertone of sorrow.

Making sure that women's voices were heard was always a priority in our cultural engagement. I am including an address I gave at the Great Hunger Museum in Quinnipiac University at the opening of an exhibition of Lady Sligo's letters. As well as talking about how I saw the role of the museum, I celebrated the fact that a woman's voice was being reclaimed from history.

Finally, in somewhat more prosaic mode, there is an address I gave at a lunch hosted by the then-Governor of Connecticut and his wife in their official residence: "The Arts: An Expression of Who We Are". I was asked in advance to be a sort of crusader for the arts, to help make the case for investment in the arts to some of the business people present, and that theme features fairly clearly in the address.

My cultural engagement definitely didn't end with retirement: if anything, it has grown more expansive and I am especially proud to be a Board member of the wonderful Druid Theatre. I consider myself immensely fortunate that my career had such a rich cultural vein and provided a professional rationale for doing what was so personally satisfying - and what I would have loved to do under any circumstances.

A Feast of Friel
Irish College, Paris
4th June 2009

It is a privilege for me to be here, on this opening evening of the "Feast of Friel". It promises to be a particularly rich feast. The Irish College has done us proud in how it has organised the event. We are greatly honoured that Brian Friel is with us in person. And the involvement of the MacGill Summer School – which organised such a successful celebration last year, on the cusp of Brian's eightieth year – has added real depth.

My role this evening is to help launch the new French translations of seven of Brian's plays. We have already had a taster of these new translations in the brilliant performance this evening by Laurent Terzieff, one of the great standard bearers for Friel in France.

As befits such a landmark undertaking, great care has been taken by the publishers, both in the writing of the prefaces and the choice of artwork for the covers.

And of course there is the translator: Alain Dellahaye. I imagine that every writer has a somewhat ambiguous relationship with his translator: like entrusting your precious child to be reared by someone else. The child remains wholly yours, but bears the recognisable imprint of another.

Alain Dellahaye faced particular challenges. Brian Friel's work is rich in idiom and regional nuance, and so much can rest on the precise turn of a phrase. In the French language, which is more standardised and has fewer regional variations, such subtleties could easily be lost. And language is not just a medium for Brian Friel, it is also sometimes the object. 'Translations' is a play all about the complexities of the clash between the Irish and English languages. How to even begin to address that in French?

Fortunately the collaboration between playwright and translator has been something really special – a remarkable partnership, with a remarkable result. Alain's work is clearly a labour of love, and his respect for the writing shine through in the sensitive translation that captures the essence and flavour of Brian's words.

When I received the invitation to speak tonight, I was somewhat diffident about accepting. There is always the question of what added value one can bring. Brian has already been crowned with laurels: as a Saoi of Aosdana, he has the highest honour in Irish cultural life. The expert speakers addressing you over the next few days will eulogise more eloquently, and analyse more deeply. But what perhaps I can do is to comment from the particular perspective of Irish Ambassador in France.

An Ambassador's job, or at least a key part of it, is to interpret his or her own country to the country of accreditation. Our interpretations generally tend to be benign, not just because that is what our profession requires of us, but because we are representing a country we love and of which we are proud. But the picture we present, if it is to be authentic and credible, needs to be a rounded and honest one. That means showing Ireland as it has been and is, not as we would want to mythologise or idealise it.

I can think of few better interpreters of Ireland than Brian Friel. At the heart of his plays of course are the individual characters, with all their particularities and idiosyncrasies: it is their storylines that make the plays live and breathe and give them universality. But for the most part, these characters are anchored in a context that is distinctively Irish. Over the span of his work, Brian Friel again and again turns his gaze on Ireland, sometimes with a tenderness that never descends into sentimentality, sometimes with a severity that – even if it does not forgive – is nevertheless tempered by an understanding of how and why our society came to be flawed.

This new set of translations will ensure that more of Brian Friel's work reaches a wider audience in this country. It will help to create a more rounded, multi-layered picture of Ireland in France – the kind of picture that takes us beyond romance, beyond indulgence, to the more complex understanding that benefits today's mature relationship between the two countries.

In addition, this new accessibility of Brian Friel's work will further enhance – not just his own – but Ireland's literary and artistic reputation in France. Our artistic reputation is of course solidly established, and successor generations stand on the shoulders of giants such as Joyce and Beckett. But it is important that France is reminded that the great outpouring of creativity which characterises our island continues, that we are producing new giants on whose broad shoulders further generations will stand.

I mentioned the universality of Brian Friel's work. Ireland may be his prism, but his subject matter is the human condition. At the heart of his work are the big themes which define human existence: time, memory, relationships, displacement, loss, the living of life in the perspective of death. Friel knows better than anyone how these themes cross all cultural and linguistic divides – they are the themes which have repeatedly drawn him back to Chekhov, Turgenev, Ibsen. And they are of course themes at the heart of the great literary and theatrical traditions of this country.

Apart from theme, there is form. How often have I seen the French word, avant-garde, attached to Friel? His technical risk-taking, his innovation – for example, in Molly Sweeney, the play we heard this evening, the separate monologues between characters who do not interact – will have a particular appeal to sophisticated, experimental, French theatre audiences.

Like all true writers, Brian Friel writes not to render service to anyone but because he must write. I would imagine he is uneasy about having labels of any sort attached. But in holding up that sometimes relentless mirror, in addressing abiding and universal questions in an Irish context and idiom, in reminding the world of the well springs of Irish creativity, he seems to me an Ambassador of his country in the best and truest sense.

Every good celebration looks forward as well as backward. This 'Feast of Friel' celebrates decades of achievement and what is yet to come. I have no doubt that, ushered in by these translations, part of what is to come will be a wider and better appreciation in France of Brian Friel's genius.

Tribute to Oscar Wilde
Père Lachaise Cemetery, Paris
20th July 2009

I know that all of us here – especially because we are such an intimate group – feel a sense of privilege. To be here, in this unique place, on this special anniversary, at this quiet morning time, is something we will not forget.

If one believes in some sort of afterlife, in spirits that live on in some way we do not know or understand, then one can assume that Oscar Wilde is witnessing us with wry amusement and I hope with some tenderness.

The tenderness, I am sure, would come from the presence of his grandson, and his grandson's wife. Because it is obvious from everything we know, that Oscar dearly loved his two boys. Nothing that ever happened could take away from that.

And the wry amusement. Oscar Wilde of course loved irony and contradiction: turning everything on its head was key to his cleverness. The essence of the epigram is the inversion of conventional wisdom.

So in witnessing us, he would no doubt have some sharp reflections on the nature of fame, of immortality. The contrast between the circumstances of his death in 1900, and the shrine that this grave in Père Lachaise has become. One can almost hear his epigrams on the subject.

And I daresay he might have a particular sense of wry amusement about my presence here. Because I am here not just as a lifelong fan of Oscar Wilde, although I am that, but also as Irish Ambassador.

The card on my bouquet reads, "from your compatriots". He might well reflect on his own ambivalent feelings towards the country of his birth, and, for a long time, our ambivalence towards him. One can speculate how much Ireland made him or unmade him. It has often been suggested that the tensions inherent in being born into an Anglo-Irish class in Ireland contributed to the duality that characterised his whole life.

But the past is at rest now, and I am here with pride as Irish Ambassador.

A grave contains mortal remains, but in a larger and truer sense, it contains the whole of a life. For it is at a graveside traditionally that the summing up is done. In the Ballad of Reading Gaol, Oscar spoke about "he who lives more lives than one". In his own case, he lived many lives, wore many different masks, was many different people.

There were so many different incarnations in his personal life. Some of these incarnations we can neither like nor admire. Some evoke our empathy and sympathy. And his writing life gave us Lady Bracknell and Lord Windermere and the other deathless characters, but it also gave us De Profundis and the Ballad of Reading Jail.

There were many Oscars – as he teased us with his own title: The Truth of Masks.

In De Profundis, towards the end, when so much had been stripped away, Oscar said that the only people that interest him are those who know what beauty is, and those who know what sorrow is. This grave contains beauty and sorrow, and it is that interplay between beauty and sorrow – those things at the heart of human existence – that draw us and so many to this graveside.

There is a line in the Ballad of Reading Gaol: "God's kindly earth is kindlier than men know." We all know that Oscar is at rest in the kindly earth of Père Lachaise.

The Literary Legacy of Seamus Heaney
Folger Shakespeare Library, Washington DC
7th April 2014

Tonight is a bittersweet experience for all of us here. It was a night intended for Seamus – a night when he would be with us in person: when we would experience at first hand his intelligence and grace, and – as we always were – be touched and transformed by the experience.

Within hours of Seamus' death, a poet friend of mine in Ireland texted me: "We all feel like orphans". I knew exactly what she meant. We had lost someone who had grounded and guided us, who had helped us more fully inhabit our humanity. Seamus was a public figure, but countless among us felt his loss in a personal way.

Some seven months later, the sense of loss remains acute. But I am so glad that the Folger has kept this date in the diary and brought us together to honour the literary legacy and to celebrate the continuity.

Seamus was intensely conscious of the Human Chain of which we are all part. And his whole life was testimony to the literary chain – he drew deeply from what went before, and taught and inspired those who came after.

Tonight, we have a vivid sense of that golden chain – human and literary – as we hear from five wonderful poets whose lives and works were intertwined with Seamus' life and work.

Our speakers this evening knew Seamus far better than I did and are infinitely better equipped to sing his poetic genius.

But before I hand you over to hear directly from them, I would like to say just a couple of things.

The first point I want to make – and perhaps as a diplomat I am particularly attuned and attracted to this – is that Seamus was at once utterly Irish and utterly cosmopolitan.

Seamus could not have been other than Irish. Not just because, as he famously told us, his passport was green. His Irishness was there in his blood and bones, his language and sensibility, in the inspiration he drew from the particular and the local.

At the same time, he was entirely cosmopolitan in the most natural and unassuming way. He was completely at home in the Englands of the Mind: with Hughes, Larkin, Elliott. He was deeply influenced by the great poets of Eastern Europe: Brodsky, Milosz, Holub, Herbert. And of course there was a very special and strong link with America: his relationships with all the beloved American poets; the happy and fruitful years at Harvard; the fact that he felt it natural that many of his papers would be at Emory University; indeed his position as an honorary member of the Board of the Folger.

His was such a graceful, well-stocked mind – truly a mind that knew no borders.

My second point is this: in what is still the early aftermath of Seamus' death, it is timely to remind ourselves of his immense capacity for joy. As a poet, of course, he explored all registers of the human heart and mind. In life, like every one else who walks this earth, he was no stranger to sorrow. But joy was at the core of it all.

In his lecture on The Redress of Poetry, Seamus examined the multiple ways in which poetry provides redress. But he took pains to remind us: "Poetry cannot afford to lose its fundamentally self-delighting inventiveness, its joy in being a process of language as well as a representation of things in the world."

And there was such joy in the life as well as in the work. I loved his answer to the penultimate question from Dennis O'Driscoll in "Stepping Stones". "Often, when I'm on my own in the car, driving down from Dublin or Wicklow in spring or early summer – or indeed at any time of the year – I get this sudden joy from the sheer fact of the mountains on my right and the sea on my left, the flow of the farmland, the sweep of the road, the lift of the sky. There's a double sensation of here-and-nowness in the familiar place and far-and-awayness in something immense."

What a way of describing these everyday, life-enhancing moments.

And joy was also part of his contemplation of death. To my mind, one of the most penetrating pieces Seamus ever wrote was: "Joy or Night: Last Things in the Poetry of WB Yeats and Phillip Larkin". Seamus contrasts the bleakness of Larkin's vision of death with Yeats: "always passionately beating on the wall of the physical world in order to provoke an answer from the other side." Faced with this choice, it was clear where Seamus stood: with Yeats, in managing – as he put it – to pronounce a final "yes".

And so, tonight, I hope we will recall the joy of the legacy. We are not, after all, orphans. Seamus is immortal in the way that all great poets are immortal. But, beyond that, and in a more particular way, his affirming spirit has withstood death. The joy that defined his life and his poetry will not be extinguished.

I look forward to a wonderful evening of celebrating the legacy.

HoCoPoLitSo Irish Evening featuring Emma Donoghue
Howard County, Maryland
6th February 2015

I am delighted to be here for the first time with HoCoPoLitSo. I know its tradition and reputation, and something of its storied history now stretching back over forty years. This Irish evening is one of the established annual milestones; the list of those honoured over the years is very impressive: a roll call of Irish literary giants.

Tonight, we are very privileged to have Emma Donoghue – a giant not just on the Irish literary scene but internationally. And I will talk more about Emma in a moment.

As it is your Irish evening, let me first talk for just a few minutes about Ireland, and my role of representing Ireland here in the United States.

I happened to be reflecting on this in the past few days. I was asked to be the patron of a major charity ball that will take place in DC next month, and we were choosing a theme for the ball. The theme we decided on was: Ireland – Legendary and Contemporary.

I think this theme really does capture the duality of our country. The legendary Ireland has a powerful hold on all our imaginations, and particularly on the American imagination. This is the Ireland of majestic, beautiful landscapes, of ancient myth, of Gaelic tradition. It's the Ireland of haunting music and an age-old reverence for words. It's the country that was colonised for eight hundred years but never lost its will for freedom, and ultimately wrested back its sovereignty.

Even if at times the image is highly romanticised, there is an essential truth embedded within the myth. Our heritage is indeed a proud one. And in presenting Ireland here in the U.S., I want to be able to validate and affirm all that is good and sometimes glorious in our history and tradition.

At the same time, I have a very strong sense of mission in representing contemporary Ireland, with all our strengths and challenges – the excitement and grittiness of the Ireland of today.

Many of you probably know Ireland well and may have visited recently. You know the more open and multicultural country we have become. You know the arc of our economic path over the past decade or so: from the intoxication of our Celtic Tiger years to the near collapse in 2008 of our property sector and banks, and now back to recovery mode, where once again we are experiencing the highest growth figures in Europe.

Things are certainly looking up in Ireland, and you can feel the optimism coming back in the air. But it has been a tumultuous decade in the life of our country. And as we begin to recover from our trauma, there is a serious interrogation of issues of identity, and values. Did we lose our soul during the Celtic Tiger years, and if so, how do we recover it?

Our cultural community, as we would expect, is at the forefront of this interrogation. As always, it is the writers and poets who are holding the mirror up to our society. And in that mirror we are seeing the evolving Ireland – imaginative, creative, still in love with words and music, but also traumatised by austerity, grappling with rapid social change, navigating our new cosmopolitanism.

I spoke last night at the opening of the Capital Irish Film Festival in DC which will run for the next few days. One of the more arresting titles that caught my eye was a short film entitled: "Me Buddy, Mohammed" – about two youngsters who form a friendship in the playground of an inner city Dublin school.

That indeed is very emblematic of the new Ireland. I think we have a very exciting period ahead in the arts in Ireland. It's a time of transition, and transition almost always sparks a bout of uncertainty. We are also facing a major anniversary next year, as we celebrate the centenary of 1916.

As some of you know, the Easter Rising of 1916 was the iconic event which led some five years years later to Irish independence. In 2016, as well as celebrating, there will be a great deal of soul searching about the journey of the last hundred years, where we have arrived, and how we position ourselves for the next hundred years. I hope and expect that our cultural community will have a very important voice in that national conversation.

And now let me come to Emma Donoghue. Emma has been her own wonderfully original and distinctive voice and her writing is of such a range as to escape any categorisation. Probably everyone here was mesmerised by 'Room', which has been so successful and been garlanded with so many awards. Her latest novel 'Frog Music' in some ways could hardly be more different – on a crowded stage, absolutely teeming with life, as opposed to the hermetic sealing of 'Room'. But it is equally original and equally mesmerising.

The sheer breadth and versatility of Emma's work is extraordinary: eight novels, a prolific short story writer, a writer of drama for stage, screen and radio, a scholar and literary historian who has published ground-breaking works of her own as well as editing two anthologies.

But even if Emma escapes all categories, I would dare to situate her a little in what I was saying earlier about contemporary Irish writing. She is a natural cosmopolitan: living for years between England, Ireland and Canada, before settling in Canada seventeen years ago. She moves easily and fluidly in time and space – back and forth between historical and contemporary settings, back and forth between Europe and North America. From her first novel 'Stir-fry', written when she was twenty five years old, to 'Frog Music', we see her questioning what it means to be a woman.

In many ways, she was ahead of her time – even when writing in historical settings, the freshness of her voice and themes makes her utterly contemporary.

And so I'm delighted to present Emma Donoghue – a narrator for our times, sometimes excavator of historical stories and legends, but always a compelling modern sensibility. I talked about Ireland: legendary and contemporary; perhaps it's not a bad way to describe Emma.

Bloomsday Reception
Embassy Residence, Washington DC
16th June 2014

I am delighted to welcome everyone here this evening. After these short opening remarks, we will have the great pleasure of hearing from television presenter Chris Matthews and from author Alice McDermott.

As you know, and you saw from your invitation, this is a very special day for lovers of Joyce. It's the 110th anniversary of Bloomsday, that famous day – 16 June 1904 – when Leopold Bloom crisscrossed Dublin. A day that is now celebrated in Dublin and around the world – hundreds of events in Dublin today and celebrations all over Asia, South America and in some of the most unlikely places.

It's also the 100th anniversary of the publication of *Dubliners* – the set of fifteen short stories which in different ways portray the lives of people living in Dublin in the first years of the 20th century.

Dubliners is in some ways a clear precursor of *Ulysses*, and there is a whole study around tracing the connections; and the early foreshadowing of *Ulysses* in *Dubliners*. But it absolutely stands in its own right. Colum McCann in his recent introduction to the centennial edition of *Dubliners* says that "it includes some of the most beautiful sentences in the English language".

Probably the most beautiful among the beautiful stories in *Dubliners* is the The Dead, and the most lyrical passage in that story is the final page and a half. The Dead is set in mid-winter, probably 6th January, on a snowy night, and is built around the relationship between the dead and the living.

I suspect there are few other Embassies where you will be invited to a party on a glorious summer day to hear tales of a snow-filled night where the shades of the dead walk among the living. But that's the Irish for you! Joseph O'Connor, the Irish novelist, wrote recently that in Ireland, "Gaiety is grief on a good day".

What Chris' reading will also demonstrate is the sheer musicality of Joyce's language, and how much it benefits from being read aloud. You will hear exactly the same thing when Alice reads the Gerty McDowell passage from *Ulysses*. I recommend you just close your eyes and listen.

Now, let me tell you about the very short passages I have chosen to read to you tonight. Some of you here are Irish-American, descended from Irish emigrants who flooded to America. Joyce was himself an emigrant, wandering Europe, from Trieste to Zurich to Paris, throughout his adult life. And I have spent a lot of my time over the past year working on immigration issues.

And so I thought I would read two short passages about emigration. The first is from Eveline, one of the stories in *Dubliners*. Nineteen year-old Eveline is on the verge of emigration, leaving her home in Dublin – a life of hard work, a dead mother, a violent father, responsibility for two younger children. She was about to go abroad with Frank, a young Irish sailor who had travelled on board ships and now had a home in Buenos Aires. Frank has asked her to marry him, and she is set to embark for this new life. But there's the pain, the trauma, the terrible pull of what is left behind:

"She stood among the swaying crowd in the station at the North Wall. He held her hand and she knew that he was speaking to her, saying something about the passage over and over again. The station was full of soldiers with brown baggages. Through the wide doors of the sheds she caught a glimpse of the black mass of the boat, lying beside the quay wall, with illumined portholes. She answered nothing. She felt her cheek pale and cold, and out of a maze of distress, she prayed to God to direct her, to show her what was her duty. The boat blew a long mournful whistle into the mist. If she went, tomorrow she would be on the sea with Frank, steaming towards Buenos Aires. Their passage had been booked. Could she still draw back after all he had done for her? Her distress awoke a nausea in her body and she kept moving her lips in silent fervent prayer.

A bell clanged upon her heart. She felt him seize her hand:

"Come!"

No! No! No! It was impossible. Her hands clutched the iron in frenzy. Amid the seas she sent a cry of anguish!

"Eveline! Evvy!"

He rushed behind the barrier and called to her to follow. He was shouted at to go on but he still called to her. She set her face to him, passive, like a helpless animal. Her eyes gave him no sign of love or farewell or recognition".

Now to contrast with that, a couple of famous paragraphs from the end of Portrait of the Artist as a Young Man. Here it's the other side of the coin, the liberation of travel abroad, the disruption that unleashes the genius, the necessity to go away to be more fully yourself. Stephen Dedalus, in many ways an autobiographical figure for Joyce, is about to depart and here are the final diary entries...

"April 16: Away! Away!

The spell of arms and voices: the white arms of roads, their promise of close embraces and the black arms of tall ships that stand against the moon, their tales of distant nations. They are held out to say: We are alone - come. We are your kinsmen. And the air is thick with their company as they call out to me, their kinsman, making ready to go, shaking the wings of their exultant and terrible youth.

April 26. Mother is putting my new secondhand clothes in order. She prays now, she says, that I may learn in my own life and away from home and friends what the heart is and what it feels. Amen. So be it. Welcome, O life! I go to encounter for the millionth time the reality of experience and to forge in the smithy of my soul the uncreated conscience of my race.

April 27. Old father, old artificer, stand with me now and ever in good stead."

So much for us all to reflect about in those two contrasting experiences of emigration.

And now I will hand you over to Chris Matthews for his reading from "The Dead". Let's set the scene: Gabriel and Gretta have come back to the Shelbourne Hotel. Under the influence of events at the party, and particularly the singing of a song called "the Lass of Aughrim", Gretta has spoken for the first time about a young boy from Galway, Michael Furey, who had died many years ago, probably for love of her. Gabriel is wracked by jealousy. Emotionally exhausted, Gretta falls asleep......

Celebration of Yeats Day/Bloomsday
The Cosmos Club, Washington DC
16th June 2015

Thank you all for joining us for this special combined celebration – our annual marking of Bloomsday, and this year also marking the 150th anniversary of the birth of William Butler Yeats, who came into the world on 13 June 1865.

At the outset of the evening, I have the sad task of asking for a moment of silence. As too often happens in life, tragedy intrudes in our joyous moments. During last night, there was a real tragedy in Berkeley, California. A group of young Irish students, over here for the summer on J1 visas, were gathered to celebrate a 21st birthday. As thirteen of them stood on the balcony of the apartment, it collapsed and they fell five stories. Six of them died, and seven are seriously injured. One can only imagine the heartbreak and grief of the bereft families. May I ask you to stand and observe a moment of silence, in sympathy and solidarity.

Thank you, and a book of condolence will be available later.

And now, let me try to switch emotional gear: from sadness to pride.

I am always proud to be the Ambassador of Ireland. But never more so than on an evening like this, when we present these two Irish literary giants: Yeats and Joyce.

I use the word "giants" advisedly. Both were towering, transformative, figures who shaped their times and refashioned the entire literary landscape. T.S. Eliot said of Yeats: "He is one of these few, whose history is the history of their own times, who are part of the consciousness of an age which cannot be understood without them." And Joyce is credited with changing the very art of writing. Yeats said of Joyce's approach: "It is an entirely new thing – neither what the eye sees nor the ear hears, but what the rambling mind thinks and imagines from moment to moment."

The two men were different in so many ways. Joyce forever the loner, the outsider. Yeats, in later life at least, the engaged and public man. Their relationship, such as it was, was not always easy. Yeats was the more forbearing of the two. Joyce relentlessly criticised Yeats for presenting an idealised Ireland, not the gritty urban reality that is the setting for Joyce's own writing.

But some qualities both men shared. They were men of passion. Yeats' unrequited love for Maud Gonne gave us some of the world's most exquisite, lyrical, love poetry. Joyce's full-blooded love for his wife, Nora Barnacle, fed his life and art, inspiring some wonderfully sensual writing that was of course considered shocking in its time.

And for both men, their passion extended to Ireland. Both spent time outside Ireland, with Joyce living abroad all his adult life, but Ireland was etched on their souls. As Joyce wandered around Europe, from Trieste to Paris to Zurich, in his head he was forever, obsessively, criss-crossing the Dublin he had left behind. Yeats struggled through different phases in his feelings for Ireland – chronicling all the momentous events of those turbulent times – but his passion was never in doubt. In one of this last poems, *Under Ben Bulben*, he commanded us:

"Cast your mind on other days
That we in coming days may be
Still the indomitable Irishry."

Finally, although both wrote so differently, they shared an intense musicality of language. Their writings are meant to be heard almost more than read. So many of Yeats' poems have been set to music – they are songs as much as poems. "Words for Music

Perhaps?" as one of his titles had it. Joyce loved music almost as much as words; he was a poet in his early days and his prose always had the cadence of poetry.

Tonight, we will try to weave some of these threads together. First, the poet Terri Cross Davis will read us the final passage from Molly Bloom's soliloquy at the very end of *Ulysses*. We will follow that with a musical segment, an Irish singer and a classical guitarist playing songs from the works of Yeats and Joyce.

Then, reflecting Yeats the public and political figure, we will have three special readers: Senator Ed Markey (let me remind you that Yeats was also a Senator), Congressman Richie Neal, who is also Chair of the Friends of Ireland, and Deputy National Security Adviser Ben Rhodes. All three are lovers of Yeats' poetry, fluent in his writings, and will share some of their favourite poems with us.

Next, a short 'play for voices', which brings the two great writers together – penned especially for this evening by our friend and scholar of Irish literature, Joe Hassett.

And, for our finale, back to music – songs that show how the two writers drew from each other's work. As we finish, our two Irish musicians will be fortified by some great local talent.

Again, thank you all for joining us. We hope to introduce, or reintroduce you to these two writers of genius, to share our Irish intoxication with words and language, and – even on a night of sadness – to make your hearts sing.

Opening of the Exhibition of Lady Sligo's Letters
Great Hunger Museum, Quinnipiac University, Connecticut
29th April 2014

I am honoured to be here this evening. I have wanted to come to Quinnipiac University since the opening of the Great Hunger Museum in 2012. The addition of the Great Hunger Institute last year sparked my interest even further. I have finally made it, and I cannot think of a more fitting occasion than this exhibition of Lady Sligo's letters.

Before saying a few words about this fascinating Exhibition, I would like to speak briefly about the Museum and the Institute.

Great Hunger Museum and Institute

Firstly, I want to pay tribute to the imagination, the generosity, and the hard work of those who brought the Museum and Institute into being. The vision and determination of President John Lahey launched and sustained the project. The extraordinary generosity of the Lender brothers made it possible. And, at the Institute, Christine Kinealy has brought huge commitment and distinguished scholarship.

Way beyond providing us with a resource or facility, I suggest that these places – the Museum and the Institute – fulfil a real and deep-seated need.

Why is this so? The Famine, after all, took place more than one hundred and fifty years ago. Generations later, in a transformed world, should old wounds still matter this much?

I suspect that most of us here instinctively grasp the answer to this question. Some wounds are so grievous, and so deep, that their imprint is indelible. The rawness has long gone, and the scar tissue has developed, but time has not erased the injury.

The need, I think, is three fold. Firstly, there is the duty of remembrance. Secondly, amid the competing narratives, there is the need to rescue the truth of what happened. And, thirdly, there is the importance of making this historical experience relevant to how we live our lives today.

The act of remembering tries to reclaim something of the particularity of the individual lives lost. To retrieve them from anonymity. To restore, even at this distance, some vestige of dignity to those who died – the dignity they were so cruelly stripped of in life.

When we contemplate the deaths of a million people, so huge a figure can leave us numbed, anaesthetised. But when we give a face or a voice – through art, or letters, or diaries, or literature – to some of those who died, they call out to us in a different way.

The duty of remembrance arises in relation to all of history's terrible and large-scale losses of life: through war, genocide, or natural disasters.

Today, there is perhaps less risk of anonymity of suffering. Mobile phones have penetrated the planet, allowing images to be captured even in the remotest places and transmitted globally in seconds.

But some things have not changed. Large-scale loss of life in the poorest parts of the earth is still underreported. Lives are still valued differently, depending on where and in what circumstances those lives have been lived out.

A life was worth pitifully little in Ireland in the 1840s; it is still worth pitifully little in many parts of the world today. The Great Hunger Museum and the Institute connect us to the human reality of Ireland in the 1840s. In doing so, they serve a wider purpose, insisting on the humanity and individual tragedy that mass statistics often obscure.

The second need I mentioned is that of rescuing the truth. This of course is always the vocation of the historian. We know that total objectivity is illusory; there is always a prism of some sort. But historians of distinction and integrity – and Christine Kinealy most definitely belongs in that category – will excavate and contextualise, and try to lead us to an honest appraisal of the facts.

The Great Hunger has been one of the truly defining experiences of Irish history: the direct experience and the inherited memories have shaped the Irish psyche over generations.

And given the emigration triggered by and associated with the Great Hunger, the experience has also shaped our diaspora – nowhere more so than in America. The famine, in all its cruelty and horror, has powerfully imprinted itself on the Irish-American consciousness. It has conditioned political perspectives, and seeped into the songs and stories.

The narrative has often been a fairly simple, elemental, one. We need our historians to continue to shine the torch, to guide us through the complexities – not to varnish the truth, or to airbrush the cruelties, but to give us a deeper understanding of how and why this unspeakable tragedy could have been allowed to unfold in the way it did.

The third need is for relevance, connection to how we live our lives today. If it is possible to speak of the Famine having any positive legacy in Ireland, it is surely one of empathy. Irish people, more than most, identify with the poor and dispossessed of the planet. This is not self-congratulatory rhetoric: our levels of development assistance bear witness.

Even through the recent period of austerity in Ireland, our level of official development assistance has remained substantially intact. In 2012, for example, we contributed 0.47% of our Gross National Income (GNI) in official development assistance. To put the figure in context: this compares with 0.37% for Germany and 0.19% for the US in the same year.

Because of the Famine imprint, dealing with hunger and under-nutrition is at the core of our development aid. Today, more than 840 million people around the world are hungry. One in three people suffers from chronic under-nutrition. Stunting is a scourge of children throughout the developing world.

I hope that every visitor to the Museum and Institute will remember those cruel statistics of our contemporary world.

Exhibition

And now let me turn to this inaugural exhibition at the Institute whose opening we are celebrating this evening. I am so pleased that this particular subject has been chosen.

I visited Westport House some years ago – still in the hands of the Browne family – and I recall very well its feel and ambiance.

And, as you might expect, I am especially pleased that it is the voice and testimony of a woman that is being heard in this exhibition.

The extent to which women have been written out of history – in Ireland as elsewhere – is now widely acknowledged. We women have generally been allocated walk on parts, appearing in crowd scenes or in cameo roles as sweethearts or muses. It is rare that we glimpse the women who have acted and achieved in their own right, rather than as support to their menfolk.

This of course is not coincidental: over the centuries, society was structured in ways that inhibited and constrained women in the roles they could play. Despite that, they certainly did a great deal more than history has given them credit for. Christine Kinealy's book, "Charity and the Great Hunger in Ireland", illuminates some of the ways in which women were able to come out of the private domain and involve themselves in relief and philanthropic work throughout the famine years.

Lady Sligo's voice interests us not just as a female voice. It is an Anglo-Irish voice, a landlord's voice. It is very much a voice of its era, imbued with the attitudes – and indeed some of the prejudices – of the era. But it is also a humane voice at an inhumane time.

I had the privilege of a short private tour of the exhibition this afternoon: the letters remain as vivid and compelling as when they were written.

And so, I congratulate and thank everyone involved with this important exhibition and I look forward to many more such exhibitions of equal insight.

More generally, I look forward to the Museum and the Institute fulfilling its double mission – to strengthen our memory, but also to stir and sharpen our conscience.

It is a large and challenging task, but we are in very good hands.

The Arts: An Expression of Who We Are
Lunch hosted by the Governor of Connecticut, Hon. Dan
Malloy, and Mrs. Cathy Malloy
14th April 2015

My warmest thanks to Cathy and to Governor Malloy for this invitation to their beautiful home. It's a pleasure to be here in Hartford for the first time, to meet you all, and also to be offered a chance to talk about something slightly different.

I so often find myself talking about Ireland's economy: today's lunch provides an opportunity to apply a somewhat different prism and to reflect on our culture: what it means to us, what it says about us, and the steps we need to take to safeguard it.

As I began to think about what I would say to you today, I googled "definition of culture" and immediately realised I was in something of a minefield. I read that there are 164 definitions of culture, and lots of battles about which definitions are more politically correct. So let me keep it simple. I think of the arts as how a society experiences itself, interrogates itself, holds the mirror up to itself.

My title gives me a very broad theme – the subject matter of a whole symposium, and so I'm going to concentrate on a few specific points. But first, maybe a little ground-clearing.

There are probably few nations whose image and identity are so strongly bound up with its arts as is the case with Ireland. Try a word association game: say the word Ireland and the chances are it will conjure up music, poetry, story-telling, theatre, dance. There is a long golden thread that links the glories of the ancient Celtic and monastic culture to the four Irish Nobel prize winners for literature over the past one hundred years.

One can analyse endlessly why this should be so. Some of the answers are undoubtedly to be found in the particular circumstances of our history. In broad brush terms, there is a great deal of heartbreak in Irish history – oppression, impoverishment, hunger – and our songs and dance helped us to survive and deal with heartbreak. And there's the tension: as the Anglo Irish culture, and the English language was forced on Gaelic speaking people, that collision of two cultures gave rise to extraordinary creativity.

And then there is emigration which was a constant in Irish history. The experience of emigration was critical in itself: so many of our great writers have been wanderers: think of Joyce and the final words in *Portrait of the Artist as a Young Man*. Stephen Dedalaus says of his mother:

> She prays now, she says, that I may learn in my own life and away from home and friends, what the heart is and what it feels. Amen. So be it. Welcome, O life. I go to encounter from the millionth time the reality of experience and to forge in the smithy of my soul the uncreated conscience of my race.

And so, there you have it – it was the very fact of emigration that crystallised a sense of our Irish identity. Sometimes we need to go abroad to recognise who we are.

And of course, as well as sparking some works of genius, emigration also spread and transmitted Irish culture worldwide – we are a country of less than 5 million people, with a diaspora of some 70 million around the world, around half of these in America. Article 2 of our Constitution states:

> The Irish nation cherishes its special affinity with people of Irish ancestry living abroad who share its cultural identity and heritage.

So, from the outset, our shared cultural identity was seen as the glue that binds the global Irish family together.

That's the backdrop. But rather than a general treatise about culture, I want to to make four points in particular:

(i) That this is a time of cultural invigoration and renewal in Ireland;

(ii) That there is an increasing realisation of how much culture contributes to our economy;

(iii) That even as we quantify the economic contribution, we cannot let that circumscribe our thinking about culture;

(iv) That we need to prioritise culture, and devote the necessary resources.

Invigoration and Renewal

Ireland is currently going through a period of self-examination, self-questioning. We had our Celtic Tiger years – those years of phenomenal growth; then a five-year period, from 2008 onward, which were a time of crisis and austerity; and then, from 2014, the beginnings of a comeback which is now increasingly taking hold and becoming entrenched. Last year, we had the highest growth rate in the European Union and growth this year is also likely to break European records.

So it has been a roller coaster – a period of disruption and change. And it's often such periods which trigger reflection about identity, values, a kind of national soul-searching. Certainly, what you see in some of the new literature and drama of the past years is a merciless examination of the hubris of the Celtic Tiger years, as well as exposing the harshness of the austerity years and the price paid by individuals and communities. To hark back to Stephen Dedalaus, something new is being forged in the smithy of our soul.

A second major impetus is that we are in a period of commemorations – the decade of commemorations. And foremost among the anniversaries is the centenary next year of the Easter Rebellion of 1916. This was a seminal event in our history: it was the rebellion which triggered the series of events which led to our independence some five years later.

This centenary is by any standards a major milestone in the life of our nation – we will mark it in significant ways both at home and abroad, including a flagship three-week festival of Irish culture at the Kennedy Center in DC. And of course, as you reach the centenary, you look in the mirror and ask yourself questions about the journey, what kind of country you have become, where you are headed.

This would be true in any circumstances, but even more so because the 1916 rebellion was so strongly associated with a cultural context and cultural triggers. 1916 was rooted in cultural nationalism: the preoccupation with words, the reverence for words – the *word* was everywhere, not just in poetry and theatre, but in the over three hundred newspapers that were circulating in Ireland between 1900 and 1922. Years later, Patrick Kavanagh said, "Ireland has a standing army of 300,000 poets". Our independence was born more in words than in rifles.

Contribution to the Economy

Passing from the existential to the more pragmatic, the second issue I want to touch on is what culture and the arts contribute to the economy.

Over the past years, there has been an increasing tendency to measure everything in terms of jobs and growth. That's perfectly understandable in our situation and we should in no way be hesitant about it.

There is huge potential in the arts and in the cultural, heritage, and creative industries to create growth and jobs. A 2011 report by the Arts Council showed that the arts provided €307m in taxes and that the wider creative industries contributed €47 billion overall to the economy, supporting 79,000 direct and indirect jobs.

Just look at cultural tourism. Failte Ireland has estimated that, in 2011, 3.5 million of our 6 million overseas visitors engaged in cultural activity and spent an estimated €2.8 billion while in Ireland.

The growth and job creation continues, expanding into new categories. For example, in our budget at the end of last year, new financial incentives were offered for film-making in Ireland. I was present with the Taoiseach late last year when he met Stephen Spielberg and Stephen was very clear as to the potential Ireland offers. Animated film is linked in with the high tech and digital sector. It's a buoyant sector. A short animated film – Song of the Sea – was shortlisted for an Oscar this year.

And the ripple effects extend far wider than can be easily calculated. The point has so often been made to us that culture is our "calling card", that it's a key way of introducing Ireland, of giving us a recognition and "stand-out" factor. Who knows how many investment decisions have had their origin in a sense of connection to Ireland's cultural richness?

Not a Commodity

The third point counterbalances the second – the challenge of thinking more broadly about culture. It can never be a commodity. It exists in freedom; it is often subversive. It is something to be valued and promoted in itself, not as an economic tool.

This was specifically recognised in the major paper on the Diaspora that the Government produced last month. Speaking of culture, the paper says "While it is recognised as a valuable calling card, branding Ireland and opening doors, it is about much than that. Through culture, Irish imagination and creativity are inspired, nurtured and expressed."

Of course, as Ambassador, I appreciate it when a piece of literature or theatre reflects well on Ireland. Sometimes it's a bit uncomfortable, particularly with Irish American audiences, when there is work subsidised by Irish taxpayers that is fairly biting in its criticism about Ireland. I can feel some perplexity on the part of audiences as to why we would be showcasing this.

But that's how art and culture thrive – respecting the integrity and independence of the artistic inspiration. We have to be ready to subsidise culture even when we may not feel comfortable with what the art is saying.

And I would argue that encouragement of free rein to the imagination has its economic benefits too. Of course this is hard to quantify. But all the time, I hear from U.S. multinationals in Ireland that the first reason they are there is for the talent – the young, educated workforce. And it's striking the same words they use all the time: flexible, creative, versatile. And I think that kind of workforce is more likely to exist in a country where the education system promotes cultural experimentation, a country that values culture.

Prioritising Culture

The final point I want to make is how we need to prioritise culture. I have spoken to you about how important the arts and culture are to our identity. I could also tell you about the resources that are being allocated. I could tell you about Aosdana, a system that honours 250 of our foremost cultural practitioners... how, for example, there is a major capital investment programme currently being carried out at the National Gallery. I could tell you about the commitment to arrest the cuts in cultural budgets.

And yet, and yet... There is a less comfortable truth. Our current President, Michael D. Higgins, is a former Minister for the Arts and there is no-one who has a more developed appreciation of the place of culture in our lives. A few weeks back, he spoke to Aosdana, the cultural group I just mentioned.

He was unsparing in his criticism about the cuts in government expenditure on the arts in recent years - cumulative cuts of about 40% in annual budgets of the majority of cultural institutions between 2011 and 2014... "That the arts are something apart, peripheral, belonging in the fringes of society is an assumption that must continue to be challenged... when we support artists, we support visible democracy... As a society, we must come to recognise that institutional provision for the arts is as important to our infrastructure as roads, hospitals and schools."

I see the same hand-wringing in Northern Ireland, as cultural budgets are also being slashed. And you can see the dilemma: at a time of cutbacks, inevitably it is easier to stop subsidising a theatre than to slash hospital beds.

There is a difference in approach to funding cultural institutions in Ireland and in the U.S., and this of course is a debate in itself. In Ireland, while philanthropy and private donations do help to support the arts, there is a strong sense that this is essentially a governmental responsibility and that our taxes should be used to ensure appropriate government subsidy. In the U.S., as you know, philanthropy plays a very important role and throughout my years in New York and DC I have been involved in very many projects to assist cultural institutions in those cities.

At least in the short term, given the differences in approach between Ireland and the U.S., I do not see private donations filling the gap left by the shortfall in Irish government expenditure. As the economy recovers, we have to put our money where our mouth is, and make sure that our budgetary choices do not consign culture to a peripheral place, at the bottom of our priority list after what are seen as more pressing needs have been fulfilled.

Given the time constraints, I will limit my introductory remarks to these four points. I know that there are many guests present from both the business sector and the arts community and I look forward to an invigorating discussion.

The early years - above, at a meeting of the United Nations High
Commission for Refugees, November 1978.
Below, with the then Taoiseach Garret Fitzgerald at the Embassy in Washington
DC, March 1984

Chairing the Commission on Human Rights, Geneva, 1999-2000. Above: On the podium with Mary Robinson, High Commissioner for Human Rights

Below: The daily attendance in the CHR meeting room, UN Geneva

Above: From the Brussels years (2001-2005): Addressing a business conference in Louvain

Below: During the Paris years, addressing a conference at The National Centre for Franco-Irish Studies, Institute of Technology, Tallaght

Above: Presenting credentials to President Chirac at the Elysée, July 2005 (with Catherine Colonna, the French Minister for European Affairs)

Below: with Prince Albert, just before delivering my speech in the Princess Grace Library, Monaco, February 2008. (Note picture of Princess Grace on easel)

Left: Getting ready to host a dinner for the Ireland Fund of France at the Embassy Residence on Avenue Foch

Below: Following an evening at the Irish Cultural Centre, dinner at Fouquet's (Joyce's old haunt) with author Colm Toibin and Pierre Joanon, Ireland's Honorary Consul in Antibes, December 2007

Above: Presenting credentials to UN Secretary General Ban Ki-moon, New York, July 2009. Below: At the "Future of Europe" panel discussion, Columbia University, New York, February 2013, with George Soros and George Papandreou.

Below: One of many statements to the UN General Assembly and its various Committees

Above: With President Obama and my partner Dr. Frank Lowe at the White House, March 2016.

Below: with Vice President Biden at the Gala opening of the "Ireland 100" Festival at the Kennedy Center, May 2016

Above: Becoming the first female member of the Friendly Sons of St Patrick, Philadelphia, March 2016. Below: Rededication of the statue of Robert Emmett, Massachusetts Ave, Washington DC, 2016

Below: "Women Rising" Symposium, Irish Embassy, Washington DC, with author Colum McCann

Above: People to whom I was honoured to pay tribute included poet Seamus Heaney and former President Bill Clinton. Below: Saying farewell on Capitol Hill, July 2017 with (left to right) Congressman Joe Kennedy Congressman Richie Neal, (now) Speaker Nancy Pelosi and Secretary General of the Department of Foreign Affairs Niall Burgess.

Wearing the green in America: Above left, Grand Marshall of the St Patrick's Day Parade, Charlotte, North Carolina. Above right, cheering Ireland's rugby team at their historic victory over New Zealand, Soldier Field, Chicago, November 2016. Below, with Irish athletes at the opening of the Special Olympics, Los Angeles, July 2015

Having fun…I was invited to throw the ceremonial first pitch at the Nationals' Washington DC Stadium, May 2nd 2017. Above: with my daughter Claire as I get ready. Below: throwing the pitch (I made it!)

Life since retirement: Top, the Bar of Ireland, King's Inns, International Women's Day 2018. Above, addressing the American Chamber of Commerce Ireland, November 2017. Below: with UN Secretary General António Guterres and members of the Advisory Group on the Peacebuilding Fund, February 2020

CLAIMING HALF THE SKY

As I explained earlier, I considered myself throughout my career to have a dual mandate - first and foremost to represent my country but, in doing so, to try also to be a standard-bearer for women. This section could well have expanded to fill a slim volume; there have been so many gender-related speeches over the years. I came across an early address that I gave to the Forum of European Women in 2002, and I responded to many similar invitations over the subsequent fifteen years. The invitations continued into my retirement to a degree that surprised me.

This duality of role mostly felt joyful and enriching; occasionally, I have to admit, it felt onerous. In my speech at University College Dublin in 2018, I quote the author Anne Enright: "The business of writing is hard enough without taking on the additional burden of gender politics". The same might be said of the business of diplomacy. But still, as I suggest in the UCD speech: "The answer, I think, lies in recognising our responsibility - it's a price we pay for the privilege of being born a woman; but trying to see it not as something distinct and separate, rather integrating it as part of who we are and how we function... definitely not letting it eat our head or our talent!"

I chose the first five speeches of this chapter because they are overview speeches, looking back at the scope of my career and distilling some observations from that experience. Although all five are from the past six years - and inevitably there is overlap because I am reviewing the same experience and mostly drawing the same lessons - I find it interesting to see a certain sharpening of tone, a steady accumulation of impatience.

I would not wish in these introductory comments to tilt the balance of what the speeches say. Time and again, I emphasised the privileges and opportunities of my career, and made clear that any memoir I might write would be the very opposite of a "misery memoir". Without adjusting that balance, or diluting that strong sense of privilege, this may be a moment to elucidate a couple of incidents that the speeches touch on more discreetly.

I gave the first of these five speeches in January 2014, in the ballroom of Iveagh House, at a gathering of the Department's Gender Equality Network. I struggled a bit in advance as to how personal and frank to be. I pushed myself to speak more openly about my personal life than I normally would. I talked, for example, of how my then husband was treated before and during our first posting to Geneva, and recalled an incident from my daughter's infancy in Washington.

But maybe I could have gone a bit further with the frankness. There is what now strikes me as a slightly coy passage. Talking about the importance of open and transparent processes, I note that "In the interest of honesty and completeness, I would add that I made my feelings in this regard clear both before and after the Secretary General appointment in 2009." My reticence in part was in deference to the presence in the audience of the then Secretary General of the Department. But, in truth, I suppose it was also because I didn't want to re-hash in public an episode from five years previously that still had not quite lost its sting.

It was late 2008, and we were approaching a moment of transition in the Department. Secretary General Dermot Gallagher had announced his intention to retire, and senior members of the Department were invited to submit their applications for consideration for the post. I agonised over whether to throw my hat in the ring but finally decided that I would. I knew that my experience to date was exceptionally well-matched to the role. And there was another element in the equation. I had spent decades pushing for more women in senior positions: how could I not apply for this top job for which my whole career had prepared me?

There had been no specifics as to how the post would be filled but the general expectation - certainly my clear expectation - was that there would be a competitive process of some kind. This did not materialise: there was a complete vacuum until, some weeks after the applications were submitted, I received a phone call from then-Minister Micheál Martin informing me that the Cabinet had decided to appoint another departmental colleague to the role (a very well-respected colleague, but one whose career experience at the time did not match mine.)

I still remember taking the phone call that mid-December day in my office at the Paris Embassy. I had serious questions to put to the Minister, and subsequently sought a follow-up meeting with him in Dublin for more in-depth discussion. I made a very clear distinction in our exchanges: I had no sense of entitlement to the post, but did feel entitled to a fair process. Beyond giving me a very courteous hearing, Minister Martin had nothing of substance to say on the thinking behind the decision. (Later on, a different government Minister told a family member of mine that, when the Cabinet had come to choose between two names, including my own, then-Taoiseach Brian Cowen had made clear he felt "more comfortable" with the other candidate. If true - and I have no reason to doubt the account - it illustrates precisely why women are likely to lose out when decisions are taken behind closed doors.)

At this remove, I feel that fate actually smiled on me when the Secretary General appointment went elsewhere. My years in New York and Washington were immensely fulfilling both personally and professionally; unquestionably my life would be much the poorer for having missed them. But that happy outcome does not rewrite history, nor reconcile me to the way in which the decision was taken. And today, one hundred years on from its establishment, the Department of Foreign Affairs still has not had a woman Secretary General…

The speech to the 30% Club, in January 2017, came three years after my address to the Gender Equality Network. If the 2014 speech had been rather qualified in its optimism, the tone in the later speech is still more sober. I describe some of the reality checks of the intervening years, especially an experience from March 2014 which I also allude to in subsequent speeches. Although I downplay the incident a bit - describing it as "minor" and"nothing seismic" - it felt decidedly unpleasant at the time.

Despite some surrounding colour, the facts of the incident were pretty simple. It unfolded during the US visit of the then-Taoiseach, Enda Kenny, for St Patrick's Day 2014, my first in Washington. Vice President Joe Biden hosted his traditional breakfast. As we circulated before taking our seats, the Taoiseach chatted with Richard Haass, the President of the US Council on Foreign Relations who had chaired political talks in Northern Ireland the previous year.

I happened to be seated beside Mr Haass at the breakfast and he mentioned that the Taoiseach had suggested they meet in New York over the next few days to continue their discussion. He asked that I call him with a time slot when there was a chance to confirm the schedule for the New York segment of the visit. Having double-checked with the Taoiseach that he had indeed suggested the meeting and wanted it to go ahead, I contacted Haass a day or two later to confirm arrangements.

These straightforward interactions triggered a cascade reaction. It emerged that the Secretary General of the Taoiseach's Department, present on the trip, had a very negative view of Mr Haass; he was angry that the meeting was going ahead and he held me responsible. When he sought me out late in the evening in the lobby of our New York hotel to vent his anger, we were unwittingly within earshot of an Irish reporter, and something of a tabloid media storm erupted.

The incident in itself was unpleasant enough, but the sexist overtones of the media coverage - and particularly the naked sexism that was evident in some of the comments attributed to government sources - was the real eye-opener. It took me a while to shrug it off. As I said, a reality check.

On the more positive side, the incident probably helped me double down on the gender agenda throughout the Washington posting. Whenever possible, I fitted in meetings with women's leadership groups as I traveled around the country. And in other chapters I recount the attempts to advance the inclusivity agenda with Irish-American organisations and our determination that women's contribution would be at the heart of our 1916 commemorations.

The keynote address I gave to the UCD Women's Leadership Conference was my first significant speech on gender issues following retirement: it was a wide-ranging speech and something of a retrospective on my career. But it also allowed me to talk a little more freely about US politics and to share a few thoughts on the #MeToo movement. My frustration at the slow pace of change shows through, and I describe how "my patience has been steadily eroding..."

Just a month later, at a dinner marking International Women's Day in March 2018, I addressed a gathering of women lawyers in the elegant surroundings of King's Inns. Re-reading the speech, I can see that my impatience is even more marked. I speculate about the radicalising effects of retirement, and also allude to research I was doing on the position of women across a range of professions. The picture from the legal profession was fairly dispiriting. A little earlier, when I was preparing for a speech I gave at the Royal

College of Surgeons of Ireland, I was equally sobered by statistics from the medical profession which illustrated precisely the same pyramidical structures.

Before we all became grounded by the pandemic in March of this year, the last speech I gave was to an audience of 500 or so women (and some men) at an annual gathering organised by the Institute of Directors in Northern Ireland to mark International Women's Day. I was asked to speak about Leadership on a Global Stage and - as well as rehearsing some of my own life experience - I tried to distill some of the leadership lessons I had absorbed at various points of my career. The day-long conference in Belfast was lively and inspiring; despite the gathering storm-clouds of Brexit, I was struck by the energy and optimism in the room.

I wanted to shift the focus slightly to finish the chapter, to touch on the position of women in less developed parts of the world. The book and movement "Half the Sky" from which I draw this chapter title are about global engagement. It was always important to me that, as we crusaded for change in our own countries, we did not lose perspective on our own position of first world privilege.

Over the UN years, I had made many speeches about the position of women worldwide, particularly ones that addressed the implementation of Resolution 1325, the landmark Security Council Resolution on Women, Peace and Security adopted in 2000. And well before that, in late 1992, I had written about my participation in an EU Mission to Investigate the Rape of Muslim Women in Former Yugoslavia. But the speeches seemed to me too specialised (or too reliant on inputs from mission colleagues) and I hesitated to broaden the scope to include a newspaper article.

So I chose this very brief speech, from May 2018, when I was asked to deliver an award at the annual lunch organised by the Women's Refugee Commission in New York. On this occasion the theme was "The Resilience of Women Refugees". It was a theme that strongly resonated with me and I was more than happy to speak to it. The fact that the woman refugee to whom I was supposed to present the award, Majida Alaskary, was debarred from entry by US immigration authorities made its own, sad statement. I read out the beautiful message she had sent, and I find it very fitting to end the chapter with Majida's inspiring words, reminding us of the real meaning of love and heroism.

Gender Equality Network
Department of Foreign Affairs and Trade, Dublin
24th January 2014

Let me confess that I had a little difficulty in framing my remarks today. My instinct was to be analytical: to try to catalogue the issues, marshal the arguments, quote the statistics. But I braked myself, at least to a degree.

Firstly, I know that this Gender Equality Network has been meeting for some time, that you have had first class presentations, that you are as familiar with the facts and figures surrounding gender inequality as I am. Secondly, I am conscious that I was invited to speak not as an expert on gender issues but as someone who has lived the experience of a woman in diplomacy – in Irish diplomacy – over many decades. Thirdly, I recall that when I set up a Women Diplomats Network during my time as Permanent Representative in New York, I said on each occasion to our invited women speakers: "Please: you must tell your own story; that is what people want and need to hear."

I regularly encountered a reticence on the part of these women speakers in New York. Most preferred to focus on the societal rather than the personal. No one wanted to come across as self-absorbed or self-congratulatory. But I pushed them and so I decided to push myself a little today - I will indeed try to make my address a personal narrative.

But before I begin, I wanted to make just a few introductory comments of a more general nature.

As we seek to navigate our way as women diplomats, we face challenges at three levels: as individuals, within our particular work environment, and within wider society. Those three sets of challenges are not fully distinct and compartmentalised; they intersect and sometimes feed off and reinforce each other. But they do have some sort of separate reality.

The barriers that exist within ourselves have been documented in legions of studies. Sheryl Sandberg's recent book, *Lean In* may not be particularly original but I found it accurate and insightful. Even if Sandberg's financial circumstances are worlds removed from ours, what she writes about – the ambition gap, the confidence gap, the myth of doing it all – chimes with our everyday experience. The question she poses – "what would you do if you weren't afraid?" – is one we should ask ourselves every day.

But addressing the internal barriers will never be enough; the external barriers have to be dismantled simultaneously.

Our work environment, of course, is this Department. And it is very heartening to see the clear commitment to promoting equality that exists. The Management Advisory Committee, led by Secretary General David Cooney and by the Gender Sub-Committee, is piloting the way. I understand that the Gender Equality Audit, drawn up by expert consultants, has set out recommendations. From the outset, the Tanaiste's political leadership on the issue has been strong and consistent.

But, unquestionably, we need to accelerate. Today's pyramidical structure – with less than 10% of Assistant Secretary posts held by women – is simply unsustainable. This is not how Ireland looks; this is not who we are. And so every lesson we can take from other foreign services, every step recommended by the consultants, needs to be seized and implemented.

The wider societal challenge is more pervasive, more amorphous, and therefore more difficult to tackle. But recognising it, and arming ourselves to deal with it, is already a step forward.

In talking today about my own career, I will touch on some of these various challenges – individual, Departmental, societal. And, without for a moment suggesting I have all the answers, I will try to tell you something of what I have learned along the way.

I joined the Department in November 1972, just weeks before Ireland joined the then EEC on 1 January '73. It was a large intake by the standards of the time: twelve Third Secretaries, of whom two were women – the late, wonderful, Clare O'Flaherty and myself. There was some comment at the time about this "big influx" of women, which left me rather perplexed. I was told that, while of course there had previously been female Third Secretaries, this was the first time there had been *two* in a single intake.

I married in 1974, and here is where the EEC entry in 1973 becomes very significant. Our EEC accession had forced the lifting of the ban on married women in the public service. Without this insistence from Brussels, the ban would undoubtedly have persisted for years further. Like generations of women before me, I would have had to choose between marriage and public service.

The early years went smoothly, even if there were some straws in the wind. When I kept my own name on marriage, the Head of Personnel at the time – otherwise a kindly and benign individual – told me that he didn't "know what game I was playing" but he supposed it was up to me.

The first real difficulties arose in 1976 when I was posted to Geneva. I found myself with the distinction of being the first married woman to be posted abroad. At the time, as now, there was a different foreign service allowance for a married and single officer, and – less formally – a rent ceiling that differed depending on whether the accommodation was for a married or single officer.

Although the relevant regulations referred to "married officer" or "single officer", our Personnel section still felt it necessary to refer the matter to the Department of Finance: should a married woman officer be entitled to a married officer's allowance? The Department of Finance was sceptical: its view was that the Regulations were framed at a time when by definition a married officer could only be a married man. Therefore, at a minimum, the issue needed to be referred to the Attorney General for his advice.

My husband, at the time an Administrative Officer in the Department of Finance, was bearing the brunt of the extremely conservative mindset that prevailed in that Department. On the question of the rental ceiling, his superior officer told him of the terms in which the debate was being conducted: "Why should a man be allowed hang up his hat in his wife's apartment, paid for the State." Shades of the old "fear isteach" mentality of rural Ireland of decades ago!

A certain amount of steel entered my soul at that time. The whole discussion was patently ridiculous and I knew that, particularly in an EU perspective, it was legally unsustainable. I also felt that, if the file went to the Attorney General, it might languish indefinitely on his desk. I lodged strong objections and finally, on the eve of my departure, I was informed that married officers would be deemed to include female married officers, and my allowances would be the same as a married man.

Let me pause here and frame the issue.

The experience had not been a comfortable one for me. What 24 year old, still feeling his or her way in the Department, wants to be branded as a trouble-maker? And, in particular, what young woman wants to risk a reputation for being strident or shrewish?

But the lesson was important. The "system" isn't always right, and we can't always wait and hope the cogs of justice will slowly turn. We need to choose our battles. But if the issue is important enough, we have to be ready to speak up and stand our ground.

Meanwhile, still across in the stone-age Department of Finance of 1976, my husband had applied for a career break to join me on my posting abroad – by definition, the first married man to do so. His application was refused right up along the line before, finally, it was granted following the personal intervention of the Minister for Finance. It required courage on my husband's part to persist against the hierarchy. We women are not the only warriors!

That first Geneva posting was interesting in a number of respects. A male 'traveling spouse' was still something of a novelty in diplomatic circles. My husband was very supportive and often cooked dinner for our diplomatic guests. He was regularly being congratulated on his selflessness and heroic readiness to subordinate his career to mine.

I had no doubt my husband deserved this acknowledgement. Yet something nagged. Lots of female spouses of male diplomats, who were equally supportive and some of whom had made similar career 'sacrifices', were not being acknowledged in the same way. And I often detected an undertone to these elaborate compliments. While praise was being heaped on my husband's selflessness, unspoken but implicit was a sense of an 'unmanly' choice, a more sophisticated expression of the naked prejudice we had experienced in the Department of Finance.

That was almost forty years ago and of course attitudes have evolved. But, even if to a lesser degree, I continue to believe and sense a societal attitude that is different in the case of male and female spouses, with a greater threat to self-esteem in the case of the male spouse. If this is true, there are knock-on effects. There will be a corresponding greater reluctance on the part of the female officer to put her husband in this position, and guilt if she feels she has done so.

I think this issue is too little understood, and it's important to identify it. Being a diplomat by definition implies service abroad; no one can expect to climb the ladder without foreign postings. Our own job satisfaction, and our progression within the Department, requires us to undertake and embrace that part of our career. Over time, in the majority of cases, this will mean finding an accommodation with our lives as wives and mothers.

Yes, we certainly need to think about working hours, child care, and those other very important issues. But we also need to consider deeply within ourselves, and with our partners, how we are going to live with our choices at a psychological level. The Department has an important role in helping to facilitate working spouses, irrespective of whether they are male or female. But, in dealing with the wider societal issue, we need to arm ourselves as individuals and within our partnerships.

The next jolt came in 1982, after I had been back in HQ for a couple of years. A post as Consul General, at First Secretary level, in the US came up and I applied for it, as did others. The posting was discussed at the Management Advisory Committee and subsequently – over coffee for members of our Division – our Assistant Secretary told us, quite openly and unselfconsciously, about what had transpired. He said a view had prevailed in the MAC that Irish America was not ready for women diplomats and that this needed to be taken into account in posting decisions. A male colleague was appointed to the Consul General post.

I found the episode very troubling: not that I or anyone else had an entitlement to this or any other post, but that such considerations should have swayed the choice. Together with another female colleague who had also been an applicant, we sought a meeting with the Secretary of the Department. I recall articulating very strongly my view that the Foreign Service must assert the image and values that define contemporary Ireland, and not try to refashion ourselves in a way that caters to prejudices, or perceived prejudices, of Irish America or any other grouping.

As the then Secretary is not here to relate his side of the story, I should say that he told us the MAC discussion had been misunderstood by our Assistant Secretary and that the posting decision had been made on other grounds.

I am sometimes reminded of that long ago conversation. I still believe, emphatically, that the integrity of our foreign policy requires that we are in all circumstances true to who we are as a people. There may be extreme cases – where, say, the laws of a particular country would make it impossible for a woman diplomat, or a gay diplomat, to function with any degree of effectiveness. But in all other cases – and this will include postings in more marginal countries – our own values will provide the true touchstone of our conduct.

Perhaps partly as a result of this bracing discussion in 1982, I was posted to Washington the following year. I stayed there until 1987, and my daughter was born in Washington in 1985.

Here, let me shift to something more personal.

I have exactly the same recollections of my daughter's infancy as are shared by every working mother: all the delights and all the conflicting pressures. One memory will never leave me: St. Patrick's Day, the Taoiseach's visit, a very long day with all hands on deck in the Embassy, one-year old Claire with a fever, plunging with her into a cold bath around midnight to bring her temperature down. I knew – or at least I felt – that I couldn't let the Embassy down, but I also felt utterly miserable: that I was falling short as a mother and as a human being.

But even if I will never forget that particular night, I think I knew even at the time that I was over-reacting. This was a routine childhood illness, nothing more serious; my daughter had been well cared for during the day. And I think there is a lesson here: we can't deny the reality of our feelings, but we have to go easy on ourselves, and not beat ourselves up unnecessarily.

I doubt there is a single address of this type without the 'guilt' word coming up. For a reason: because it's everywhere: this over-developed, misplaced, female propensity to feel guilt. Of course none of us is perfect, but we are sane, responsible, decent people trying to make the best choices we can. Let's make those responsible, balanced choices – and then live with them.

In 1987, I returned to HQ on promotion to Counsellor. At this stage, I had been thirteen years as First Secretary, including a couple of years as acting First Secretary. The Department had entered inter-Departmental competition for a brief period in '86–'87, and I won my promotion through a competitive interview process. It was the only Counsellor post filled from that year's competition and I felt myself very lucky.

But I felt more than that. There was at the time – as there is now – a bottle neck from First Secretary to Counsellor and it felt like getting through the eye of a needle. Nevertheless, prior to the interdepartmental competition, First Secretary colleagues more junior than me had already been promoted to Counsellor through decisions of the Management Advisory Committee. I respected those who had achieved this promotion, but it was certainly not self-evident what accomplishments or aptitudes had seen them promoted ahead of myself and other colleagues. And, whether or not it was a relevant factor, these were male colleagues promoted by a male MAC.

I always considered the '87 promotion as a watershed in my career, and the question remained open for me as to whether I would have had to wait years longer if I was dependent on a decision of my own MAC. Perhaps not – and it was indeed a decision of the MAC that saw me promoted to Assistant Secretary in 1991. But the '87 experience led me to believe that women are likely to fare better in more open, structured, competitive, processes than in decisions taken behind closed doors.

I am well aware that interview processes carry their own risks and potential for unconscious bias. But I would prefer any day to take my chances in these more transparent processes. And that applies at every level – in the interest of honesty and completeness, I would add that I made my feelings in this regard clear both before and after the Secretary General appointment in 2009.

When I arrived back as Counsellor in '87, I came to a busy Anglo-Irish Division, which was working through the implementation of the 1985 Anglo Irish Agreement. It was an exciting and invigorating time, and in many senses a Division in transition. There were still residual traces of earlier attitudes, when not just had Irish America been regarded as macho territory, but dealing with political figures in Northern Ireland had in some ways been seen so too.

It was definitely time to evolve, and I was glad to be there at the time of evolution and to be part of it. Today of course, Anglo-Irish Division is a very different place, with a strong female presence at senior level. But, more generally, the risk of stereotyping or clustering – certain jobs being seen as more male-oriented and others as more female-oriented – requires constant alertness.

In '91, I was promoted to Assistant Secretary and Head of Administration and was in that role for a further four years. We pushed out a number of boundaries, including our first experiment with interview boards for internal promotions within the Department.

Overseeing the recruitment of Third Secretaries is one of the responsibilities of Administration Division. There was a puzzling aspect of what was happening in the early '90s. More women than men were applying, but proportionately considerably fewer women were making it through the preliminary written general knowledge testing. We were losing too many women at the first hurdle.

We worked with the Civil Service Commission to try to figure out what was happening. The answer, we found, lay in a degree of unconscious bias in the multiple choice questions – there were, for example, sports related questions which would fit far more readily with traditional male interests.

And here let me say something in parenthesis: how often have we women sat around while our male colleagues, or male politicians and civil servants, bonded over forensic analysis of soccer or GAA results? Of course, we don't begrudge this interest, and may sometimes share it – particularly for the major GAA fixtures – but there is something amiss if it becomes workplace currency to an alienating degree.

Once the problem with the general knowledge questions was diagnosed and fixed, and they became more gender neutral, we started to see women coming through in proportionate numbers. So there's a lesson here too: if outcomes are skewed, the inputs and process need investigation to see where along the line the problem is occurring. The answer may not be immediately obvious, but if one keeps digging, it will be found.

My first posting abroad as Ambassador was to PMUN Geneva. I would offer just one vignette from those years.

In 1999, I was elected to chair the UN Commission on Human Rights. It was a profoundly satisfying year but an extremely busy one. At the end of the year, there was a final session where I made my valedictory speech and handed over to my successor. Because I wanted my then 14-year-old daughter to understand the importance of the cause, and why I had seen much less of her in the course of the year than I would have wanted, I invited her to the session.

I was so touched and thrilled by her pride. Although probably not for her, in my head at least, it was a turning point. I could see that my daughter was beginning to grasp the trade-off that is involved in juggling motherhood and career. She understood the worthwhileness of what I was doing professionally. Her pride that day helped move me on from a sense that career achievement equals family cost. I came to realise that one of the great unsung rewards for all the effort is that, one day – and probably much sooner than you think – your child or children will understand your choices and very likely applaud them. I offer this to help and encourage those of you still at the coalface.

Going to Brussels in 2001 as Permanent Representative brought the next big shock. I had no idea before I arrived that I was the first woman Permanent Representative from any member state of the European Union. It seemed unthinkable that this could still be the case, over forty years on from the foundation. As I took my seat in Coreper, the Financial Times wrote: "She made history by sitting down."

Right through our Presidency of the Union in 2004, and the accession of ten new member states in May of that year, I continued to be the only woman Permanent Representative. It was only in my final year, when a new colleague from Luxembourg arrived, that I finally had female company at the table.

My Coreper II colleagues were highly experienced and professional diplomats and I cannot say that I was ever conscious of sexist treatment. But it often did occur to me whether the discussion on occasion might have been less tortuous, whether there might have been less locking horns and more focus on results, had we had some kind of gender balance around the table. Coreper requires grit and strength and endurance but that doesn't mean it needs to be a bull-pen.

And this brings me to the point that is so often, and so rightly, made: gender balance is not just about what is just and right but what it effective. It seems fairly obvious that key decisions are not best made in boys' clubs. And we in Ireland should understand that better than most: we saw where testosterone-fuelled decision-making brought us in 2008.

It is deeply disappointing that, a decade later, there are still only two female Permanent Representatives from the 28 EU member states. And the External Action Service too seems to have been born with a birth defect: women are seriously under-represented at Ambassadorial level. All of us will be scrutinising the filling of top EU positions later this year, and one hopes there will be strong female representation. Of course it's not just a question of externalising the responsibility to EU institutions: member states have to own their own choices in terms of who they send to Brussels – to Coreper, to the Commission, to top jobs in the other key bodies.

Subsequent to Brussels, my postings have been in Paris, New York, and now in Washington.

By the time I went to Paris, my marriage had ended some years earlier. It can be quite daunting as a single person to take on the heavy entertainment responsibilities of a major bilateral post. The tradition in such posts has been very much the married male Ambassador, with a supportive wife who carries a considerable share of the burden on the social front. The Department, and the country more generally, owe a great deal to DFA spouses; I am the first to say how important it is that their contribution be acknowledged, valued and supported.

But the mould is changing: we can expect in the future to see more single Ambassadors, more unaccompanied Ambassadors, more same sex couples. We all need to get used to more diversity, and those of us who are single need to get comfortable with multi-tasking. Insofar as there are any residual stereotypes, it's time we said goodbye to them.

I want to say a quick word about the experience at the UN in New York, even if it represents something of a gear shift from the earlier points I have been making.

One of the greatest satisfactions at the UN was the scope to work on gender-related issues. Ireland can take pride in all we are doing in that regard: the strong gender dimension of our development policy; our support for UN Women; our work on women, peace and security. I felt honoured to give voice to Ireland's values and priorities. Also, in two separate appointments as Co-Facilitator, I had the opportunity to put a strong gender stamp on the wider UN work.

Doing this work at the UN brings a sense of urgency and a sense of perspective. The problems and challenges for women worldwide are enormous – too great a burden as victims and too little recognition as actors. It is important for us to be reminded that, real as they are, ours are first world problems. We need to hold on to that wider vision, and to recognise the obligations that come with it.

I am now almost five months into the Washington assignment, and I am still struck by the resonance of my appointment as Ireland's first woman Ambassador there. Not just young Irish women I have encountered, but so many women of an older generation too, have expressed a vivid sense of pride. When I see how many women feel affirmed by this appointment, it reminds me forcibly just how critical it is that our diplomatic service should be reflective of our country as a whole.

I might add that serving as a woman Ambassador in Washington feels very liberating. Women hold a high percentage of the top posts in the State Department, and the Department organises periodic get-togethers for female Ambassadors. Just last week, I was very happy to attend the swearing-in by Vice President Biden of the new Ambassador for Global Women's Affairs, Catherine Russell.

And so this is where I have arrived; these are some of the threads of my career narrative. They are of course only that – threads and glimpses. I have dwelt on some challenges, but these have never obscured the enormous pride and satisfaction. I know how privileged I am to have had such great assignments, and now to be in Washington. If I ever write my memoir, it will be the very opposite of a "misery memoir" – it will be a celebration of the privilege and opportunity all along the way.

In concluding, I want to come back to these intersecting circles – the individual, the workplace and the wider society – and to present just one final thought.

We have an increasingly sophisticated understanding of how we, as women, are shaped – sometimes misshaped – by our societies. But through our collective choices we too shape our societies.

Some years back, in 2005, in a Graduation Address to the International School in Brussels, I tried to express this to the young people beginning to fashion their lives. Speaking about the disempowerment of women in our society, I said:

"If we are to make space for women at the top, then society will have to be restructured in a way that secures a better work/life balance for us all. But women too must rise to the challenge. Of course it's our right to prioritise and our priorities will probably shift in different phases of our lives. For myself, I would say unhesitatingly that my role as a mother is absolutely central to my life. But I also know this: if we women consistently prioritise the personal over the professional, and the personal over the political, then we cannot legitimately complain if the hands on the levers of power are male hands."

Let us by all means be clear as to what the Department's responsibilities are, and how a more equal society needs to be constructed. But let us also not overlook our own responsibilities, nor ever underestimate our power to fashion our own choices.

"Diplomacy, Diaspora, Diversity"
Annual Conference: The 30% Club Ireland, Dublin
25ᵗʰ January 2017

I am very glad to be here, and to have received this invitation to address your gathering. Some clever person in the 30% Club chose this wonderfully alliterative title: "Diplomacy, Diaspora, and Diversity", and it gives me a broad canvas to address a number of issues.

Let me make one thing very clear at the outset. I speak as someone who has had tremendous opportunities in my professional life. For almost forty-five years, I have had the enormous privilege of serving Ireland at home and abroad – always in interesting places, at fascinating times. Every day, I am grateful for that privilege and opportunity.

I could easily and effortlessly spend my allotted fifteen minutes this evening speaking about the enormous progress achieved in the decades since I joined the Department of Foreign Affairs. And all of it would be true. The Department today is almost unrecognisably different from the institution I joined in 1972. Today's management has a strong commitment to gender equality. Recommendations of a gender audit, carried out a few years ago, are being conscientiously implemented. Almost 30% of our heads of Mission are female, and a recent round of promotions to top level posts had a very healthy success rate for women candidates.

But I believe what's most important on occasions such as this is to jolt ourselves out of any tendency towards complacency. So I will largely concentrate this evening on the road still to be travelled.

There is one question I want to touch on at the outset: "Does it matter that there should be gender balance in diplomacy?" As you might expect, my answer is unequivocally yes – it does matter. I could put forward various rationales. In general, I assume it's the common currency in this room that a more balanced workforce leads to better decision-making. But more specifically, I could posit a view that we would have a more collaborative, more consensual, less bellicose world if women had an equal share of top diplomatic and foreign policy posts.

That might indeed prove to be the case but, as of now at least, we don't have a solid evidential basis to support such a thesis. In fact, there is interesting research about the minority of women in top foreign policy posts feeling they need to battle stereotypes, perceptions of "softness", and therefore being propelled towards more hawkish positions. What we don't know is whether, with more women in these posts, and absent the stereotypes and women feeling they had to react against them, behavioural patterns might be different. So, the jury is still out on that.

The basis for my answer is much simpler. Diplomats – and especially Ambassadors, who are among the most visible diplomats – should look like the people they represent. It's normal; it's healthy; it's how it should be. Remember a couple of years ago when Canadian Prime Minister Justin Trudeau came into office, and was asked to explain the logic of the 50/50 gender breakdown of his cabinet. His answer could not have been more succinct: "Because it's 2015". And so I don't think we need to over-claim or engage in special pleading. Women represent 50% of humanity; we should have a 50% stake in decisions that affect the future of humanity. It's really that simple.

Does this matter to people? In my experience, it does – a lot. As you heard, I was the first woman to represent Ireland in each of my five posts as Ambassador, and when I went to Brussels in 2001, I was the first woman Ambassador, ever, from any member state of the Union – and this over forty years since the Union was founded. Everywhere I've been, but especially in my current post, again and again I have had women come up and tell me how happy they are to have a woman Ambassador. They notice; they feel affirmed; it matters.

And I think there is an important general point here. People connect with what they can identify with. One could express it as a mathematical equation: Representivity equals relatability. And isn't this what all our institutions – government or business – are looking for: a sense of connection with our citizens or clients?

Now let me get to the main focus of what I want to say this evening: the extent to which problems still persist.

First, a few statistics – or rather one stubborn statistic that keeps recurring. For all the undoubted progress made, the fact is that women in our Department still hold only 15% of the posts at most senior level. And our Foreign Service is not in any way aberrational. When I look around me in DC, although the number fluctuates slightly at any given time, about 15% of the Ambassadors are female. And the same is true of the women Ambassadors to the United Nations in New York: the ratio there too has hovered around 15% over the past years.

Perhaps this is the moment to say a word about pipelines, because it's such an important issue. As I said earlier, the picture in our Department is certainly not static; things are improving and unquestionably – based on recruitment patterns in recent years and the cohorts of very able younger women moving through the ranks – things are bound to get better. But I'm always sceptical of any easy reassurance about pipelines. The fact is that they can let you down. I have seen this in the civil service and I'm sure the same is true in the private sector. For all sorts of reasons, pipelines are very prone to developing leaks. So it's critical to diagnose what's causing these leaks and to move very actively to reinforce and protect the pipelines.

As I suspect is true of many professional women, I am more

comfortable talking about issues and statistics than drawing on personal experience. But I think it's important to share a sense of how it actually feels to be part of that 15%.

Three years ago almost to the day, I addressed the Gender Equality Network in my Department (and yes, it's so good that we have such a Network). Especially given the coincidence of dates, I thought it might be of interest this evening to juxtapose what I said on that occasion with my perspective today, informed by three further years at the coalface.

When I spoke three years ago, I thought it would be helpful, especially for my younger colleagues, to talk about some of the challenges I had experienced throughout the years. I spoke about the "marriage ban" which existed since the foundation of the State right up until Ireland joined the European Union – the ban which meant that women were systematically ejected from the public service, civil service, Foreign Service the day they got married. I talked about the legacy of that ban for those of us who entered the Foreign Service in the early '70s: how we lacked female path finders or mentors.

As it happened, when I was posted to Geneva in 1976, I was the first married woman diplomat to serve abroad in the history of our Foreign Service. Faced with a rear-guard action from the Department of Finance, I had to threaten legal action to secure a married officer's allowance and rental accommodation suited to a married officer. And throughout most of the intervening decades – even if things slowly but steadily improved – there were still recurring struggles to assert equal rights to postings and promotion.

When I gave that address to my colleagues in January 2014, I certainly didn't minimise the continuing challenges or suggest that all the battles were behind us. But my conclusions were essentially upbeat, feeling that the path ahead was now clearly signposted, and that we were poised for the next push. I also described how liberating it felt to be in DC, where there were a significant number of women in senior positions in the State Department and across the Obama Administration.

Within a couple of months of giving this speech, I had a reality check. Mid-March 2014, St. Patrick's Day. The Taoiseach's programme in DC had gone well and our delegation had arrived in New York. A minor incident intruded: I had arranged a meeting which the Taoiseach wanted; there was a misunderstanding with one of his senior officials, and an exchange of words followed which was overheard by a journalist. There were some overblown media headlines over the next few days before the whole thing receded.

As I said, nothing seismic and it would scarcely be worth recalling had the incident not brought some pretty shocking sexism to the surface. References appeared in the media to my being "too big for my boots, to my "Prada" shoes, (let me interject here that I have never owned Prada shoes in my life; and I don't know anyone on a civil salary who has!); how I looked and how I dressed.

It was a jarring – but perhaps salutary – reminder of the attitudes that professional women still have to contend with.

Over these past three years, I have also had reason to adopt a rather more nuanced view as to how good it was for senior women in the Administration in Washington. I came to know a number of these women well, and to hear their stories. Just a couple of vignettes.

I hosted a reception recently for a distinguished senior woman official, head of one of the major US scientific and environmental agencies. As it happened, she had an Admiral on her staff, a man who reported to her, who was also at the reception. They both told me, with a degree of amusement but underlying seriousness, about a strategy they had developed over the years. He would always accompany her on official networking occasions, at her shoulder, fully uniformed and badged. This was important, they explained, as a signifier of status. Otherwise, she would risk being side-lined, since the unspoken but prevailing assumption on these occasions was that people of consequence in the room – the people one needed to direct oneself towards and impress – were male.

I have, from time to time, experienced something along these lines myself in DC (where, unfortunately, I don't have the benefit of an Admiral at my shoulder!). No issues at all when people know in advance it's a woman Ambassador. But otherwise, come into a room with a man at one's side; someone will say, "Here is the Ambassador", and the chances are that hands will be outstretched to greet the man.

In other words, for Ambassadors (and I would suspect the same is true for CEOs and Board Chairs) the default setting is male. And clearly the only thing that's going to change that is critical mass. Everyone here obviously knows that – since you're in the 30% Club – but it bears repeating over and over.

Another vignette; this time relating to women in the White House. Even under the equality-conscious President Obama, it seems that all was not quite as it should be in the earlier years of his Administration. In key White House meetings, the women – over time – came to feel that male voices were disproportionately carrying weight. They got together and analysed what was happening and why. They agreed to develop a conscious practice of "amplification": when one woman made a cogent point, other women would deliberately support it and credit her: "As Mary said …"

I think most of us are familiar with this particular syndrome, but it was something of an eye opener that it was still an issue – even in the Obama White House.

The ultimate reality check came with the Presidential Election.

Of course I am not going to make a political speech here this evening. Our Embassy works in an entirely bipartisan way in Washington. I have met President Trump, and had the honour of attending the Inauguration last Friday, and it goes without saying that we will be working towards a fruitful and forthcoming relationship with the incoming Administration. But you could not have lived through this campaign in the US without being struck by the sexism and misogyny that accompanied it.

Seeking to elect a woman to the White House is constantly referred to as the effort to break the "ultimate, highest glass ceiling". Based on what I have seen, I'm inclined to think this ceiling is more reinforced concrete than glass!

The title of my talk also encompasses the diaspora, so let me say a word on that subject. My interaction with Irish America has been one of the most enriching aspects of my posting: their love for and loyalty towards Ireland never ceases to inspire me. The diaspora comprises many interwoven strands and there is no single catch-all characterisation. Some of the organisations are progressive; others are rooted in an earlier vision of Ireland and perhaps an earlier vision of America.

Since my appointment, I have had a series of courteous and mutually respectful but honest exchanges with the Friendly Sons of St. Patrick. The Friendly Sons have been an all-male organisation since their foundation in 1771. In the majority of their branches, the main annual activity is the St. Patrick's Day dinner. Frankly, it falls so far short of how a joyful and inclusive St. Patrick's Day could be, when hundreds of men gather for a celebratory dinner and shut the door on women.

Early last year, I was delighted to receive a communication from the Friendly Sons of St. Patrick in Philadelphia – the cradle of the organisation – informing me that they had decided to revise their policy of nearly 250 years and to admit women members, and inviting me to become the first female member.

There was a wonderfully positive, celebratory evening in Philadelphia when I was admitted to the Society, along with other women. And this led to one of the most cherished moments of my DC posting. At the White House reception on St. Patrick's Day last year, when President Obama addressed the guests, he warmly referenced my admission to the Friendly Sons and went on to quote an excerpt of the speech I had given in Philadelphia: "To quote Ambassador Anderson: There are no second class citizens; there are no children of a lesser God".

As I said, a lovely moment – and important to remind ourselves that, when one keeps knocking on doors, they may eventually open.

Moving from the personal anecdotes back to the issues, I would make three points before concluding.

Firstly, we need to ensure that there is a balanced, clear-eyed identification of the problems. The constraints on women's advancement are threefold: attitudinal issues for women themselves, workplace issues and societal issues. And each set of issues needs to be comprehensively addressed.

Throughout my posting in the US, I have time and again addressed women's groups – not just in New York or DC but in more far-flung places like Missoula, Montana, or Anchorage, Alaska. The problems that keep coming to the fore in these discussions are the ones that women experience in their own psyche: the confidence issues, the limits we place on our aspirations, the trade-offs between ambition and likability, the guilt of working mothers.

These issues are absolutely real and absolutely need to be addressed. Of course we have responsibilities as women to fashion our own futures. But we also have to remember: *it's not all on us*: I worry sometimes that – at least in the US – women will drown in self-help books while letting employers and governments and the media off the hook.

Secondly, and very briefly: my title was about diversity but, given the focus of today's meeting, I have treated this in terms of gender diversity. But diplomacy of course will be enriched by diversity in all its forms. We represent a rainbow of people: male, female, gay, straight – and, in an increasingly multi-ethnic nation, let's all look forward to the future Ruth Neggas of Irish diplomacy.

The third point is one that I want to leave you with. Particularly in my current post, but in previous ones too, one of my core responsibilities has been protecting and promoting Ireland's image and reputation. Our success in so many areas depends on this, but it is vital to our economic performance. Again and again we talk about our talent—and all our feedback from the key economic decision-makers, the corporate heavy hitters, suggests that this is indeed one of the most compelling elements of our FDI offer. Particularly in the period ahead as we are buffeted by Brexit, and the increasing likelihood of some type of corporate tax reform in the U.S., image and talent will become more than ever important.

So what is this image we project? It is one of a modern, progressive, country with a dynamic and flexible workforce. In other words, a "cool" Ireland, in the American sense. Implicit in all of this is an image of Ireland that has women, in critical mass, in senior echelons of business and in the board rooms. That's part of the very definition of modernity. And so we need to walk the talk – especially as the competition heats up on every front, we need to make sure that the reality matches this projection of ourselves.

One that note, let me finish and repeat my thanks for this invitation to address you, and to applaud the good work of the 30% Club. Although I retire from the Foreign Service this summer, this is a cause I will continue to support, in whatever capacity in the future – there is just too much unfinished business.

Women's Leadership Conference
University College Dublin
8th February 2018

It's good to be here, to be talking about this important topic, and to feel the energy and drive and sense of purpose in the room.
I am privileged to have been given a 40 minute speaking slot, which allows me to be fairly expansive. I'm going to divide up my time – first talk a bit about my own career in the Department of Foreign Affairs and then move on to offer some reflections on issues surrounding women's leadership today. There is such a broad canvas to cover; I am conscious that – even with this time allocation – I will be glancing off some issues pretty briefly, and hopefully we can probe a little further in the short Q&A session.

There is one caveat I place at the outset. I don't claim to be one of those leadership gurus who can offer seven points for success or ten tips to get to the top, or whatever. Real life is messy and complicated and for women today its especially messy and complicated. I'm still working through the questions myself - my thinking continues to evolve and I certainly don't have have all the answers. What I can offer is my own experience, some of what worked for me, and a few thoughts about the way forward.

Career
So let's dial back to November 1972 when I joined our foreign service. Hard to believe that it's just over forty five years ago – a generation and a half. I had turned twenty the previous July, had graduated in History and Politics from UCD, and was very ready to embark on exciting new horizons.

I had spent three years, 1969 to 1972, at UCD and although I don't claim that I would have been considered a student radical, I had absorbed some of the intellectual excitement of the late 60s and early 70s. The anti -Vietnam protests in the US, the student uprising in Paris, had their admittedly much more muted echoes in UCD.

We emerged, most of us still tentative and unsure of ourselves or where we were going, but with a disposition to question authority and not be cowed or overly awed by hierarchy – a disposition I would still regard as a fundamentally healthy one. And the young women among us had at least a nodding acquaintance with the canon of feminist authors, from Simone de Beauvoir and Betty Friedan onward, which subsequently stood us in good stead.

The Department of Foreign Affairs in 1972 was a fascinating place. It had a robust intellectual life, with lots of articulate and confident – and of course predominantly male – officers. Women diplomats were still a bit of a curiosity. The marriage ban, which existed until Ireland joined the European Union, meant that generations of women were lost to the civil service and foreign service. We trickled in slowly: my intake in 1972 was considered highly unusual in that there were two women among the twelve recruits. To my knowledge, this had never happened before – and there were a few dark mutterings about "women taking over the place".

In general I found the Department an invigorating and welcoming workplace, and certainly there was no culture of prejudice or harassment. But inevitably, with such a skewed gender balance, the paradigm was male, the default setting was male. Women were expected to adjust, fit in, and get on with it.

There were pin pricks of irritation from time to time - I recall that in 1974, when I got married and chose to keep my own name, our Personnel Officer told me he "didn't know what game I was playing". More serious issues arose in 1976 when I had my first posting abroad and was the first married woman to be posted. I have chronicled elsewhere some of the difficulties and the fight I had to wage to get a married officer's allowance and married officer's accommodation – problems that I attribute more to the dead hand of the Department of Finance and its distinctly macho culture at the time, than to closed minds in our own Department.

And so on it went – on the one hand interesting, substantive and stretching jobs and an immense amount of fulfilment, and yet intermittent reminders that the playing field was still, at least to some extent, tilted. One such reminder came in the early 80s, when a man was appointed Consul General in Boston ahead of better qualified female candidates, and it was informally explained to us that the decision reflected Irish-American difficulty, or perceived difficulty, in relating to women diplomats.

And there was a further sharp reminder in the mid '80s when, at the crucial promotion to Counsellor Level, the all male Management Committee promoted more junior male officers ahead of me, on no grounds that were either apparent or explained. I subsequently secured that key promotion through inter-Departmental competition, confirming my sense that women are more likely to benefit from open and transparent decision making processes than decisions emerging from behind closed doors.

Things gradually improved over the years, as the number of women diplomats slowly grew (although the structures remained very pyramidal, as they still are) and the times grew more enlightened. My career proceeded apace: I worked for four years in our Anglo Irish Division and a further four years as Assistant Secretary General in Corporate Services.

My first posting as Ambassador was to the United Nations in Geneva. The six years I spent there taught me a lot. Through my work on human rights and development issues, I became much more deeply conscious of the shameful inequalities and injustices experienced by women in many parts of the developing world. It didn't make our first world challenges any less urgent; indeed if anything it threw up patterns where one could see similar underlying factors at work, even if the degree and manifestations differed. But it did bring perspective, and brought home the importance of global solidarity among women. Throughout the intervening years, the painful awareness has remained with me that - despite all the challenges - the conditions we women in the developed world take for granted are beyond the imagining of millions of women worldwide.

Four other postings as Ambassador followed: to the European Union, to France, to the United Nations in New York and then to Washington. I have spoken previously about my posting to the EU and my shock on arriving in Brussels in 2001 to discover that I was the first woman Ambassador – or Permanent Representative, as it is technically known – from any member state of the Union. And this in over 45 years of the existence of the EU, or what evolved into the EU.

Let me just say here in parentheses that last year was the 60th anniversary of the signature of the Treaty of Rome, the founding Treaty of the European Union. There were celebrations and exhibitions to mark the anniversary and I found myself contemplating the photos of the original Treaty signing ceremony. There is one photograph which shows some 50 or 60 people in the meeting room that day. Scanning the rows of men to find any woman, I eventually landed on one figure in the back row who might have been female – it was difficult to tell. Not at all surprising for 1957, but hard to explain where things still stood in 2001.

Back to my own posting. As it happened, Ireland had the EU Presidency in the first half of 2004, when the EU enlarged from 15 to 25 members. As Ambassador, I was chairing Coreper, the key decision-making group which brings together all the Ambassadors on a weekly basis. And yes, when enlargement happened we were joined by 10 male Ambassadors, so I was now one among 25. This situation continued until fairly shortly before I left Brussels and Luxembourg sent a female Ambassador.

Fast forward through the years in Paris, New York and Washington. All great postings, full of challenge, and I was very privileged to have them. But every so often, there were the reminders of the price you pay for being a woman, including, at times, the kind of media coverage back in Ireland that would never have arisen in the case of a male colleague. Whenever such incidents occurred, inside or outside the Department, I tried to deal with them in firm but measured ways, making my feelings clearly known to the relevant decision-makers but focussing on getting on with the job in an even more determined way.

In New York, as Ambassador to the UN, I was back in contact with the issues affecting women around the world: issues of inequality and marginalisation, the appalling toll of sexual violence in conflict. I am happy to say that it was, and is, Departmental policy that we maintain a strong focus on gender issues. But additionally – especially with only about 15% female Ambassadors to the UN – I felt a strong personal sense of mission to draw attention to these issues whenever the opportunity arose: in speeches, in various tasks I undertook at the request of the President of the General Assembly, in setting up a network for women diplomats that I will mention again later.

During my time in Washington, the same statistic recurred: about 15% of the accredited Ambassadors were female. Washington, as you might imagine was a very demanding posting, with a busy agenda on the economic, political, and community and cultural fronts. There was inevitably a fair bit of comment about my being the first female Ambassador from Ireland. I was anxious that this would not be just a label, or an easy way of introducing me, but would actually count for something.

And so throughout my posting I made a sustained effort to address the residual sexism in some of the Irish American organisations. I also made a point of addressing women's groups both in DC and in my travels around the country – I benefited immensely from these exchanges and I recall some terrific conversations in places like Missoula, Montana, and Anchorage, Alaska. And we ensured an overall gender consciousness in all our Embassy work: for example, when it came to the 1916 centenary celebrations, which were a massive focus in the US throughout 2016, we incorporated a strong emphasis on the role of women in the Rising, the lead up and aftermath.

I make these points to underline my belief that, if you are a woman in a senior position, you have in a sense a dual mandate: to perform at your very best level in all aspects of the job but also to stay alert to, and engage in, the gender equality agenda.

I will admit that this isn't always easy, especially in a very stretching job, and there are times when one feels a bit weighed down by the sense of a double responsibility. The wonderful Anne Enright wrote a piece a little while back about her experience as the First Laureate of Irish Fiction, which included the following:

"The business of writing is hard enough without taking on the additional burden of gender politics. Listening to arguments about gender makes men mildly defensive and takes very little of their time. If you are a woman, making these arguments will eat your head, your talent and your life."

Anne was writing this slightly tongue in cheek, and of course it's not entirely fair to men, certainly to some men. The fact is, and her article provides the backdrop, the three major addresses she gave as Laureate were all about the female voice, heard and unheard. But still, I would accept that there is a grain of truth in what she wrote. The answer I think lies in recognising our responsibility - it's a price we pay for the privilege of being born a woman - but trying to see it not as something distinct and separate, rather integrating it as part of who we are and how we function …. definitely not letting it eat our head or our talent!

Now, before I share some reflections on all of this, I think it is important to update you briefly on the present day situation in the Department of Foreign Affairs. The structures as I mentioned remain pyramidical, with 70% men and 30% women at the most senior level: Assistant Secretary upwards. But this still represents significant progress over recent years, and I sense a real commitment to building on that progress: the Department now has a Gender Equality Plan and Diversity Plan together with a dedicated Sub Committee of the Management Board to oversee implementation. So absolutely no grounds for complacency but at the very least a forthright acknowledgment of the challenges.

Reflections

I promised I would share some reflections about women and leadership.

Firstly, a general point about leadership, that applies to woman and men. I think that to rise to a senior position in any organisation, to become a leader, means being truly committed to what you are doing and to believe in its essential worth. I valued public service highly – I felt I could look in the mirror and tell myself that I was serving my country, serving Irish people, and trying to do some good in the wider world. Of course one can have an equal sense of validation in many other careers. But whatever your chosen walk of life, you have to believe in it, or else you will always be withholding something. It's that conviction that drives you forward, that means you don't begrudge your time or effort. So if any of us don't feel that about what we are currently doing, it's time to think seriously about finding ways to move on.

Another point. I take it as common ground among us - and therefore I won't labour the point - that society, and business, and policy making generally, benefit from diversity in decision making. As we well know, this is about what's smart as well as what's right. But for today's talk, I propose to take this as a given and to concentrate primarily on the issues as they affect women.

When it comes to women's leadership, I think there are three sets of issues that need to be looked at: behavioural and approach issues on the part of women themselves; workplace issues; and wider societal issues. Of course they are very much interrelated and any compartmentalisation is somewhat arbitrary – women's behavioural patterns didn't develop in a vacuum and the workplace is a microcosm of wider society. But as a way of analysing and reflecting, I think it's useful to break the issues down to some degree.

Issues for women

The behavioural patterns and traits that hold women back have been analysed in umpteen books and studies: the self-doubt, the perfectionist standards to which we hold ourselves, the guilt to which we are prone.

Everything I have experienced and encountered tells me that these confidence issues are near universal ones for women, irrespective of nationality or status. I recognise them in myself and I have heard about them from so many other women that I have respected and admired over the years. I mentioned the group I set up when I was Ambassador to the UN in New York - an informal group of women Ambassadors to interact with younger women diplomats from across all missions to the UN. We invited high level women from the UN to address us, women such as Michele Bachelet, who went back to Chile to serve a second term as President, and Susanna Malcorra who went on to become Foreign Minister of Argentina. Truly impressive and distinguished women. And I can tell you the same themes surfaced in all their presentations: the personal effort required throughout their careers to assert themselves, the battle to be taken as seriously as their male colleagues, the struggles they had with themselves along the way.

However senior or junior we are, most of us have lived these experiences. Take the familiar female syndrome in meetings – we are reluctant to take the floor first, or early on; we will wait to hear what others have to say and then intervene if we feel we have a well thought out, well rehearsed point that will genuinely add value. So we wait, and when we're finally ready, the meeting is running out of time, or people's attention span is already strained, or that key point we were saving up has been made by someone else.

This confidence issue surfaces everywhere. Remember the point that PM Justin Trudeau made when he met with Taoiseach Leo Varadkar for the first time in Dublin last year and the question came up about women in the Cabinet, and why the Taoiseach had not followed the Prime Minister's 50/50 example. There was comment about the insufficient pool of female parliamentarians and PM Trudeau said: "If you ask a woman to step forward and run, her first question often is: Really, do you think I should, do you think I can, do you think I am qualified enough? If you ask a man to run for politics, his first question is: Well, what took you so long?".

Here's what I think about confidence. I think it is something we can all achieve but it needs a lot of work. You can't just apply it like a layer of paint. There's an in depth process and a more superficial process. The in depth process requires a serious conversation with yourself, or a series of these conversations. What do you want out of life? Do you want to try to shape things and change things? Do you want to be someone who makes things happen, or someone to whom things happen? Because if it's the former – we have no choice, we have to develop confidence. And once we have made the decision, then we can go on to develop the tools and techniques – the props if you like – that will help us project as more confident people.

We also have to battle the propensity to guilt. I recall very distinctly one moment nearly 20 years ago that was a kind of turning point for me. During my time as Ambassador in Geneva, I chaired the UN Commission on Human Rights for a year. It was one of the most difficult, challenging but ultimately rewarding things I ever did. I was only the fourth women to chair the Commission, the first having been the great Eleanor Roosevelt way back in the 1940s.

The chairing role came to our regional group only once every five years and it was a big honour to be offered it. But I almost said no – mainly because I already had a very busy day job as Ambassador and I was concerned that my then 14 year old daughter would see so little of me in the course of the year. At the last moment I braked myself – how could I legitimately complain about women's marginalisation if I was myself unwilling to take on such a role when offered? So the planned no became a yes: the experience of chairing was a tremendously enriching one for me, and my daughter not just survived perfectly well but was proud of what I was able to achieve as Chair.

I don't want to be simplistic. Not all dilemmas are as easily or happily resolved as this one — sometimes our personal circumstances just leave us no choice but to turn an opportunity down, and we can't beat ourselves up about that either. But the lesson stayed with me: if something is intrinsically worthwhile, and you believe in it and want to do it, try in every way you can to make it happen.

Workplace issues

So let's accept that most of us have issues we need to work on. But, and this is an absolutely crucial point, let's not get things out of perspective. It's not all on us. The last thing we need is women drowning in self-help books while letting employers and governments off the hook.

So a word about the workplace.

We need a conversation - a whole series of conversations - about gender proofing the workplace, whether it's working schedules or general modus operandi. I think it would have been pretty healthy, for example, in that exchange between Taoiseach Varadkar and PM Trudeau that I mentioned earlier, if one or other of them, beyond pointing to women's confidence issues, had also talked about the need to examine their parliaments as places where women genuinely feel they can contribute on an equal basis. Certainly some women politicians don't feel this about Dail Eireann. Joan Burton for example spoke recently about "feeling the sighs" of male colleagues "when women are - in inverted commas -"going on". Women get interrupted a lot more and men chairpersons, by and large, can be a lot more snappy when women are speaking".

So yes, there is a problem if there aren't enough women in the Dáil to provide the pool from which a gender-balanced cabinet can be drawn, but it's essential to dig deep and try to have a real understanding of why this is so, and what can be done about it.

Some of the workplace issues are blindingly obvious – the persistent pay inequities in some sectors, the pyramidical structures with massive gender imbalances on boards and in C suites.

But there is a whole slew of other workplace issues that are somewhat less obvious but present very real barriers to women's advancement. And the more you read around the subject the more you realise that it stretches across all professions. There is the data from the arts sector and the academic and media sectors. There are well documented studies across the medical profession about the steeper obstacles facing women in medicine. Studies about the marginalisation of women economists. And the financial services sector sometimes seems in a league of its own.

Set against this wider backdrop, I think it is fair to say that the diplomatic profession offers a degree of protection. There is respect for the office – the fact that you are representing your country – and undoubtedly the title of Ambassador provides you with a certain carapace.

But of course there is no immunity. When women Ambassadors are in a 15% minority, you are the exception not the norm. For most people doing a quick word association exercise, say Ambassador and it probably conjures up a silver-haired gentleman. It not infrequently happened to me that, if people didn't know there was a female Ambassador, and I entered a room with a male member of my team, the hands of greeting were automatically extended to my male colleague and the assumption made that he was the Ambassador. Now, just when have any of us seen that happen in reverse?

People often ask me what it was like working in such a male dominated environment as for example I did during my time at the EU in Brussels. Well, I think it was only in retrospect that I recognised a certain burden that went with it. I want to make this absolutely clear: my colleagues were senior experienced diplomats; we treated each other with respect; I was definitely not patronised -and would never have allowed myself to be.

But there was undoubtedly a macho quality to some of the exchanges, a kind of verbal gladiatorial combat at times. A more balanced gender make-up would have made for a different style and culture. I fitted in and adapted because I had to – Ireland had key national interests at stake in many of the debates and it was my job to advance and defend those interests in the most effective possible way.

It was some time afterwards that a parallel occurred to me. I moved on from Brussels to be Ambassador in France. My French is quite fluent although I would not describe myself as bilingual. But I got used to making speeches and handling all sorts of public engagements through French. It was only after I got to New York, as Ambassador to the UN, that I rediscovered the ease of making speeches in and operating through my own language. It felt like I was back swimming in my native waters again, able to concentrate entirely on the substance of what I was saying, knowing that the language would come fairly effortlessly.

And it struck me that in these male-dominated work environments that's what it's like for the men – they are swimming in their native waters. For us, no matter how fluent we become with the language and style, there is always that additional effort. You adapt, and mostly you scarcely notice the effort, until you sense the liberation when you find yourself back in a more balanced environment. It's the burden of being in the minority – and of course it's true of any minority. While I have never walked in their shoes, I would imagine that it's also what people of colour feel when they work in a predominantly white workplace.

Clearly, the only satisfactory and sustainable way forward is to achieve more balanced workplaces. Reaching that outcome is a huge and complex challenge - and not something I can begin to do justice to in my talk today. But in a couple of sentences: it is going to require a combination of approaches: legislative action, cultural change, building pipelines that actually work - which means monitoring and protecting the pipelines so that they don't develop leaks along the way, as they are highly prone to. And it absolutely requires a whole hearted involvement of men, including in a far more balanced distribution of parenting and domestic duties than is the case at present.

But in the meantime, until we we get to that point of balance, women need workplace strategies which help us to survive and flourish. Firstly, we need to be informed and clear-eyed analysts so that, if we experience discrimination – overt or more subtle – we can recognise it for what it is. Secondly, after the recognition, there is the question of reaction and response. There are of course core values that must be respected, lines that cannot be crossed. If any such lines are being crossed, then all available remedies inside and if necessary outside the workplace must be deployed.

But, falling short of that, we often find ourselves in greyer areas where it's harder to calibrate one's response. I know, and respect, the viewpoint that toleration of minor transgressions can lead to or help create a permissive environment, where major transgressions are more likely to occur. My own approach has been slightly different; rather than trying to fight all the battles, I chose to engage on what I saw as the more significant ones, tuning out things that I regarded as more minor irritants. Whatever our approach or our choice, the key point is that it should be a conscious, empowering one.

Thirdly, and you will infer this from what I have said before, I believe that in navigating some of the more subtle obstacles in the workplace, gender solidarity is an important tool and asset. The objective is clearly not to privilege one gender over another, but to try to ensure there is a genuinely level playing field. Take for example the "amplification" approach. In a classic example, where a woman makes a point at a meeting, and it is echoed by a male speaker, and subsequent speakers endorse "John's point", then the female speakers need to consciously and emphatically refer to "Mary's point". Just one example of the many ways we women can validate each other.

Societal issues

To finish, then, a word about some of the wider societal issues, of which as I said the workplace is a microcosm. So much of what we struggle with, in the workplace and beyond, is the essential power paradigm: the dynamics of power, how power is distributed. Mary Beard, the British classicist, addresses the issue forthrightly in her recent book: "Women and Power: A Manifesto". Tracing the silencing of the female voice back to Greek and Roman antiquity, she is quite clear that power "is coded as male....our mental, cultural template for a powerful person remains resolutely male."

Powerful women continue to have to grapple with stereotypes. We saw this played out in technicolour at the 2016 Presidential election in the US. As Ambassador, I had a ringside seat for that campaign. The causes of Hillary Clinton's failure and Donald Trump's success will be the stuff of analysis for a long time, and it would be simplistic and reductionist to explain it exclusively in terms of sexism and misogyny. But of course sexism was a factor. The expectations of, and tolerance threshold for, both candidates were radically different.

If Donald Trump were a woman – with the same temperament, the same track record, the same behavioural patterns – it is simply inconceivable that she would have been elected. If Hillary Clinton were a man, there would still have been a fatigue factor with the Clintons, criticism of lack of vision, of excessive pragmatism and no doubt much more. But the male version of Hillary would not have had to deal with endless gauging of his likability, whether he smiled enough, whether the timbre of his voice was off-putting, and I doubt that he would have been seen as co-responsible for spousal infidelity.

And all of this applies even if you take Donald Trump out of the equation. Think back to the campaign for the Democratic nomination. One example: Bernie Sanders and Hillary Clinton both tended towards a high decibel level at their rallies, but it was heard differently. As one journalist put it: " When Bernie yells, it shows his dedication to the cause. When she yells, it's interpreted in a very different way: She's yelling at you." In other words, a passionate man translates to an angry woman.

While I didn't join the Women's March in Washington the day

after the Presidential Inauguration – it would have been incompatible with my role as Ambassador – I had a chance to engage with my daughter and her friends who came from New York to be part of it. I felt the energy and determination, and also the anger.

That energy and anger is now translating into action, and we see an exponential increase in women engaging in electoral politics right across the US. Organisation such as Emily's List are almost overwhelmed by the flood of approaches they are receiving. There is no guarantee as to where all this will lead - anger does not of itself offer a meaningful or saleable agenda- but one senses at least the possibility of transformative change.

The passion is also manifesting itself in the #MeToo movement and one of its spin-offs, the "Time's Up" Campaign. It feels as if a match has been lit and lifetimes of latent frustration are coming to the surface. Some of what has emerged has been truly shocking, even to those of us who felt we were inured to shock.

I confess to feeling conflicted about aspects of the #MeToo movement – for me, as for some other women of my generation, there are at times uncomfortable suggestions of victimhood and disempowerment. But speaking to my daughter and women of her generation, and reading what they have written, has helped me towards a better understanding.The movement is essentially about solidarity, about demonstrating the scale and pervasiveness of what has been going on, and trying to ensure that those who have the courage to speak out are not isolated and stigmatised. I have also been heartened to see the ripples of the movement spread outward, to embrace less privileged women who work in highly vulnerable situations.

Certainly we can brace ourselves for a backlash, and the legitimate debates about tactics among women who share the same essential goals, will undoubtedly be exploited by those who want to retain the status quo, who fear the loss of power and privilege. I hope we can withstand the backlash, and that the movement does not fragment along generational or class lines. Because this I do know: we need to retain the sense of urgency. It is time for women to be impatient.

I am a diplomat by instinct and experience. This often means achieving or accepting change by increments. How often I have said to myself or to my staff: "60% of something is better than 100% of nothing". I am not going to lose that willingness to work for incremental change, to bank it and build on it.

But my patience has been steadily eroding faced with the slowness of change. It is profoundly dispiriting to do the math, and see how long it will take to achieve gender parity in key areas if we continue at the current pace of change.

I think back to what I and my cohort believed in when we were 20 years of age, the change we believed was on the horizon. We felt ourselves to be trailblazers, on the cusp of a revolution. Too often, along the way, it felt as if we had turned into Sisyphus.

Yes, there has been change and it's important that we measure and acknowledge it. But there has to be steep acceleration and real momentum. We all saw those "Time's Up" buttons that were handed out at the Golden Globes and elsewhere - a sharp and no doubt effective message. But the button I would like to distribute would have a slightly different caption: not so much " Time's Up" but "It's Time". Because it is time and long past time.

And that of course is why occasions like today are so important. I have no doubt the exchanges throughout the day will prove a fortifying and energising experience for us all. My congratulations to UCD for organising it and my thanks to all of you for being attentive listeners.

Bar Council of Ireland Dinner Celebrating International Women's Day
King's Inns, Dublin
8ᵗʰ March 2018

It is truly a privilege to be here with you on International Women's Day and to be invited to give this address. I have a deeply ingrained respect for the legal profession. Particularly through my human rights work over the years, I have seen how societies are defined by the quality of their legal systems, and how the rule of law provides the foundation for healthy societies. So yes, I am genuinely glad to be here.

And I have also had the honour of coming to know personally some of the extraordinary women in the Irish legal profession. Any roll call is invidious but one has to mention of course our two women Presidents, Mary Robinson and Mary McAleese, whom I saw close up as they represented Ireland with such distinction abroad. I also want to recall the trailblazing Mella Carroll, the first woman on our High Court - Mella was such a redoubtable character and I came to know her during my Geneva days, when she was involved with the International Labour Organisation.

And our most recent woman appointee to the Supreme Court, Mary Finlay Geoghegan, who is here tonight. I know Mary from our days at UCD. Back then, Mary exhibited the same ferocious intelligence and enviable poise which has marked her stellar career. And there are of course so many other women who have done,and are doing, such honour to their profession and their gender.

As you see from my CV, I retired about seven months ago after a forty five year career in our foreign service. Indeed, as I retired, I was told by our Personnel Service that I was the longest serving diplomat in the history of the Irish State. I think that such longevity says something about my passion for the career!

Since my retirement, I have spoken to various audiences on a range of topics, and have fairly regularly been asked to address gender issues. And so I have reflected quite a bit on my own career, the changes and challenges for women diplomats, the current perspectives. I have found myself, in these talks, vacillating between optimism for the future and impatience about the glacially slow pace of progress to date. The result tends to be an "on the one hand, on the other hand" kind of speech. As judicious lawyers, you will be very familiar with that kind of approach.

Tonight, on International Women's Day, it is tempting to go for the more celebratory version. And I could certainly speak to you in that vein for the next twenty minutes. Here's how it would go. I would start by drawing the backdrop: late 1972 when I joined the Department of Foreign Affairs, just weeks ahead of Ireland's accession to the then EEC. Emerging from the dark days of the marriage bar in the civil service, which deprived us of generations of able women, into the more enlightened period thrust on us by European social legislation. The slow but steady upward ascent for women diplomats, from near invisibility to the current situation where 55% of the entry grade are female and, just last year, we reached 30% female representation at the most senior level. And I could point to the milestones in my own career, culminating in five hugely satisfying and substantive postings as Ambassador, all of them where I was the first woman to be appointed to that position.

And then in this celebratory speech, I would go on to note the the achievements for women in the legal profession. The unprecedented numbers of young women qualifying as solicitors and barristers. Today's situation where we are seeing increasing percentages of women judges at every level, right up to Supreme Court level. The unique situation we had until recently, and which I spoke about with such pride during my Washington years, where women in Ireland held all the top posts in the justice area: Minister;

Chief Justice; Attorney General, DPP, Garda Commissioner

All of this would be genuine and heartfelt. The advances for women are real and measurable. And in my own case, I have often said that if I were ever to write my memoirs, they would express a profound gratitude for the opportunities and privileges I have had; gifted with ambitious parents and a solid education, with the good fortune to have begun my working life at a time when the country was undergoing transformative change, and new horizons and new opportunities were opening up for women.

But in all honesty, despite this unquestionable progress and my personal sense of privilege, I have felt less and less inclined to give this celebratory speech and less and less satisfied with the "on the one hand, on the other hand" approach. Instead, over the last while, I find myself wanting to focus more single-mindedly on the road still to be travelled.

I ask myself whether retirement has had a radicalising effect, whether - freed from the constraints of diplomacy - I can allow myself to express things that might have been more difficult to articulate while still in the career? Or is it because, speaking to different audiences, I find myself seeing more clearly the patterns affecting women and holding them back across a range of different professions and sectors of society?

These may well be elements, but I actually think this growing sense of impatience and urgency is reflective of something wider, and perhaps particularly influenced by my recent period in the US and the fact that I return there regularly. It feels as if something is really changing there - that a deep sense of frustration among women, which has been simmering for decades, is now coming close to the boil.

Let me stick with the US for a moment. There is no doubt that the 2016 Presidential election campaign, and the election of Donald Trump, acted as a catalyst. I said before - and indeed said it while I was still serving as Ambassador - that it would have been inconceivable for a female version of Donald Trump to have been elected. Imagine a Donna Trump, with the same personal history, the same temperament and behavioural patterns; she would never have got to first base.

And let's take a male version of Hillary Clinton; he would have met some of the same criticisms as she did - too pragmatic, a bit unexciting, around too long - but would have been spared the endless commentary about appearance, timbre of voice, and that so important but hard to define quality of "likability". If ever one needed an illustration of the trade - off for women between being respected and being liked, then one had it in spades in this campaign.

I am not for a moment suggesting that the election was only about sexism and misogyny, but they were ingredients in what proved a fairly toxic mix. And the double standards apply even if you take the controversial figure of Donald Trump out of the equation. Bernie Sanders was strong on passion but short on analysis and workable solutions, and I do not believe that a female version would have had the same traction. And even if we go back to the 2008 election: I am a great admirer of Barack Obama, but I strongly suspect if there were a female version of Obama - able, cerebral, but notably inexperienced - the response back in 2008 would have been: great Vice President material, and in time she will make a good President. What the late Inez McCormack described as the "doctrine of unripe time" as it applies to women.

The Women's March, the day after President Trump's inauguration, brought somewhere between two and five million people on to the streets in cities and towns across the United States. The question was whether the palpable anger would translate into an agenda for action. There are clear signs that this is happening: women are signing up in unprecedented numbers - an avalanche of women - for political training and to run as candidates for electoral office. If even a modest percentage succeed, it will significantly alter the gender map in US political life. And the #MeToo movement, even if triggered by a somewhat different set of factors, draws on the same well that I referred to earlier: that slow burning frustration among women that has taken on a new increment of urgency.

Back closer to home, one senses that something similar is taking hold. Of course we do not have a catalysing figure like Donald Trump, or anything close. But cable news and social media do not respect national boundaries. And certainly any flame of discontent crossing the Atlantic finds no shortage of fuel in Europe.

Yes, there has been identifiable progress but it has been so painfully slow. Here in Ireland, we are marking one hundred years of women having the vote. But it was still celebrated as a modest victory at the last General Election when the share of women in the Dail went from 16% to 22%. Wherever one turns - the arts, academia, the media, the civil service, the financial services sector, the prestige professions, the corporate sector generally - we find women underrepresented, comparatively underpaid, or clustered in the lower tiers of what remain pyramidical structures.

The causes of this imbalance are the stuff of endless debate. We women have subjected ourselves to microscopic self analysis. We are well aware that we have issues to address: insufficient self confidence, a reluctance to take ownership of our ambitions, guilt levels that can be corrosive, and a perfectionism that can be punishing. I recognise these issues in myself and in so many other women I have encountered; I have spoken about them and shared panels with women who have written insightful books about them. They are unquestionably real issues that hold us back and we need to work on them.

But this isn't even half the story. No matter how brilliant the self help books - and Sheryl Sandberg and others have written excellent ones - they won't provide all the answers. We can " lean in" until we develop hunched shoulders, but that may be all we develop unless the wider issues are also addressed. We have to focus on the societal and structural context in which we women make the choices we do.

Looking through a very wide lens, I find it always enlightening to examine attitudes that are deeply imprinted on our culture. I was fascinated to read recently a short work by the British classicist Mary Beard - a compilation of two lectures under the title "Women and Power: A Manifesto". Tracing back to Graeco-Roman times, and through the 2000 intervening years, she concludes that power "is coded as male......our mental, cultural template for a powerful person remains resolutely male".

Her first lecture, The Public Voice of Women, strikes me as particularly interesting for women barristers since the essence of your role - at least as we outsiders perceive it - is getting to your feet in public or semi- public settings. The lecture explores, through two millennia, what Beard describes as the "culturally awkward relationship between the voice of women and the public sphere." In Roman times, when very occasionally women did speak in the forum, they were by definition not real women, but were seen as androgynous. Here's one Roman anthologist describing a woman who, defying all convention, defended herself in court: "She really had a man's nature behind the appearance of a woman."

Reading it, I thought of the conscious androgyny of the wigs and gowns and the black and white garb of judges and barristers. And reflecting on that long tradition of public speaking as a projection of male authority, I thought about perceptions of authority, even today, in our respective professions. In any word word association exercise, say the word Ambassador or Senior Counsel, and for most people what immediately comes to mind is an image of an elegant middle aged gentlemen. I read recently this comment - by a woman of course - that stuck with me: "I used to love the word 'gravitas.' Now I think it's male code for "not like us" at the highest level".

So it's useful to remind ourselves that, when we insist that gravitas can also come in a skirt and high heels, we are battling two thousand years of cultural conditioning.

In any event, from that very wide lens and long perspective, to something much more specific. I want to come back to an issue I touched on earlier: the pyramidical structure across so many of the professions - the strong representation of women at entry level, compared to the much thinner air, in gender terms, at the top. It is true across most professions and it is certainly true of diplomacy.

I mentioned that I was the first woman in each of my five postings as Ireland's Ambassador. More astonishingly, when I became ambassador to the EU in 2001, I was the first woman from any Member State to be accredited as Ambassador - and this in forty five years since the foundation of the Union. In my last two postings, at the UN in New York and in Washington, the overall ratio of female to male ambassadors hovered around 15%.

And, as all of you well know, the pyramidical structure is true of the legal profession also, with only 16% of Senior Counsels female and persistent under representation of women at the top levels in law firms. I imagine most of you will have read that telling article by Elizabeth Fitzgerald in today' s Irish Times which points out that, at the top six legal firms in Ireland, women account for 64% of the non- partner solicitors and only 33% of the partner level positions.

The more optimistic would probably find reassurance in current patterns: feeling that, once the women are there in sufficient numbers at entry level, it is just a matter of time before the pipeline takes them to the top. The sceptics would take a somewhat different view. With more women coming into these professions, inevitably there will be some progression. But pipelines haven't proved that reliable to date. They have shown themselves highly prone to developing leaks, and unless there is conscious reinforcement, we cannot be confident that these leaks won't continue.

It is instructive to look at where exactly these leaks develop. Typically, across the professions, where we see the funnel narrowing in favour of men tends to be around the late 30s, early to mid 40s. In career terms, this mid 30 to mid 40 decade can be a make or break one: a decade of high expectations, high performance, high achievement. And for individuals or couples who choose parenthood, it is also likely to be a decade of births, toddlerhood, early schooling. Hugely rewarding, but also hugely demanding.

"The Mommy Track". It is an expression I detest. I am not sure if the expression is more prevalent in America than in Ireland, but over there at least I have heard it used regularly and quite unselfconsciously. Many of those using it would insist it is non-pejorative, simply denoting a choice to scale back work demands so as to balance career with the demands of young children. In practice it means opting for something with shorter or more predictable hours, sometimes moving to what is seen as a more family friendly work environment.

Fair enough. Parenthood is indeed precious and wonderful, and worth sacrificing for. And we are often reminded nowadays that a career is a marathon, not a sprint. It's possible therefore to slow down at certain points and then pick up the pace subsequently. But there is one big point that gets far too little attention. I have never, ever, heard a reference to "The Daddy Track" and I doubt such a term exists. Some fathers of course are incredibly supportive of their partner's career choice and ambitions, and are ready to pick up the slack on the home front, but this definitely is not seen as a routine choice. Indeed Anne Marie Slaughter has written about "the halo effect" for Dads carrying out this role.

There are no simple answers to the question of how to accommodate intensive career demands and intensive parenting demands, when both coincide. Robust support systems, affordable creches, work flexibility, all play their part. But there also needs to be more explicit support and encouragement - at governmental and employer level - for more equal sharing of parental responsibility. Because society - and that means all of us - needs to adjust to a parenting track rather than a Mommy track. And only when that happens will attitudes begin to evolve, and will we begin to see the working parent issue addressed in a far more serious and meaningful way.

Speaking about being serious, that's exactly what I want to address as my final point. It's time for us to insist that governments and institutions and employers walk the walk of equality. Of course it's good to have the right slogans and mission statements, but what really counts is delivery. What are the metrics telling us? To what extent is gender equality being prioritised vis a vis other priorities? These are questions that are being pressed by my colleagues in the Department of Foreign Affairs and across other Government Departments. And if I may take licence to speak as an outsider, they are also legitimate questions for the Bar Council and for law firms.

I assume that the Bar Council as a whole must be concerned by the fact of having a cadre of Senior Counsels that is 84% male. The question is just how meaningfully the issue is being addressed. I don't think anyone can simply assert that that this is a profession of self employed people where everyone, female and male, has to stand on her or his own two feet. Standing unsupported on your own two feet is mostly a myth. If young barristers can't make ends meet for a number of years, then the chances are that parental support is buttressing an elite system. And similarly, if the system is structured in a way that is blind to the demands and responsibilities of parenthood, then - society being what it is- women barristers will disproportionately pay the price. So I hope that some kind of radical thinking is underway by the Bar Council as a whole, including looking to other jurisdictions and examining whether their approaches offer even partial ways forward.

The same radical thinking is required from law firms. From what one hears anecdotally, the big law firms still have an expectation of extraordinarily long hours being worked as a matter of routine. There are obvious questions of efficiency - and in the US at least, clients are railing against the tyranny of "billable hours" - but my concern for this evening is the differential gender impact.

In my generation at least, we grew up with that Harry Truman dictum stored somewhere in our subconscious: "if you can't stand the heat, get out of the kitchen". If the heat was getting to us in the workplace, it was because we weren't tough enough, determined enough. But of course there is another way to look at it: if the kitchen is chronically overheated, then there is something structurally wrong with the kitchen, and alarm bells should be ringing.

We all have crisis periods at work, when it's all hands on deck for as long as it takes, but there is something amiss in any institution that has a culture of consistently and routinely expecting its employees to work punishingly long hours. Such an expectation is hardly fair to any employee, but it's a particularly difficult balancing act for those trying to mesh work and parental responsibilities. And here again - society being what it is - women will be disproportionately affected. Some will vote with their feet, and won't be around to be considered for top tier promotion. And some who do stay around may be felt not to have done the heavy lifting required, and therefore will be less likely to make it through the funnel to the top level.

As has often been said - and as these work/life issues amply illustrate - a society that is fairer to women is a society that is fairer to everyone. And that of course is one of the reasons why men as well as women should be on the front lines in battling for these causes. But that is the subject for a whole other talk, and I am afraid my time this evening is running out.

In wrapping up, I hope no-one is too disappointed if this speech has been a little short on celebration and long on the challenges still to be addressed. But I think it's a time for impatience and a time for urgency - there is a tide out there and we don't want to miss it. Incremental change of course is not to be discounted, but it has delivered at far too slow a pace, and in 2018 we need to be pressing for qualitative change.

In my own case, yes, there is a small jab of pride at some of the firsts in my career; who wouldn't enjoy having a little footnote in history? But I also know that women should have had these opportunities long before, and I eagerly look forward to a future when we won't have to count firsts and calculate percentages because equality will simply be a fact of life and a fact of the workplace. But right now, that situation seems very far away. There is still a mountain to climb - we may have established a solid base camp, and have the summit firmly in our sights, but it will still require a great deal of effort if we are to successfully scale it.

As a very final word: here's one thing at least to celebrate - that we can all come together for an evening like this, that we have brilliant organisers who made it such a great event, and that we can all leave here this evening, not just having had a thoroughly enjoyable time, but feeling ourselves re-committed, re-energised, and ready for the next big push.

Women's Leadership Conference
Insitute of Directors Northern Ireland, Belfast
6th March 2020

It is a great pleasure to be here today. I enjoy every opportunity to come back to beautiful Belfast, and I have been inspired and energised by the wonderful speakers we have heard from throughout the day.

The subject on which I have been asked to speak is Leadership on a Global Stage. It's a large and challenging topic and provides me with a very broad canvas. Given the day we are celebrating, I want to approach it - at least to some extent - through a prism of women's leadership. And I would like to leave you at the end of my talk with three broad propositions:

Firstly, in our fractured world, leadership - enlightened, purposeful, and empathetic leadership - has never been more important.

Secondly, it is imperative that women assume an equal role in that leadership. This is fundamentally an issue of fairness and empowerment but beyond that it's also about securing the quality of leadership our times require.

Thirdly, despite the undoubted progress, the challenges confronting women in assuming a global leadership role remain formidable, and we need a corresponding sense of urgency and determination.

I would be quite happy to spend my speaking time today focussing on those three broad propositions, but the organisers have been clear that they would like me to talk about my own career trajectory and experiences. And they are probably right; it does give a grounding and context to what I want to say. So let me open this up by giving you a sense of my long experience in the Irish foreign service.

I joined the Department of Foreign Affairs in late 1972. At the time, I was the youngest ever entrant at diplomatic level and when I retired in 2017 I had become the longest serving diplomat in the history of the Department. Along the way there were a number of firsts from a gender perspective. When I went to Geneva in 1976, it was the first time in our service a married woman diplomat had been posted abroad. In each of my five posts as Irish Ambassador, it was the first time a woman had held those posts. And when I was posted to Brussels in 2001 as Ambassador to the European Union - or Permanent Representative as it is technically called - I was the first woman from any member State of the Union to serve in that role. This in an institution that had been founded in 1957!

Throughout those forty five years as a diplomat, my job was to develop, articulate, and advance Ireland's interests and values on the international stage. Even if the substance of the role varied immensely from one posting to another, that was always the central and defining mission, the golden thread running through it all. Dealing with the wide range range of issues crossing my desk - political, economic, consular, cultural - there was a single touchstone question: how do I best serve my country?

But side by side - and absolutely not in contradiction - with that, was the fact of my gender. Early on, I came to realise the extent to which gender is a conditioning factor that fundamentally shapes your life: who you are, how you process and respond, and how society perceives you. Being a woman diplomat came with its own complexities. But it was never something I wanted to erase or downplay; I was not interested in projecting as an honorary man.

Being the first or one of a minority of women in a certain role always felt to me both a privilege and a responsibility. A double responsibility really. There was a constant sense that, while my male colleagues were being judged exclusively on their own performance, I had to account not just for my individual performance but for wider inferences being drawn about my gender. And that can often feel motivating but sometimes inhibiting. The second responsibility was one of solidarity - trying to support and keep faith with other women on a similar journey, particularly younger women coming behind.

I want to come back to that word "privilege" that I mentioned a moment ago. As I have said so often before, if I were ever to write my memoirs they would be a celebration of opportunities offered, trust placed in me, finding myself in fascinating posts at consequential times. Above all, having the extraordinary honour of representing the Irish people on an international stage. And I often reflect on that dictum attributed to Napoleon about preferring lucky Generals to good Generals. I was certainly lucky in my timing; a beneficiary of the enlightened policies of free education introduced in Ireland in the 1960s and later, a direct beneficiary of Irish accession to the European Union in January 1973.

I want to pause on that point for a second. Especially as we all grapple with the implications of Brexit, there is a debt that I think needs to very explicitly acknowledged. It is impossible to overestimate the liberating role of the EU for Irish women of my generation.... ending the marriage ban for women in the public sector, requiring equal pay and maternity leave. Had it not been for Ireland joining the EU when it did, I would not be standing here today. I would have been another statistic among those legions of Irish women ejected from the public service on marriage.

So yes, there has been a great deal of privilege and a good measure of luck. But I wouldn't be presenting a full or honest picture if I airbrushed the more difficult moments along the way. So I'm going to touch on a few of those moments too.

My career broadly falls into two halves: the first twenty or so years of advancement through the ranks, and then the next twenty five or so at senior level.

As I said, I joined in late 1972, just 20 years old and fresh out of College. Like many young women of my generation, I was imprinted with the activism and nascent feminism of the late 60s. We were bright-eyed and optimistic, certain that the world was changing and we were riding that wave of change. We soon encountered some reality checks.

Two out of my group of twelve entrants in 1972 were women and there were mutterings about "women taking over the place". When I got married in 1974, and kept my own name, the Personnel Officer said he " didn't know what game I was playing". When I was posted abroad in 1976, I had to threaten legal action to get a married officers' allowance. In the early 80s, back at HQ, a couple of us women applied to be appointed Consul General in Boston; when a lesser qualified man was appointed, there were informal explanations about having to take account of the macho nature of Irish America. And so it went....

Looking back, I would say that some of these early experiences were character forming and perhaps leadership forming. My backbone certainly stiffened along the way. I learned some important lessons about standing up for yourself, calling it out when you see discrimination. Lessons too about picking your fights carefully. I realise that, especially in the #MeToo era, attitudes are evolving and there is a legitimate view that letting smaller things go ultimately may risk legitimising larger transgressions. But my approach has always been to shrug off some of what I considered more minor irritants and stand my ground if I felt a line was being crossed.

Let me fast forward to the second half of my career, the almost twenty five years that I served at Assistant Secretary General and later Deputy Secretary General level. The major part of this period was spent in five Ambassadorial posts. Two of these involved accreditation to the United Nations, first in Geneva and later in

New York; there were also postings as Permanent Representative to the European Union, which I mentioned earlier, Ambassador to France, and finally Ambassador to the United States.

Again, I was being challenged and stretched in every post. I was broadening my horizons, learning new skills, playing on large stages - so many ingredients that are important for leadership. The perspective that I gained during my years at the United Nations will stay with me for life, and it is no accident that I have remained involved with the UN after retirement from the foreign service.

It is now 20 years since I chaired the UN Commission on Human Rights but some of the memories from that year of chairing are burned into my brain. Amid all the very real challenges that we in Europe or the US face, particularly we women, I try never to lose sight of the fact that these are first world challenges. It's not to minimise them, or relieve us of the responsibility of confronting them, but to remind ourselves of the broader solidarity we owe to those around the world who are infinitely less privileged than ourselves.

My experience, particularly in the multilateral posts, left me with many reflections about leadership. I had opportunities to see close up how power and influence are wielded and how much reputation matters and needs to be safeguarded. I spoke about these issues in a speech I gave during the New York years. I talked about how "Power implies a demonstration of strength, a flexing of muscles......influence relies more on a capacity to persuade. Power speaks with a loud voice; influence adopts a softer tone." And I reflected too on how a state's most precious asset is its reputation....recalling that quote from Shakespeare: "I have lost my reputation; I have lost the most precious part of myself".

I was speaking about the UN stage but I think the reflections are equally applicable to leadership issues and challenges in almost any context.

Over the years, I also came to understand more about empathy. Chairing various processes at the UN and also in the EU, I saw how successful negotiations almost always depend on win-win outcomes that allow all sides to walk away with their dignity intact. And a large part of creating those outcomes depends on deep listening skills. Of course it's not just about listening. You have to do your homework so that you fully grasp the background and context to what people are saying. And you have to exercise your judgement, and sometimes your boldness, as to when and how to confront people with the need to compromise. But your chances of success are so much greater if you have done the deep listening that enables you to truly understand where people are coming from and the latitude they may be persuaded to exercise.

And so I have always resisted the kind of binary approach that associates strength with male leadership and empathy with female leaders. We need a blend of both. Empathy is not in contra distinction to strength; it is part of what makes you strong.

In my bilateral posts in France and the US, as I observed and reported on political developments, I absorbed other lessons about leadership. In France, Nicolas Sarkozy was President for much of my time there - his intelligence was never in doubt but questions about his integrity impaired his ability to lead. And in the US, the first three years of my accreditation were during the Obama years and the final months during the Trump Administration. In a particularly acute way, I saw how issues of character and reputation came to the fore - how quickly a country's leadership can unravel when the elements that established that leadership are called into question; how the high ground can be abandoned and soft power squandered.

So yes, these later 25 years were a time of extraordinary growth in learning and experience. And my understanding of the challenge of being a professional woman also deepened over the years. Some things had certainly moved on. Over the decades, the Irish public service and foreign service incrementally became much more welcoming environments for women. Within the diplomatic service, women diplomats were joining in increasing numbers and working their way through the ranks. There was more enlightened leadership and greatly increased gender sensitivity. Today's figures are worth sharing: women now account for 25% of Heads of Departments and 30% of Heads of Mission. A huge change from the near invisibility of the early years but still a way to go.

As I carried out my role as Ambassador in the various posts, it was impossible not to notice the gender conditioning in the wider interactions. When you are in a senior position, to a degree at least you have a layer of protection that isn't necessarily there when you are more junior. But the reality checks that I spoke about earlier don't go away.

The default setting for Ambassador is still male - and that's hardly surprising. In both of my last two postings, in New York and Washington, the ratio of Ambassadors was roughly 85% male and 15% female. If people weren't briefed in advance that there was a female Ambassador, there would not infrequently be an assumption that I was the Ambassador's wife. Or I might walk into a room with a male colleague from the Embassy and hands would be immediately outstretched to greet him as Ambassador.

These were what I considered pinpricks. But as a female leader you also have to prepare yourself for some tougher slings and arrows. And your seniority is never going to protect you fully - maybe indeed it's what exposes you. Even during my last assignment in Washington, there was a sobering reminder of the extent to which sexism is still alive and well.

During my first year there, in the course of the St Patricks Day celebrations, I carried out an instruction of the Taoiseach which some people in his entourage were unhappy with. The whole episode ended up with unattributed briefing to the Irish media to the effect that I was "too big for my boots", comments about my "Prada shoes" (need I add that I have never owned Prada shoes!), people opining to the media as to whether or not I was the Diva of the Department.

You can't control these things; all you can control is your response. You wouldn't be human if you didn't find some of it hurtful. But I think the only response is to try to rise above the pettiness and focus on what matters. Certainly for me, it reinforced my determination to represent Ireland to the very best of my ability but also to double down on the particular responsibility I felt as a woman in a position of leadership.

I mentioned earlier the responsibility of solidarity. In both Geneva and New York I had co-founded networks of women diplomats - in New York especially, our focus was on younger women from countries where there might have been few women role models. Throughout my time as Ambassador to the US, I addressed women's groups not just in DC but in more far-flung places like Missoula, Montana, and Anchorage, Alaska. And when I saw vestiges of discrimination in some segments of Irish America, I tried to address it in clear terms and help lead change.

When you attempt to sow the seeds of change, you obviously hope and work for the best possible outcomes. Sometimes the seeds will fall on stony ground and may never germinate. Sometimes, it may take years and you won't be on hand for the flowering. But sometimes, if you are lucky, there will be moments of reward and reinforcement: occasions when you can feel and savour change and know that you were part of it. For me, one such moment was when, after nearly 250 years of being an all male Organisation, and some fairly forthright appeals on my part, the Friendly Sons of St Patrick in Philadelphia opened their doors to women and admitted me as the first female member.

The pride in that moment was amplified when President Obama referenced it in his St Patrick's Day address in the White House that year and went on to quote from my speech in Philadelphia: "As Ambassador Anderson said, there are no second class citizens; there are no children of a lesser God."

Before finishing, I want to return now to those three propositions I set out at the beginning of my talk.

Firstly, the need for leadership in these fraught and fractured times. No one in this room needs me to spell out the risks that confront us - the rise of populism and nationalism, the straining at the guardrails of democracy, the undermining of the principles and structures that have defined and underpinned the western liberal order. What is at stake here goes well beyond the confines of our conference today. The shifts are about competing political and economic visions, the unstoppable advance of technology, the existential threats posed by climate change. But leadership unquestionably matters: an erosion of trust in leadership gives licence and space to demagoguery and lowest common denominator politics.

Secondly, women must play an equal role in that leadership. The proposition may seem self evident to everyone here today but it cannot be said often enough or with sufficient sense of urgency. There is a whole cascade of reasons why this should be so. First and foremost it's a simple question of societal fairness: women represent over 50% of humanity, and there are entitlements that flow from that.

But beyond that, there are the proven benefits of having diverse voices in decision making: optimum outcomes will not emerge from echo chambers, but from vigorous debate involving multiple viewpoints. And finally there is the question of what specifically women bring to the table. Of course not every woman leader is going to be an exemplar of leadership, and we don't have to put ourselves through contortions to try to prove this. But I believe women's life experience has made them better attuned to collaborative forms of leadership: to considering a wider range of views, and bringing coherence to differing sets of needs and priorities. And these qualities are at a premium in these fluid and fast-changing times.

My third proposition is about the scale of the challenge women still face in assuming their rightful place on the global stage. There are indeed some statistics that look better than ever and definite reasons to take heart. We can catalogue the advances on our own island and internationally we can think of leaders of the calibre of Angela Merkel or Jacinda Ardern, or the changing of the guard signified by Ursula Von Leyen taking over as President of the EU Commission and Christine Lagarde taking the helm of the ECB.

I am a firm believer in acknowledging and celebrating every advance. But let's be clear. If we are measuring glass half full or half empty, it is way below half full. In almost any domain we choose to talk about - politics, business, the top levels of academia and the professions - women are seriously and sometimes massively underrepresented at the top. And we can't delude ourselves that the future will take take care of itself: the pipelines that are supposed to take women to the top are too often sputtering and leaking.

The challenges facing women are multifold. Most of us know that we still have work to do on ourselves. We recognise the confidence gap, the perfectionism, the self questioning and self doubt that can hold us back. It's a conditioning we drank in practically with our mothers milk.

But as I have so often said, it's not all on us. We can lean in until we're hunched over but things won't change unless and until there are deeper changes within the workplace and in wider societal attitudes.

There are the more obvious workplace challenges we are all familiar with: offering family friendly policies and talent development policies that equip both female and male staff to be credible candidates for the top jobs. And then there are the more insidious ways in which prospects for equality are eroded. For example: the "greedy workplace" - the demand, particularly in some of the most prestigious professions, that staff are always on, always available. In theory it's gender neutral; in practice, studies show that women are disproportionately absorbing the burden.

And then there are the deep seated societal attitudes. One of the most illuminating books I read in recent years, and have mentioned in some recent speeches, was *Women and Power* by the British classicist Mary Beard. She traces how from Graeco Roman times power and authority have always been coded male. As she draws out the implications over the millennia, one feels a stab of recognition on almost every page. Her analysis could be applied almost anywhere. Limiting myself to just one example, it's been pretty depressing to look at both the last and the current US Presidential election campaigns through the gender lens.

Most obviously and most unequivocally, It is simply unimaginable that a female version of Donald Trump would ever have been elected. But it's also worth taking a look on the Democratic side in the current campaign. From the very beginning, there has been hand wringing about whether America is ready for a woman President - and it seems it isn't. And here's a quote about leading candidate Bernie Sanders from a recent New York Times editorial: "Much of his appeal... lies in his grouchy I'm-not-here-to-make-friends pugilism." Does anyone seriously believe that a woman candidate projecting grouchy pugilism would stand a chance? Of course not; women everywhere still find themselves in the double bind of having to simultaneously signal both likability and authority.

And so, as we celebrate the advances, let's also be forthright about the challenges: not to dishearten ourselves but to ensure we are clear-eyed and determined as we navigate the way ahead.

I would like to wrap up with a recollection of a visit I paid to Washington DC a couple of weeks back. One of my current roles is as a Board member of the Institute for the Study of Diplomacy at Georgetown University in Washington. The Institute presents an award annually to to an outstanding practitioner of diplomacy. This year, our award recipient was Maria Yovanovich - those of you who follow US politics will remember Maria as the US Ambassador to Ukraine who was recalled last year by President Trump, and who testified at his impeachment hearing in defiance of a gagging order from the White House.

I went to the award ceremony both to pay tribute to what Ambassador Yovanovich had done and also to hear her address on the subject of Diplomacy Today. She spoke about the challenge of doing what's right, about the importance of courage and integrity, about the need for a personal moral compass. Being ready to speak truth to power. Holding on to one's dignity in undignified times. And of course it was all the more resonant because of the recent demonstration of how she and other public servants had lived those values.

It was a talk about diplomacy but I think it served also as a lesson in leadership. For me, it was an affirmation of the profession in which I had served for so long. I felt a real sense of pride in public service and - despite all - an optimism about the road ahead.

Once again, I am delighted to be here. Particularly as Northern Ireland navigates its way through the acute challenges of Brexit, there is need for leadership that is visionary and bold, as well as wise and generous-spirited. Today's conference demonstrates that these qualities are available here in abundance.

Presentation of Voice of Courage Award
Women's Refugee Commission Annual Lunch, New York
3rd May 2018

There has never been a more apt time to celebrate the resilience of women refugees.

"Resilience" is a beautiful word. As we know, it signifies toughness, strength, endurance, the ability to overcome setbacks and get back on your feet again. Choosing to be an author rather than a victim.

I suspect that for most of us in this room, the words "resilience" and "women" pair very naturally together. We have learned coping skills from our mothers and grandmothers. We have witnessed the contributions of women activists in our communities. We have seen how women friends pull each other through adversity.

But our culture has told us a different story. Across so much of our art, and literature, and religion, we have absorbed the narrative and imagery of female fragility, female passivity, female victimhood. Strength is coded male; and weakness is coded female.

This tension between our lived reality and cultural messaging has simmered for a very long time. But in the past year, it finally feels as if something fundamental is shifting. Some powerful waves are coming together - creating a kind of riptide, with the potential to sweep away long standing societal structures.

As a new landscape begins to emerge, solidarity among women worldwide - and among all who believe in equality - is more than ever critical. I would like to quote a few words that speak to that solidarity.

This year, we are marking the centenary of the vote being granted to women in Britain and in Ireland. Last week, a statue was unveiled in London. It commemorates leading suffragist Millicent

Fawcett; she stands there, holding a banner inscribed with these words: "Courage calls to Courage Everywhere."

I love these words. They seem to me to validate every individual act of bravery, recognising that all are mutually reinforcing, and asserting a kinship among all who demonstrate courage at different times in different places in different ways.

The particular courage calling to us today is the strength and resilience of women refugees. Their stories play out far from the headlines. The circumstance of their lives could hardly be more different from ours. But their voices reach us clearly. And their message resonates powerfully: that, despite all, they will prevail; that those who have destroyed their past will not succeed in robbing them of their future.

Their courage deserves an answering courage. It requires of us that we in our turn fight for decency and humanity in our own societies, that we take a stand against the stridency of those - in the United States, Europe and elsewhere - who want to close their hearts and close their borders.

At this point I had hoped and expected I would have the honour of introducing you in person to an extraordinary woman, Majida Alaskary. I am saddened that, despite the major investment of effort by the Women's Refugee Commission and others, it has not proved possible to secure the documentation for Majida to enter the United States to receive her award. It serves as a reminder, if we needed it, of the barriers and obstacles that stand in the way of even the best and bravest.

So instead I will read to you some words from Majida. I know you will be humbled and moved by her story. She has had to flee her home not once but twice. Despite being granted asylum in Greece, she has chosen to remain in Samos with the newly arrived refugees, helping them adjust and guiding them towards recovery of their innate dignity and strength.

Ladies and gentlemen, here are the words of a truly inspiring woman, a 2018 Voice of Courage Award recipient, Majida Alaskary:

"Thank you to the Women's Refugee Commission for this award. I wish I could be with you in New York today.

I am very honoured, but I am just one person among many.

For the past two years, I have lived here on Samos island in Greece, providing translation services, tutoring refugee children, and volunteering with the Red Cross.

Since I have asylum, I can leave whenever I want.

Unlike the women I see every day, it is my choice to stay. But like them, I know what it means to come to a new country as a refugee and to have to start your life over.

When I was a girl, my family fled Palestine for Syria. I had a good life there for many years. I became a journalist, sharing the truth of what was happening in that country with the world.

My mission is to see women as people, not numbers waiting to see a doctor or to get food. To see them for their own cultures, their own needs, their own strengths. To see them as themselves.

What refugee women want and need more than anything else is respect, a chance to start again, to work, to be seen as human again.

The happiest time for me is when I go to the port to say goodbye to women who are leaving the island. They are excited and looking to the future.

So I would like to accept this award on behalf of all the women I work with every day. Thank you all very much."

PAYING TRIBUTE

When a community wants to pay tribute to one of its revered figures, it is natural that it should look to the serving Ambassador for involvement. Because while the homage is personal, the Ambassador is also speaking - at least to some degree - on behalf of the country she or he represents. Over the years, I have been honoured to convey recognition and appreciation to many exceptional individuals.

Mostly, the homages have been to the living but sometimes to those who have gone before (a speech at the statue of Robert Emmet belongs in another chapter).

I am including a short selection of these speeches here, all of them from the Washington years. Shaking up the chronological order of delivery, I begin with tributes to two US Presidents, John Fitzgerald Kennedy and Bill Clinton.

The launch of the year-long programme to mark the centenary of the birth of President Kennedy was fittingly held in the Kennedy Center, the National Cultural Center in Washington which he and Jacqueline Kennedy had helped establish and which in the aftermath of his assassination was designated a living memorial to the President. The ceremony brought together key strands of the President's life and legacy, and speakers included the astronaut Buzz Aldrin, the Peace Corps Director, and the head of the Environmental Protection Agency. The President's grandchildren were present and his grandson Jack Kennedy Schlossberg spoke eloquently.

I was moved that the President's special connection to Ireland was being recognised and honoured. And since the event coincided with the Ireland 100 Festival which was underway at the Center, I had an opportunity to comment on this "special symmetry, as the fates again weave together stories that were so interwoven in life".

I wanted to capture the particular grace of President Kennedy, the depth of the connection with Ireland, and the special magic of that June 1963 visit. But even in that setting, and on that occasion, it seemed important to stop just a little short of hagiography. I struggled a bit and settled for: "More than fifty years have passed, and time has eroded some of the innocence of those days. The historians have given us a more nuanced picture of the President and his times..."

The tribute to Bill Clinton came easily. We were not gathered for a summation of the former President's life and career; that is for future historians. I was very happy to embrace my task of presenting an award to the President for his vital and catalytic role in the peace process in Northern Ireland. About that, there is no need for equivocation or nuance.

The introduction of Senator George Mitchell came at a gala dinner marking the 90th anniversary of Commonweal Magazine - a highly respected Catholic publication whose mission is "to provide a forum for civil, reasoned debate on the interaction with contemporary politics and culture." Influenced by the nature of the organisation, I found myself drawing on some Biblical language and imagery to try to describe the role of peacemaker. I had also recently read Colum McCann's book *Transatlantic* - Colum is a friend of mine and also very close to George Mitchell, around whom *Transatlantic* is woven - so Colum's lyrical words found their way into the speech.

In quite a different vein, I am also including two tributes delivered in much less formal settings - both honouring dedicated trade unionists whose life's work was on different sides of the Atlantic.

In my first posting to Washington ('83 to '87) I had the title, among others, of Labour Attaché, and I have had a life-long respect for the goals and values of trade unionism even if sometimes qualified by reservations as to tactical choices.

A film honouring Inez McCormack, the late Northern Ireland trade unionist and first female President of the Irish Congress of Trade Unions (ICTU) - "A Challenging Woman" - was shown in Georgetown University in April 2015. I wanted to pay tribute to Inez and to her defining causes of social justice and feminism.

The previous year I had spoken very briefly at an eightieth birthday tribute organised by the labour movement for John Sweeney, President Emeritus of the American Federation of Labor and Congress of Industrial Organizations (AFL-CIO). John Sweeney and Tom Donahue - good friends of each other when I first knew them in the '80s, both dominant figures in the US trade union movement, but who sadly parted ways subsequently - were both extraordinarily kind to the young and inexperienced diplomat I was in the '80s. My enduring regard for Tom finds expression in the Flax Trust speech in an earlier chapter in this collection.

There is a roll-call of other names, people whom I held in affection and great respect and to whom I was honoured to pay tribute on various occasions. But I will leave these speeches to their memories, and mine.

Launch of JFK Centenary Programme
Kennedy Center, Washington DC
29th May 2016

It feels entirely fitting that the programme of events marking the centenary of the birth of President Kennedy is being launched in the course of the Ireland 100 Festival. There is such a special symmetry, as the fates again weave together stories that were so interwoven in life.

Let us state it loudly and clearly and simply: John Fitzgerald Kennedy loved Ireland beyond any other country except his own, and we loved and cherished him in return.

I want to take you back to President Kennedy's four-day visit to Ireland in June 1963 - a visit that was emblematic of so much, one that is forever written on our hearts and stored in our memories.

John Fitzgerald Kennedy came as a member of our extended family, someone whose eight great-grandparents had all emigrated from Ireland. He came as the first sitting President of the US to visit our country, and the first foreign leader to address our Parliament. He came in all his youth and vigour, with all his grace and optimism, his spontaneity and wit.

He arrived with us in buoyant mood, fresh from that immortal speech in Berlin, ready to embrace his ancestral homeland. He found in Ireland even more than he could have imagined. There are experiences - in the words of Seamus Heaney - that come at us "sideways, and catch the heart off guard, and blow it open". President Kennedy indeed had his heart blown open during those four days. As one of his closest advisers put it, he was "never easier, happier... more completely himself than during those days."

For our part, we loved who he was and what he stood for. It went way beyond the charm and the ease and the eloquence. We were delighted that, when he addressed the Irish Parliament, he quoted Joyce, and Benjamin Franklin, and Parnell; Yeats, Grattan, John Boyle O'Reilly, and George Bernard Shaw. But, beyond the wonderful felicity of language, it was the deeper notes we listened to, and that continued to vibrate long after he left our shores.

The young President instinctively connected with us. He understood both our pride and our vulnerability, our dual identity as ancient country and young nation. He rejoiced in the shared past, but his eyes were firmly fixed on the future. He held out a vision of who we could be, of the destiny we could reach for, of where that quintessentially Irish "combination of hope, confidence and imagination" could lead us.

More than fifty years have passed, and time has eroded some of the innocence of those days. The historians have given us a more nuanced picture of the President and his times. And we have become in some ways a different country - more mature, more diverse, fully at home within the European family even as the bonds with America continue to strengthen.

But the deep and true notes from all those years ago continue to vibrate today.

Now more than ever, we need President Kennedy's vision for the world and for America. A world that values multilateralism and understands the strength of soft power. An America of ambition and confidence, its windows wide open to the world, continually renewed and refreshed by the exchange of ideas and interplay of cultures.

As he left Ireland, President Kennedy promised to come back in the springtime. The poignancy of that unfulfilled promise has stayed with us throughout all the intervening decades. But now, in the late springtime of 2016, as we commemorate our own important centenary, the artists of Ireland have made the journey in the reverse direction. They have brought their music and songs and words to the Kennedy Center, and as we hear them echo throughput this majestic building, it feels as if a circle is being closed.

Always, in Ireland and wherever green is worn, President Kennedy will have a special place in our hearts.

Introduction of Former President Bill Clinton,
Lifetime Achievement Award Recipient,
Irish America Hall of Fame Luncheon, New York
30th March 2016

It is probably the very definition of a redundant task to introduce the Honorable William Jefferson Clinton to an Irish or Irish-American audience, because of course absolutely no introduction is required.

But I am truly honoured to be asked to say these few words. No recipient could be more worthy of the Lifetime Achievement award, and it is all the more resonant and meaningful for being conferred in this momentous year, as we commemorate the centenary of 1916.

I returned just yesterday from the commemoration ceremonies in Dublin over the Easter weekend: ceremonies that were moving and dignified, and appropriately reflected the pride of a nation. The themes of the commemoration - remember, reconcile, re-imagine - are ones that chime precisely with President Clinton's own involvement on our island.

Indeed, a happy chord was struck on the first day of the visit home, last Thursday. I was accompanying a US Congressional delegation, and our calls included ones on the newly elected Ceann Comhairle, or Speaker, of the Irish Parliament. As he greeted us in the entrance hall of Leinster House, the Speaker proudly pointed to a photograph on the wall: a photograph of President Clinton addressing the Oireachtas on 1st December 1995.

Today, we are honouring the former President's central and catalytic role in the peace process in Northern Ireland. But, in a world so fraught with strife and instability, we are also recognising the qualities that are at the very heart of peacemaking and peacebuilding. I would suggest three qualities in particular that defined Bill Clinton's approach.

The first is leadership.

It was not at all obvious that a former Governor from Arkansas, on becoming President, would prioritise Northern Ireland. On arrival in the White House, there were so many other claims on his attention. And there were many who advised that Northern Ireland as a cause was hopeless, or thankless, or even - in the view of some - inappropriate. But the President grasped the potential, and was ready to take a calculated risk.

He had also made a campaign promise.

In the Irish language there is an ancient and honoured rallying cry: "Beart do réir ár briathar" - action in accordance with our word. Bill Clinton exemplified that, when he might very easily have found a rationale to do otherwise.

The second quality is engagement: hands on, up close and personal.

There were two mutually reinforcing elements at work here - the President's passion, and his extraordinary grasp of nuance and detail. There were the public moments, hugely symbolic and meaningful, and the private moments of empathy and encouragement.

In those dark mid-winter days of 1995, we had the first visit by a sitting American President to Northern Ireland. No one who witnessed those extraordinary scenes in Belfast and Derry will ever forget them. The symbolic switching on of the Christmas tree lights, the bonding with the huge crowds, communicating so urgently the belief in a better future.

And all the countless private moments, empathising with and comforting the victims, encouraging the actors from all sides, willing them on, cheering them on. Combining the power and prestige of the Oval Office with the personal warmth and persuasive skills of the man who held the office.

President Clinton gave us the great gift of George Mitchell as personal envoy but much more than that - he was always there at the end of a telephone line, never more so than during those final fateful 24 hours leading to the Good Friday Agreement, when he stayed up all night to help push things over the line.

And the third quality, persistence: sticking with it. Knowing that peacebuilding takes time and patience; that the the spark, once kindled, has to be nurtured; that long after the media caravan moves on, lives have to be painfully rebuilt and hope and vision sustained.

Bill Clinton simply never let up. He visited our island three times while in office. In March 2014, almost 20 years on, he was back again in Northern Ireland, with John Hume on the Peace Bridge in Derry. Once again, entreating the politicians from all sides: finish the job, finish the job.

Throughout the years since leaving Presidential office, his door has always been open for counsel, encouragement and always his continued insistence: finish the job.

I mentioned a moment ago the visit to Dublin with the Congressional delegation this past weekend, and our encounter with the Speaker, the Ceann Comhairle, on the first day. My last engagement with the delegation was the State Reception in Dublin Castle on Sunday night. As we stood chatting in St Patrick's Hall in the State Apartments, a former Minister reminisced about the State Dinner held for President Clinton in that hall in December '95. She recalled one of the most moving moments of the evening when, following and echoing the President's speech, an Irish tenor sang "You'll Never Walk Alone".

That too is a promise kept. Twenty years later, we do indeed know that we have never walked alone.

And so, today we want to express our thanks to President Clinton, we want to recognise his work on our island as one of his proudest achievements, and in a world so desperately in need of peacemakers and peacebuilders, we want to recognise the qualities it takes, and which he has so compellingly demonstrated.

Commonweal 90th Anniversary Dinner: Honouree Senator George Mitchell
New York
27 October 2014

I am delighted to join you this evening.

I pay warm tribute to Commonweal on your 90th anniversary. Never has your mission been more relevant, nor the conversations you promote more necessary. At this time of change and renewal within the Catholic Church, the kind of reasoned debate you champion is essential to light the way forward.

There is no honouree whom I would feel more privileged to introduce than George Mitchell.

Senator Mitchell embodies so much of what I admire about this great nation.

He is quintessentially American in his background. The Arab-American community proudly claims him as one of their own. Most of us in Ireland would consider him to be a member of the Irish-American family. But I doubt that he thinks of himself in any hyphenated way. "I am an American," he has said. "Proud to be a citizen of what I believe to be the most open, the most free, the most just society in human history".

George Mitchell was not born with a silver spoon in his mouth. His mother was a textile worker. His father was a janitor. He earned his success by hard work, by quality of mind and quality of character.

His career has been rich in achievement: a distinguished lawyer, a much lauded legislator, an activist in many important causes. He has chaired prestigious groups and committees, and been conferred with some of the highest honours this country offers. A man who has applied his talents generously and widely, a man for all seasons.

But tonight, I want to talk about George Mitchell as a peacemaker. If I view his achievements particularly through a Northern Ireland prism, it is not simply because I am the Irish Ambassador. The Senator himself has said that his three and half years in Northern Ireland were the longest, most difficult years he has experienced; and that the outcome was the most gratifying achievement of his public life.

For those of us growing up in Ireland some decades ago, attending Catholic schools, there was a requirement that we learn long tracts of the Bible by heart. The Beatitudes had a particular poetry. And so, from a very young age, these words had a lovely familiarity to me:

Blessed are the peacemakers
For they shall be called the children of God.

Through the years, the words continued to resonate. I spent much of my career on United Nations work, most recently as Ambassador to the UN in New York. Three critical interwoven tasks - peacemaking, peacekeeping, and peacebuilding - were at the heart of my concerns there. I developed a profound and abiding respect for those who are practitioners at the coalface.

George Mitchell is universally acknowledged as one of the most successful peacemakers of the past decades. His role was pivotal in achieving the Good Friday Agreement. While he makes a point of sharing the credit with others, without his leadership there would not have been an outcome.

Reading the Senator's book, *Making Peace,* helps to get the measure of the effort and of the man. And Colum McCann's novel, *Transatlantic,* distills the truth of that time in an unforgettable way.

The attributes I mentioned before - hard work, quality of mind, quality of character - were tested to the full. Patience, perseverance, determination. A sense of timing. Above all, fairness and integrity. In his book, Senator Mitchell recalls agonisedly asking himself at key moments: "What's the right thing to do?"

That touchstone question for all of us: "What's the right thing to do?"

Peacemaking, as we know, is not a business for the sentimental or dewy-eyed. It requires astuteness and clear-sighted analysis - the rigorous intellect that George Mitchell so obviously has. But it requires more than this.

Let me evoke another Biblical reference: "And now these three remain: faith, hope and love, but the greatest of these is love."

George Mitchell could scarcely have survived the three and a half years of gruelling work in Belfast without faith and hope. But I doubt that he could eventually have succeeded without what I would define as love.

By love, in this context, I mean a deep sense of connectedness and empathy with one's fellow human beings.

George Mitchell's empathy with the people of Northern Ireland shines through every page of his book. The sixty-one children born on the same day as his son, Andrew. The lovely fifteen-year-old Claire who lost her sight in the Omagh bombing. The two elderly grey-haired women who embraced him, tears flowing down their faces, on his final day in Belfast.

At the core of it all is the individual, the man or woman in whose shoes any of us might walk if our life circumstances had been a little different. Grief, as George Mitchell understood so well, makes no distinction; it wrings each human heart in the same way. In *Transatlantic*, Colum McCann gives us this sad litany:

"How many times has he heard it? How often were there two ways to say the one thing? My son died. His name was Seamus. My son died. His name was James. My son died. His name was Peadar. My son died. His name was Pete. My son died. His name was Billy.

My son died. His name was Liam..."

The same litany can be replicated in so many parts of the world. Palestinian and Israeli: "My son Mohamed, my son Jacob." Sunni and Shiite, Hutu and Tutsi, and on and on and on. My daughter, my son, my child.

Northern Ireland is still a place of fragile peace, of much unfinished business. The talks currently under way have had a difficult start and are of uncertain outcome. No one suggests that things are perfect.

But so much has changed, and - at the very least - people aren't dying. George Mitchell helped to staunch a river of tears. He delivered a transformative Agreement, from which there will be no going back. And beyond Northern Ireland, he helped the world to believe in the possibility of peace.

For all that he has achieved, and especially for the qualities of mind and character on which those achievements have been built, George Mitchell deserves this Catholic in the Public Square Award.

Film and Panel Discussion on Inez McCormack: "A Challenging Woman" Georgetown University, Washington DC 8ᵗʰ April 2015

I want to thank Melanne Verveer and the Institute for inviting me to make some brief remarks.

This was a moving and inspiring documentary. It captured Inez in a very vivid way: her values, her causes, her grittiness. And it also captured the feelings she inspired in others.

Many of you here in the room knew Inez far better than I did. I met her only a few times, but I relate so much to what she stood for.

Her great causes were social justice and feminism, and of course the two were intertwined because many of the most deprived - the cleaners, the house help, auxiliaries - were women.

There are just a few points I want to make: firstly, how tough those causes were, and how tough she had to be in pursuing them; secondly, the importance of trade unionism in pushing a rights-based agenda; and thirdly, the fact that these causes are unfinished business.

Throughout the decades that Inez was waging her crusades, it was tough - tough for a trade union activist, and doubly tough for a woman. Northern Ireland, during the conflict and as it emerged from conflict, was a macho society. And both trade unionism and politics were particularly macho domains.

It was an absolutely classic situation of peacemaking and peacebuilding. During my UN days, when I had a lot to do with peacebuilding around the world, I saw the same paradigm everywhere - those who wage the wars are those who get a seat at the negotiating table. And as the women have mostly not been on the streets, but trying to keep hearth and home together, they get excluded. And the marginalised, the socially deprived and excluded, the kind of people that Inez cared most about, don't get much of a look-in either; they are simply not seen as stakeholders.

And that's why Inez had to be tough. She was a warm and deeply caring person but she certainly wasn't cosy and cuddly. As I said, I met her a few times in the '80s when I was heavily involved in dealing with the McBride Principles here in the US and later, working in our Northern Ireland Division in the late '80s, dealing with fair employment issues in Northern Ireland. She was quite stern, assertive, a challenging woman - as she had to be.

I saw where she said to the film maker: "Don't make me into a saint: I want to continue to be effectively annoying when I am gone."

The second point relates to the importance of the trade union movement as a non-sectarian force, when there were few such forces in Northern Ireland. The unions were also well-connected internationally and had particularly good relations with the American labour movement. That's part of what helped to give a face to the McBride Principles. So we should absolutely not underestimate the importance of Inez's role as a trade union leader.

The third point relates to unfinished business. Women still have to push to have their voices heard, to be considered players. And though there's so much that's good and positive in Northern Ireland, there are still hard-to-reach communities who aren't seeing much of a peace dividend. And of course, there's more unfinished business. Inez always championed a rights-based approach, and the Good Friday Agreement envisaged a Bill of Rights. We are still waiting for a Bill of Rights, and it would still be very worthwhile.

Inez accomplished an enormous amount, and left a huge legacy from her decades of work. But part of her legacy, as she wanted, is to continue to challenge us - to continue to have her voice ringing in our ears.

Tribute to John Sweeney, President Emeritus, AFL-CIO
Eightieth birthday celebration, Washington DC
30th July 2014

I know there will be many tributes to John, for all his extraordinary work as a trade union leader, a lover of Ireland, and a promoter of peace on our island.

I think one simple sentence in his biography says it all. "The son of Irish immigrants, Sweeney grew up in a union family." That's it: Ireland, and the unions, were and are in his DNA. They have been his life's work.

But I am here tonight not just to applaud what he has done for Ireland, important as it is.

I am here because of my huge personal regard for John.

I have served for a year now in my capacity as Ambassador, and I value the friendships I have made. But I value even more the friendships that are decades old, that long predate my becoming an Ambassador.

Thirty years ago, I was here as a young diplomat: from '83 to '87. We were a small Embassy, and I was multi-hatted. I was Trade Attaché, Agriculture Attaché and Labour Attaché.

I was young and junior and finding my way. John at the time was already a big cheese: President of the Service Employees' Union.

But he treated me with the same degree of courtesy and care as if I were much more senior in the pecking order. He and Maureen spent time with me, professionally and socially. John marked my cards, taught me a lot, and acted as guide and mentor.

Some years later, when I became Ambassador to the UN and ILO in Geneva, and John had now reached the dizzy heights of President of the AFL-CIO, we connected again. And, some time after that, when I was Ambassador to France, John and Maureen and I got together in Paris.

You can imagine how happy I was to meet up again in DC. So I am here to give testimony to a friendship, to a man - and a couple - who are kind and caring, who took a bright-eyed young diplomat under their wing, and showed me every kindness and respect.

That's what I call a great guy.

Thank you John. Thank you Maureen.

ENGAGING WITH IRISH AMERICA

Managing the relationship with Irish America is a particular challenge. The diaspora is in many ways our grounding and our strength, and of course we want a vibrant and positive engagement that reflects this. But the relationship is always nuanced, and inevitably there will be times when it veers towards tension or mistrust. That is not a question of fault or mismanagement. It is simply a reality, reflecting the different ways in which contemporary Ireland and Irish America have evolved.

The fact that I was Ireland's first female Ambassador to the US, succeeding a long line of male Ambassadors, added a new ingredient to the mix. For many, it was something to celebrate - and I will particularly cherish some of the quieter moments, when silver-haired women that I encountered in Irish-American community centres beckoned me over and whispered their delight about finally having a woman Ambassador. But it was rather more complicated with the long-established organisations, some of them still clinging to traditions that would not have survived in today's Ireland.

I found some of the interactions personally quite difficult - trying always to demonstrate the courtesy that is owed to Irish America; warmly and deservedly applauding the immensely worthwhile work that is done at community level and sometimes in national or state campaigns, while trying to stay true to myself and to the values that I felt should be upheld by an Ambassador representing modern, inclusive Ireland.

I had an overall positive relationship with the AOH/LAOH and the fact that we soldiered together on immigration issues gave us an important common cause. I was not in sympathy with the structure and membership criteria. There are two separate but interconnected organisations (the Ancient Order of Hibernians for men and the Ladies' AOH for women) and for both, to be a Catholic is a qualifying condition for membership. But I knew that any change in the religious requirement, if it were to come at all, lay in the distant future. And the LAOH at least was moving towards proper partnership - it had begun its life as a "Ladies' Auxiliary" but had made significant strides in status and confidence.

I had very regular interaction with the AOH/LAOH in informal as well as more structured settings. The big set-piece occasions were the biennial National Conventions; the first during my tenure was in St Louis, Missouri in August 2014 and the second in Atlantic City, New Jersey in July 2016, and I addressed both of them. I am including the Atlantic City speech here as I think it gives a good flavour of the interaction.

As the speech makes clear, there was important common ground: not just our shared work on immigration but a genuine appreciation for how the AOH/LAOH had organised their ceremonies for the 1916 centenary. But the nuances are also evident. In the Brexit section, there is a concern to brake the support which was already emerging in Irish America for a very early Border Poll. And the final section - "a Time of Renewal" - tries to encourage some rethinking in Irish America: "It means embracing equality and inclusivity; creating an environment that is generous and open, where all daughters and sons of Ireland feel equally cherished; and where young people will feel they can grow and breathe and connect to what it means to be Irish in the 21st century."

There were times when I felt weighed down by the traditions prevailing in some segments of Irish America. I recall, for example, a trip to Savannah, Georgia, in the run-up to St Patrick's Day 2014.

Savannah organises a very impressive St Patrick's Day parade, with major celebrations the weekend before which include Mass at the beautiful Cathedral followed by a march to the Celtic Cross. At the Saturday night dinner, I was seated beside the Grand Marshal designate and casually inquired as to how the Grand Marshal is chosen. He began matter-of-factly reciting the criteria: "must be male, must be a practicing Catholic...". My partner Frank, also at the table, told me later that my jaw visibly dropped as I took this in!

By contrast, it felt like a breath of fresh air when I was talking with the Irish Network-USA, a recently-formed organisation of mostly young, many Irish-born, people in the US. I was always delighted to speak at their annual gatherings, which brought together their individual chapters from across the US. I am including here my remarks to their conference in Boston in November 2015 - notably more relaxed and informal, more at ease, than my address to the other organisations.

And then there were my interactions with the Friendly Sons of St Patrick, which deserve a subsection all their own. I spoke annually to the Friendly Sons of St Patrick in Washington, DC; I decided to include all four speeches here as they trace the arc of our interaction. But the centrepiece of the section is my address to the Friendly Sons in Philadelphia, on that joyful night in March 2016 when I was admitted at the first woman member of the Philadelphia Society.

The relationship with the Friendly Sons in DC was rocky from the start. It is an all-male Society but there is an established annual tradition of an "Ambassador's Reception" - one occasion in the year when the members bring along their wives and female guests. I did not want to disrupt the tradition, but there was a delicate advance discussion about the terms of my attendance. I was clear that I would need to speak (by tradition, the Ambassador stood in the receiving line but did not address the gathering) and I would want in my remarks to address the issue of membership. These terms were accepted, and so I prepared with some care for attendance at my first reception in October 2013.

To my recollection, this short speech of October 2013 is the only one in the entire collection that I sent to Dublin for advance clearance. Arising from some interviews I had given around the time of my appointment to DC, there had already been some minor media headlines about my view of male-only organisations in Irish America. I wanted Dublin on board for what I would say and - especially given what I knew to be ambivalence at HQ - I appreciated that this approval was forthcoming.

I tried to couch the speech in positive terms, expressing my respect for the work and legacy of the Friendly Sons, and for the non-sectarianism it had embraced from the outset. In calling for the organisation to open its doors to women, I drew on my personal experience, and explained my particular difficulty with the appropriation of St Patrick's Day for all-male celebrations.

It was not a comfortable speech to deliver. Not surprisingly, the reaction was mixed: some of the audience applauded; others stayed ostentatiously silent. This awkwardness continued over the next three years as I spoke at each of the annual events. The reception of my speech was usually tepid but courteous - the exception being one year when a particularly irate gentleman approached me immediately after the speech and loudly berated me for my "secular, feminist" views. (The Society President, who was by my side, did not respond.)

It was one of the happiest nights of my four-year tenure in DC when, in March 2016, the Friendly Sons in Philadelphia - the organisation's original and most hallowed branch - finally admitted women members. As I said in my speech: "there is a fittingness to this evening, a fundamental sense of rightness". A photograph of that evening captures the exuberance: in evening dress (it was a gala, black-tie event) and wearing the Friendly Sons blazer, I am raising my arm in a celebratory salute.

The speech that I made that evening was a joy to write: some speeches are cranked out laboriously; this one just flowed. And of course the pleasure was magnified when, only days later at the St Patrick's Day celebration in the White House, President Obama made reference to the occasion and quoted from my speech.

I have to say that I took particular pleasure in wearing the blazer I had been given in Philadelphia as I attended my final reception with the DC Friendly Sons in October 2016. I was frankly relieved that this would be the last time I had to go through this annual ritual - a relief that I suspect many of the membership felt too. My speech on that occasion continued to mix praise with exhortation, trying to encourage a reflection on what it means to be a responsible custodian of tradition.

I mentioned earlier what I knew to be the ambivalence in Dublin. Some Departmental colleagues shared my views; others did not. I want to summarise fairly the viewpoint of the latter group: they felt that it is for Irish America to define its own traditions and that we should avoid tensions with organisations like the Friendly Sons, whose membership includes people of influence and whose annual St Patrick's Day galas provide important networking opportunities.

Because of this unresolved difference, visiting Ministers and even Consuls General basically did their own thing - some were happy to attend all-male Friendly Sons dinners and other stayed away as a matter of principle. (The line could be a little blurred when all-male gatherings extended an *ex officio* invitation to a female office-holder; for my part I was clear that I would not attend such events as a kind of honorary man.) Before leaving DC, I proposed again to Dublin that we try to come up with a more coherent approach.

After my retirement I saw that the issue once again came into focus. My own views have not wavered, but I understand and accept that an opposite viewpoint can be genuinely held. What I find disingenuous is to hear an argument made that it is better to attend these events and "engage in debate" - such an argument might be more persuasive if those who embrace it had ever actually spoken up at the Friendly Sons occasions they attended.

In wrapping up this introduction I want to make a final, important point. Speeches are moments in time and do not capture the breadth of a relationship. All over the US, and often outside the structures of established organisations, there were many, many relaxed and warm occasions of interaction with our diaspora - people of worth and decency, whose commitment to Ireland always made me feel grateful and humble. More so than the big set-piece occasions, these are the encounters that will stay in my heart.

AOH/LAOH Biennial National Convention
Atlantic City, New Jersey
12th July 2016

It is a privilege to be invited to address you this morning. I retain warm memories of the gathering in St Louis in Summer 2014 and I have greatly enjoyed the close working relationship with the AOH and LAOH over the intervening two years.

I would like to focus in my remarks on three specific issues: (i) immigration reform, (ii) the aftermath of the British referendum, and (iii) how we might build on the experience of the 1916 centenary celebrations in the U.S.

First, however, a word about the context in Ireland.

These past couple of years have been good to Ireland in many ways. The economic recovery has gathered pace: we have had the fastest growing economy in Europe for two years in a row, and are firmly on course to hold on to that record in 2016. The economic indices are uniformly healthy – output, exports, foreign investment, tourism, are all showing record growth. And the most important figure, the unemployment rate, continues to drop steadily and is now under 9%.

Those of you visiting Ireland recently will have felt the uplift. I was there last month for Vice President Biden's visit, and the buzz and the optimism was palpable – a real sense of the country getting back on its feet again.

At the same time, we have absolutely no basis for complacency. The election results in February showed how bruised many people feel by the austerity of recent years. Serious questions are being asked: how fairly was the burden of sacrifice distributed, and how evenly is the recovery being experienced? The challenges facing the new Government are considerable, particularly given current uncertainties in the European and global environment.

Immigration Reform

We all know the extraordinary warmth of the relationship between Ireland and the US. There is no doubt as to President Obama's special feelings for Ireland, and the Vice President has just spent six days with us: the longest visit to a single country he has made throughout his two terms in office. We are lucky to have a Speaker of the House – Paul Ryan – who is proud of his Irish roots. And the Friends of Ireland in Congress remains a committed and robust group, whose advice and support we greatly value.

And yet, immensely positive through this picture is, there is one area of continuing deep frustration: the lack of progress on immigration reform. We have knocked on so many doors; we have made our case over and over; we have felt ourselves on the verge of a breakthrough only to be set back again; and for months now, there has been an extended stalemate as the November elections cast their long shadow. The Supreme Court decision last month, which stymied President Obama's executive action on immigration, was another grievous blow.

I am conscious of how deeply this frustration is felt in the community. All of us know people who are affected, who are trapped in their lives in the shadows, and who, every single day, feel and live the consequences of Congressional inaction.

As we try to predict the future, we have to soberly remind ourselves of the repeated setbacks and disappointments of recent years. Clearly there are no certainties: over the past months of the Presidential campaign, the anti-immigration rhetoric we have heard in some quarters has been shocking.

But yet, quite apart from any appeal to generosity of spirit, one has to hold on to the belief that logic, common sense, economic self-interest, will ultimately prevail. The November elections will hopefully prove a catalyst. Many of our contacts point to 2017 as the year of action, and suggest that Congress may finally be ready to legislate in the course of next year.

If things are indeed to move in 2017, now is the time to lay the groundwork. As far as the government and our diplomatic network are concerned, I can pledge that no effort will be spared. The Taoiseach and Ministers will continue to raise the issue at every opportunity; we will monitor the Presidential campaign platforms and robustly make our case to whatever Administration emerges; and we will continue to try to energise and enlist Members of Congress to our cause.

Brexit: Aftermath of British Referendum

All of you will have been following the outcome of the British referendum on 23 June, and I know that the implications for Ireland will be uppermost in your minds.

The "leave" decision is clearly not the outcome we wanted, or that the Irish government campaigned for. But it is the outcome we all have to deal with – with regret certainly, but without rancour, and with respect for democratic decision-making. Rather than "what ifs", the challenge for our Government is to ensure that Ireland's interests are protected in the protracted negotiations that lie ahead, as Britain moves towards withdrawal from the European Union.

Two things are crystal clear: firstly, Ireland will remain a deeply committed member of the European family. There is absolutely no ambiguity or hesitation on that score. Despite its imperfections, the European Union is our chosen home and has provided the setting and support system which has allowed us to develop and prosper over more than forty years. A very recent opinion poll in Ireland showed that 86% of those polled felt that Ireland should remain in the EU; only 9% believed we should follow the UK exit.

The second point is equally clear. Given the unique ties between our neighbouring islands, Ireland's interest lies in having a future relationship between Britain and the EU that is as close and constructive as possible.

British withdrawal will undoubtedly have profound implications for Ireland's economy, and it will take time for the full ramifications to become clear. But the implications for Northern Ireland lie at the heart of our concerns, as they do for all of you here.

There is a particular complexity about the referendum outcome – the fact that England and Wales voted to leave the European Union while majorities in Scotland and in Norther Ireland voted to remain. The Irish Government does not underestimate the level of disquiet felt by many people in Norther Ireland at the prospect of losing their connection to the European Union. Inevitably, and appropriately, a debate is under way about how this reality is to be factored into future discussions and arrangements.

For our Government, the priority is clear: we do not want a situation where the border between the two parts of our island hardens. We have come too far, and too much has been sacrificed, for that to be allowed to happen. The focus of the Government's efforts will be to protect all the progress achieved through the Good Friday Agreement and successor agreements, and build on it further. Even after the UK leaves the EU, the Good Friday Agreement will remain the foundation stone for relations on the island of Ireland, and both the Irish and British Governments have again made clear that they are fully committed to its principles and institutions.

Some of you will have heard calls for a new Border Poll, on the basis that the referendum outcome has created a new context for moves towards reunification of our island. I have read attentively the AOH statement on this issue last week.

The Government's position with regard to a poll has been set out in considerable detail by our Taoiseach, Enda Kenny, and

Foreign Minister, Charlie Flanagan. As I indicated earlier, the concerns underlying these calls are well understood, and those concerns must be addressed in the forthcoming negotiations. Nevertheless it is our belief that such a poll could be divisive at this time, that there is very little possibility of it being won in any event, and that it would distract from the absolute priority of protecting the gains of recent decades.

We believe that the immediate priority should be for the two Governments and the Northern Ireland Executive to work urgently and intensively together to find solutions to the various challenges that a UK exit will present. That work has now commenced and I anticipate that there will be intensive engagement over the coming months between the administrations in Dublin, Belfast and London.

I know that Irish America, and the AOH-LAOH, will continue to follow with close attention all developments in the course of these critical negotiations over the next two and a half years or so. Let me assure you that – while we may not always reach the same conclusions – we will be ready at all times to engage in dialogue with you, to hear your concerns, and to share perspectives.

Building on Centenary Commemorations

The third issue on which I would like to touch is the 1916 centenary commemorations, and how we can build on our work together.

I want to say how impressed I was by the work and dedication of the AOH and LAOH in marking the centenary nationwide. I was with some of your leadership in Dublin over the Easter weekend. The ceremonies were extraordinarily meaningful for us all, and those of us who gathered outside the GPO on Easter Sunday will never forget the emotion and dignity of that day.

A few weeks later, I was privileged to participate in the Mass and commemorative ceremony organised by the AOH-LAOH in

New York on 23 April. That too was a huge organisational achievement, and it was a day that will live in our collective memory.

Throughout these past months, we have had a range of ceremonies in DC and right around the nation where many of your members were organisers and participants. In DC, the rededication of the statue of Robert Emmett was another important shared moment.

These centenary commemorations have been immensely important in honouring the 1916 legacy and helping us to examine our one hundred year journey. But beyond that, I believe that the experience of coming together to mark this centenary has been extraordinarily valuable of itself. We have all been energised and inspired by the partnership, and by the strengthened sense of purpose and identity. In the second half of this year, I would propose that we reflect together on how we can build on this experience.

In this decade of commemorations, spanning 2012 to 2022, there will be other centenaries that we may wish to mark, and it will be important to establish which of these is most meaningful to Irish America. But the reflection I have in mind goes beyond that. We have seen the energy that is generated when we come together around common projects, when there is a sense of connection to something larger. Let us consider how we might distil the essence of this, and examine whether there are ways we might apply that same energy and spirit in other shared causes and endeavours.

A Time of Renewal

This reflection on how we build on the centenary leads me to a final, wider point about maintaining the weight and influence of Irish America.

As we know, America is home to some 35 million people of Irish descent. The pride of these daughters and sons of Ireland is legendary – a legitimate pride based on everything that Irish people have contributed to the building of this great country.

We are heirs to a great tradition, and have carved out a unique space. There is every reason for confidence that this tradition will continue, and that the voice and views of Irish America will continue to resonate strongly.

At the same time, our stocktaking and strategising must take account of evolving realities. With the demographics in this country changing, the percentage of Irish Americans in the overall US population is shrinking. And as avenues for legal immigration from Ireland have narrowed over recent decades, there are markedly fewer first and second generation Irish.

Especially against this background, the challenge for Irish America is one of constant renewal – valuing our roots and our past, but being ready to rethink and reimagine. This is what our forebears did: taking the emigrant ship, reinventing themselves in their new homeland, adapting and changing with each generation.

And this is also what is required today, if we are to ensure that Irish America remains vibrant and future-focused. It means embracing equality and inclusivity; creating an environment that is generous and open, where all daughters and sons of Ireland feel equally cherished; and where young people will feel they can grow and breathe and connect to what it means to be Irish in the 21st century.

Faced with so many issues of substance, your Convention clearly has a very packed agenda over the coming days. I wish you a very productive conference, full of satisfaction and challenge, drawing strength from all your many achievements, and ready to write the next chapter.

Irish Network-USA National Conference
Boston, 6th November 2015

I am delighted to be here in Boston to join you all for the third Irish Network-USA national conference. I am proud to say that I have been to each of your national conferences so far and I look forward to keeping up that tradition next year.

I have to tell you that I genuinely look forward to this event in my calendar each year. I am fortunate to have an opportunity to travel to many parts of this great country as a central part of my job as Irish Ambassador – including last week to the West coast, where I accompanied our President, Michael D. Higgins and Mrs. Sabina Higgins, during their very successful visit to Washington State and California – but attending the IN-USA national conference is a real celebration for me.

The fact that your organisation is wide open to all is, I believe, one of the key reasons that Irish Network - USA resonates so clearly, particularly (though certainly not exclusively) with a younger generation of Irish, Irish Americans and friends of Ireland.

When I meet and engage with Irish Networks around the US, I see a real reflection in the leadership and members of the modern Ireland of the 21st century which is open, which is outward looking, which is tolerant, which is generous, and most of all which is inclusive.

That is no small thing and I warmly applaud you for it.

My presence here this morning in Boston is a clear reflection of the extremely high regard in which your work is held by the Irish Embassy in Washington D.C., by our network of Consulates across the United States and indeed by the Irish Government.

We are with you and we will continue to be with you as you develop, expand and enhance the Irish Networks around the United States.

Engagement with the Diaspora

I think that it is fair to say that this last year has seen a real step change in the Irish Government's approach to and engagement with our diaspora around the world.

Building on the appointment in July 2014 of our first ever Minister for Diaspora Affairs, Jimmy Deenihan T.D., the Government published in March this year a new policy document entitled "Global Irish: Ireland's Diaspora Policy", which is the first clear statement of the Government's policy on the diaspora.

With up to 70 million people around the world claiming Irish ancestry and heritage – around half of them here in the United States – this new policy document seeks to drive and foster diaspora engagement by supporting, connecting with, facilitating, and recognising the diaspora. The vision set out in the policy is of "a vibrant, diverse global Irish community, connected to Ireland and to each other".

The document sets out a range of planned actions including: a Global Irish Civic Forum – the first instalment of which took in Dublin Castle at the beginning of June, drawing an attendance of around 200 participants, including I know, some of you in this room; a Global Irish Media Fund, an Alumni Challenge Fund, and a Fourth Global Irish Economic Forum – which I look forward to attending in Dublin later this month.

This year has also seen the first ever Global Irish Parliamentarians' Forum take place in Dublin, drawing together a group of Irish-connected parliamentarians serving in national parliaments and state assemblies in Australia, Canada, France, the UK, and I am delighted to say the US was also very well represented.

Image and Identity

The particular theme I want to talk about today is image and identity. It's a cross-cutting issue which brings in a number of other themes. I want to talk about the positive aspects, as well as some of the challenges.

The first point is that there is probably no other country with an image or brand that is more positive than Ireland's here in the US. Of course it's about the almost 40 million Americans of Irish descent, and the legacy that is so important and deserves to be honoured.

But my focus is very much on trying to get people to connect with contemporary Ireland. The kind of open, multicultural, tolerant, generous society we have become. This was best typified in the same-sex marriage referendum earlier this year which opened a lot of people's eyes to the new Ireland.

I think that some of this is hard for more conservative strains of Irish America to understand. We see the backlash in relation to the St. Patrick's Day parade in New York. And it is sometimes not easy for the longer established Irish American associations to adapt.

I am always conscious that Ireland and Irish America are not one and the same, and that Irish America is shaped by its own distinctive history and influence. There is a need to tread softly. But at the same time, it's important always to be proud of the Ireland we are, and the Ireland we are striving to become. The more I can connect Irish America with the reality of Ireland today, the better I feel about it. It's ultimately not healthy that there should be dissonance between the two.

And the whole immigration issue is relevant here too. As you know, there have always been two strands to our campaign on immigration. Firstly, it's about getting status for the undocumented – because we all know the misery that comes with being undocumented, living your life in the shadows. And it's deeply, deeply disappointing and frustrating that Congress has refused to move on this.

The second aspect relates to getting some kind of pathway for legal immigration. This too is very important for all sorts of reasons, but also because the lack of new blood from Ireland is having an effect on Irish America. Less than one fifth of 1% of Green Cards issued annually go to Irish people. It means that you don't have the oxygen coming in to freshen up the pool.

Of course we want legislative change, but we also want to build up all the people-to-people contacts. I am particularly interested in the education sector, and trying to increase the number of young Americans who spend a semester or longer in Ireland. And in the other direction, we want to keep the numbers up in the J1 programme. Currently about 7,000 young Irish people come to the US each summer – that's about 8% of our entire third-level student population.

The bottom line is that we want to do everything we can to keep the oxygen flowing, people being able to take up jobs here, young people studying and visiting in both directions, getting away from stereotypes and exposing Americans and Irish America to contemporary Ireland.

The second area where I want to talk about image and reality is the economic area. Again, I think that our image is extraordinarily positive, based on the realities on the ground. We are out of the economic crisis and well into the recovery phase. We have the fastest growth rate in Europe: 5.2% last year, likely to reach 6.2% this year.

But it's still worthwhile sounding a couple of cautionary notes. We've had enough of the hubris, and we have learned a lot of tough lessons the hard way. So, yes, it's a great story but let's not hide the human cost of it all.

Another aspect of image is our reputational risk on the tax front. We know that Ireland offers a very attractive overall package for FDI: talent, tax, English-speaking, etc. But the more we succeed, the more some circles – whether in Congress, the media, or wherever – will attribute it exclusively to our 12.5% corporation tax. We need to stand our ground judiciously on that – not to be overly defensive but to correct some of the misstatements that are made.

The third area I want to touch on in relation to image and identity is the centenary celebration in 2016.

I see this centenary year as a wonderful opportunity both to honour the past but also to examine the present and set our compass for the future.

I have said repeatedly that it's about not just 1916, but about the 100-year journey. It's a time to celebrate, but also to interrogate.

Our Embassy and our six Consulates are working on a programme that will have hundreds of events right across the country, involving a wide variety of partners, and I know that many Irish Network chapters are deeply involved.

So, in terms of image, I think this is a once in a generation opportunity and it's a tremendous privilege for us all to be part of it.

In wrapping up, let me reiterate that there is a full and exciting shared agenda with the IN network. We are delighted you exist, that you are growing so fast, and that you can embody and represent today's Ireland. I look forward to a great year ahead of continuing to work closely together.

Annual Ambassador's Reception,
Society of the Friendly Sons of St. Patrick, Washington DC
15th October 2013

Firstly, let me express appreciation for your hospitality and warm welcome. I know this annual reception is a courtesy extended to Irish Ambassadors over many years, and it is a pleasure to meet members of the Friendly Sons together with your spouses and partners. I also appreciate that, in what I gather is a departure from the usual practice, you have invited me to address you briefly this evening.

This is a Society of long and distinguished lineage. The Washington chapter is 85 years old this year, and you in turn are an offspring of the original chapter founded in Philadelphia over 240 years ago.

The Society can take legitimate pride in its achievements over so many years. The roll call of speakers at your annual St. Patrick's Day dinner is truly impressive. Through the decades, that roll call has included many distinguished speakers from Ireland – Presidents, Taoisigh, Ministers and diplomats – testifying to the regard in which your Society is held. With your long established Scholarship Foundation, you have worked to encourage educational exchanges between Ireland and the United States and to promote reconciliation in Northern Ireland.

But perhaps your greatest badge of honour is the non-sectarianism that you embraced from the very start. Indeed, the original founders in 1771 saw it as one of the defining characteristics of your Society. You were so far ahead of your time in that regard. As Vincent Burke says in his history of the Society: "The Friendly Sons were a trailblazer in what the world now acclaims as the ecumenical movement".

When I met with your President and Secretary shortly after my arrival here, I expressed my respect and appreciation for this work and legacy, and I now happily do so again. But I went on to make another point in our conversation, one that I would also like to share with you this evening.

I am very privileged to be Ireland's seventeenth Ambassador to the United States, and the first woman in that role. Since taking up duty, I have been struck by how my appointment resonates with Irish women, and indeed with Irish people more generally – how much it is welcomed as a statement about the kind of Ireland we have become: a modern, inclusive Ireland where women are slowly but surely assuming their rightful place.

I believe this statement about modern Ireland also finds a resonance with our Irish American family. We can all rejoice in the increasingly rich and vibrant relationship that is developing between Ireland and its diaspora. And as the relationship deepens, it seems to me more than ever important that our diaspora should connect with contemporary Ireland.

As someone who is deeply committed to representing modern, inclusive Ireland, I have been very open in advocating to your President and Secretary that the Friendly Sons should end its all-male status and open its membership to women.

I think that sometimes it is hard for those on the inside to understand how it feels to be on the outside. Perhaps therefore, in frankness and in friendship, I might evoke my own memories of the period in the mid-80s when I was posted here in Washington as a young diplomat. Decades later, I still recall how jarring it felt to be excluded from your St. Patrick's Day festivities to which all my colleagues at the Embassy were invited. I know that, over the years, other female diplomatic colleagues have felt the same way. And I assume that what we felt was shared by very many other women, perhaps even by some in this room tonight.

Why did we – and do we – feel this way? I suspect there are rather few people – male or female – who would not accept that there is scope, in some circumstances, for groups that are gender-specific. Indeed, I am myself happy to be a part of support and mentoring networks for professional women.

But I would suggest that the Society of the Friendly Sons is different. A very large part of your purpose is to mark and celebrate our national day. In different venues across the country, the Friendly Sons dinner is the premier event on or around that special night. This should surely be the most inclusive of times. As the Irish family gathers to celebrate its Irishness, women belong inside the room – joining fully and equally in the talk and laughter, the connecting and networking.

Today's Ireland is an exciting, dynamic, fast-changing place. It is true that these past few years have been sobering, and we have had to draw on all our resilience as a people. But there is now a national conversation under way that is bracing and invigorating.

We are eagerly inviting our diaspora to join fully in that conversation: to help us both to distill what is best from our past and to rise to the challenges ahead. And we especially need the energy and generosity of spirit of Irish America.

I come back to my earlier point: openness is such an important part of what the Friendly Sons stood for at the outset. Your mission statement is admirably written. It sets out as one of the purposes of this Society: "… in every way to stimulate and strengthen better relationships between all people".

And perhaps I could return to that word "trailblazer", to which your Society rightly lays claim in describing its ecumenical origins.

I would personally love to celebrate with you a new chapter in your trailblazing history. Those of us who are proud daughters of Ireland would be so happy to recognise ourselves in the name and reality of your Society.

Thank you again for holding this reception in my honour this evening and for giving me the opportunity to open this conversation with you.

I wish you all a wonderful evening.

Annual Ambassador's Reception,
Society of the Friendly Sons of St. Patrick, Washington DC
21st October 2014

I am happy to be back with you for a second time and to have this opportunity to meet and greet the Friendly Sons, together with your spouses and partners.

This time last year, when I attended your reception, I was in my first months as Ambassador in DC. It has certainly proved to be an eventful year on all fronts.

The Past Year

The headline change of course has been the improvement in economic circumstances in Ireland. After the years of austerity and sacrifice, recovery is now finally under way. The forecast is for 4.7% growth this year – truly impressive by European standards. Our borrowing costs are way down, the unemployment rate is reducing, consumer confidence is returning.

Right throughout these past difficult years, the economic relationship with the U.S. has been a powerful engine for recovery. Now, as our economy takes off, all the indicators remain immensely positive. Investment flows between the two countries have never been healthier, trade is flourishing, and tourism is at record levels.

It has been an exceptionally busy year for all of us at the Embassy. We have welcomed a range of Oireachtas and Ministerial visitors to the US. As always, the annual highlight was the Taoiseach's visit around St. Patrick's Day. Experiencing it for the first time as Ambassador, I was struck again by the extraordinary access that Ireland enjoys here in the nation's capital.

As well as setting down roots in DC, I also had the opportunity during my first year to travel to a dozen or so cities right across the US – all the time seeking to promote our economic and political agenda, and to connect with our vibrant diaspora. Each visit was a learning experience for me: after fourteen months in the post, I am more than ever conscious of the depth and richness of the Irish contribution to this country, and the unique ties that so strongly bind us together.

It has been a year both of looking back and looking forward.

In the last weeks, the Embassy organised a series of events around the 90th anniversary of diplomatic relations between Ireland and the US. In addition to providing a great opportunity for celebration, the anniversary events offered fascinating insights into the thinking which guided policy making in those early years.

Important as it is to ground ourselves in the past, our strongest focus has been on strategic planning for the future. Earlier this year, following considerable reflection, the Embassy produced a paper on Challenges and Opportunities in Irish/US Relations. The Paper reviewed a plan originally drawn up five years ago, and has helped set the compass for the next five years.

This Review exercise strengthened our sense of purpose, bringing into relief the many challenges we continue to face: further improving the economic relationship, lobbying for immigration reform, continuing to ensure a positive American engagement on Northern Ireland, and strengthening the cultural relationship.

Irish America/Friendly Sons

Given the make-up of the attendance here this evening, perhaps I might share a passage of the Embassy's review paper as it relates to Irish America.

Our paper strongly affirms the role and importance of Irish America and emphasises that our Irish American diaspora will remain a resource of incomparable benefit. We underline the two-way, reciprocal, nature of the relationship with Irish America. We also discuss diversity; let me quote a couple of paragraphs:

"Irish-America is diverse and multi-faceted; there is no single identikit. And, like all diasporas, the Irish-American family will continue to evolve in its own way, shaped by its own particular set of experiences and influences. This diversity and distinctiveness of Irish America needs to be recognised and valued.

But constant interaction and two-way communication are essential. The homeland of memory, or the "Ireland of the mind", will always exert a powerful pull. It should not, however, displace today's realities. Just as we in Ireland need to recognise and respect the diaspora perspective, it is important that Irish America understands the evolution that is taking place in Ireland and is fully aware of the values of contemporary Ireland."

Against this backdrop, I would like to revert to an issue that I raised here last year – because, in truth, it is an issue that is inescapable in our conversations and interactions with the Friendly Sons.

In my first engagement with you, at last year's reception, I set out the respect I have for all the achievements of the Friendly Sons over the two centuries since your organisation was founded.

In particular, I said that the non-sectarianism which your organisation embraced from the outset stands as a true badge of honour.

Speaking as openly and honestly as I could, I went on to advocate that the Friendly Sons should end its all male status and open its membership to women. I shared my own personal experience – the sense of exclusion when, as a young diplomat here in the mid 80s, your doors were closed to me as I wished to join in the St. Patrick's Day festivities on an equal footing with my male colleagues.

This type of issue was very much in our thinking as we crafted the passage on Irish America in our Review paper.

We understand of course that Irish-America is not a

transposition of Ireland. We recognise that you are shaped by your own experiences and influences. We know the pull of tradition, and how it can seem to offer solidity and reassurance in a world of sometimes jarring change.

But, as our Review states, it is important also that Irish America is fully aware of the values of contemporary Ireland.

Inclusivity is at the heart of these values. As we define the kind of people we want to be, the kind of country we want to become, inclusivity is a touchstone. Even if we struggle to get there, and all too often fall short in turning aspiration into reality, the commitment is genuine and strong.

There can indeed be a tension between defending established tradition and adapting to twenty-first century values. We see that tension played out in so many different situations, both at home and abroad. Here in the U.S., we need look no further than the debate under way in New York about participation in the St. Patrick's Day Parade.

Each of us faces our own responsibilities. The challenge of fashioning the new Ireland belongs to the people of Ireland; the choices are theirs. In Irish America, the challenges and choices fall to you – the leadership and membership of Irish-American organisations. But just as we in Ireland benefit from your input, I hope that you will grant a hearing to those of us who greatly value and care about Irish America, and who genuinely respect the legacy and past achievements of organisations such as yours.

I understand that a discussion about future direction has begun within the DC chapter of the Friendly Sons, and I wish you well in taking that discussion forward.

And so, let me finish on a note I sounded earlier this evening – looking back and looking forward, honouring the past while setting our compass for the future.

We in Ireland will need to rise to that challenge in a very

particular way in 2016, the 100th anniversary of the Easter Rising which paved the way for Irish independence. We will want to keep faith with the historical reality of 1916, as well as celebrating the 100-year journey and the point of arrival. I look forward to engaging with Irish America as we plan how to mark that iconic year here in the U.S.

Again, I thank you for your hospitality and your welcome to me this evening. I am glad to bring such good news from Ireland and I look forward to a further year of recovery and renewed prosperity.

Annual Ambassador's Reception,
Society of the Friendly Sons of St. Patrick, Washington DC
20th October 2015

I am very happy to join you this evening for what is now my third Ambassador's reception with the Friendly Sons, together with your spouses and partners.

I am conscious that this evening is primarily a social occasion and I will not detain you too long. There are, however, a few issues I think worth touching on.

Economy

Firstly, an update on the economy in Ireland. Many of you may have visited in the course of the year and all of you, I am sure, stay closely in touch. You will have seen that the economic recovery has gained real pace and momentum. So much so that, in 2015, we are on target for more than 6% economic growth, the strongest growth rate in the European Union.

This growth rate, in the aftermath of the crisis of 2008 and the years of austerity which followed, is a tremendous boost for the country. There is a real sense of the recovery taking hold. Exports and FDI and tourism are all powering ahead, and it is hugely encouraging to see the growth in domestic demand and consumer confidence. Unemployment is still far too high, but it's on a clear downward trajectory – compared to 15% unemployment in 2012, we are now at 9.4%.

So I think it's fair to say we are back with a spring in our step. Too bad that our valiant rugby team was stopped in its tracks on the way to the World Cup final – a lot of us are still smarting from Sunday's defeat by Argentina! Such small setbacks aside, however, one can sense the increased buoyancy and returning optimism.

But, even if we are firmly back on our feet, it is very far from being a return to the Celtic Tiger years. Firstly, too many people are still hurting from the years of austerity, and we are still grappling with a major public debt overhang. Secondly, none of us wants to go back to the hubris of the Celtic Tiger era. We have learned some tough lessons in the period since 2008, and learned them the hard way. This time, things must be different – our recovery must be real, sustainable, with a firm foundation of values. We are determined to build a society that continues to incentivise success, but also one that is inclusive and fair, true to our better selves.

Celebration of the centenary

The second point I want to touch on – and it's not unconnected to the first point – is next year's celebration of the centenary of 1916. I know that all of you appreciate just what an iconic year 1916 was in Irish history: the year of the Easter rebellion, setting in motion a series of events which ultimately led to the Irish independence in 1921.

The centenary will be marked in a very high profile way in Ireland throughout next year. And given the tremendous resonance of the centenary for Irish America, we want to mark it in an appropriately high-profile way on this side of the Atlantic too. There are ambitious plans for events right across the US; here in DC our flagship event will be a three-week "Ireland 100" festival at the Kennedy Center. The festival promises to be a wonderful showcase of Irish cultural talent – theatre, music, literature, dance – and I hope we will see many of you at the various events.

One point I think is very relevant in terms of how we mark the centenary: this will not just be an opportunity to look back. Of course there will be a great deal of reflection about the seminal events of 1916 and the one hundred year journey that has brought us to where we are. But, even more importantly, it will be a time to look at where we have arrived and how we go forward; a time to set our compass for the decades ahead.

And so, in addition to the stocktaking that has been triggered by the financial crisis and its aftermath, there is also this unique opportunity offered by the centenary. Both are coming together in an invigorating and exciting way. It is a time for re-evaluation and renewal, a time for forging a new Ireland for the 21st century. And, happily, there is every sign – as we saw with the referendum on same sex marriage earlier this year – that this new Ireland will be a place that is more open, more inclusive, and more generous.

Irish-America: Inclusivity

And to my third and final point. I know that Irish America will mark the 1916 centenary with a deep sense of pride and connection. The contribution of Irish America, in the lead up to the Rising and throughout the century since, truly deserves celebration. And as the community looks back with all that justifiable pride, I hope that – just as we in Ireland see the centenary as a time of renewal – Irish America too will approach it in the same way.

There are signs that this kind of renewal is happening. Next year, for example, the St. Patrick's Day parade in New York, will be different. For the first time it will include an Irish LGBT group. The organisers have decided that the time has come to opt for a more inclusive approach, while respecting all the Parade's proud history over more than 250 years.

I see other signs of renewal too.

In addressing you at the two previous Ambassador's receptions, in a spirit of friendship and respect, I have shared my sense that the time has come for the Friendly Sons to open its doors to women members. You will understand how gratified I was to receive a letter a few weeks back from the President of the Friendly Sons in Philadelphia, telling me that the Organisation there has decided to admit women members. In the President's own words: "245 years in waiting was long enough." The vote to change the by-laws was carried with 90% in favour, and the President has invited me to attend their annual dinner in March when the first women members will be admitted.

As you all know far better than me, Philadelphia was the cradle of your organisation – it was there that the Friendly Sons were first established, on St. Patrick's Day in 1771. And perhaps where Philadelphia led all those years ago, it can still lead.

As custodians of your own rules, you will of course take whatever decision you see fit. But I would simply make one point: as we enter this centenary year, there was never a more appropriate time to dismantle those barriers – of gender, or religion, or sexual orientation – that survive from earlier and different times.

It is my hope that an open and inclusive Irish American family can share a wonderful celebration of the centenary, cherishing the rich legacy of the past but also positioning ourselves for these new times and a new future.

Gala Dinner,
Society of the Friendly Sons of St. Patrick, Philadelphia
12th March 2016

This is a very special night, whose resonance extends well beyond this room and well beyond Philadelphia. It is one of these rare occasions when we feel the ground shift, and witness the arc of history bend a little.

Tonight, after 245 years as an all-male organisation, you have opened your doors to women members.

I feel immensely privileged to become the first woman member of your Society, in the company of twenty distinguished women who are also today admitted to membership.

It is a source of particular pride that I am only the second adopted member of your Society. I am informed that I follow in the footsteps of George Washington, who in 1781 became the first – and to date the only - adopted member of the Society. There can hardly be a more exclusive club: a membership of two, with the other member being George Washington!

I express my deep appreciation to your President, Joseph Heenan, for his enlightened leadership and to your membership who last September, by an overwhelming majority, took the landmark decision to admit women members.

There is a fittingness to this evening, a fundamental rightness about it. So much chimes together: this city, this Society, this important centenary year.

Philadelphia is a city founded on a vision – William Penn's vision of religious tolerance and brotherly love.

It is a city which writes history – the city where it all began, the city where the Declaration of Independence was adopted two hundred and forty years ago.

It is also a city which bears powerful witness to the unique ties that bind Ireland and America. Let us recall with pride that when the Declaration of Independence was signed in Philadelphia in 1776, three of the signatories were Irish-born.

Five years before signature of the Declaration of Independence, the Friendly Sons of St. Patrick were formed in Philadelphia. Your city is the cradle of this organisation; the Philadelphia Society is custodian of the traditions, keeper of the flame.

As Friendly Sons, you are heirs to a proud history. For nearly 250 years, your Society has brought men of Irish ancestry together, buttressing and affirming their pride in their Irish identity. You have a long and worthy tradition of philanthropy, evidenced by the grants and scholarships you continue to fund, which have touched and changed the lives of many.

From your foundation, you were ahead of your time in one key respect. From the very beginning, you have been consciously and deliberately non-sectarian, embracing Catholic, Protestant and Dissenter. In the words of Thomas Moore, for so long printed on your dinner menus, and which you have honoured and echoed throughout the years:

"Shall I give up a friend I have valued and tried

If he kneel not before the same altar with me?"

Tonight, the embrace you extended to men of all religions over so many years is finally extended to women.

From one generation to the next, all of us recognise that we stand on the shoulders of those who have gone before. And who among us doubts that the shoulders of women have borne just as much weight as the shoulders of men?

"Irish Philadelphia", published in 2012, sets it out: "The sons of the famine immigrants became merchants, loom fixers, stevedores, locomotive mechanics, and skilled tradesmen. The daughters of these famine immigrants worked in mills, garment factories, nursing wards and domestic service." These women, and those who followed them, were just as courageous, resilient and indomitable as their menfolk.

We feel the shades of these generations of women thronging the room tonight.

I said at the outset that our gathering takes place in a special city but also at a special time.

There could not be a more fitting year for your Society to take this step forward. 2016, as we all know, is a momentous year, centenary of what is perhaps the most iconic year in Irish history.

This is a year to reclaim the spirit and intent of the 1916 Proclamation. And that spirit and intent, remarkably for its time, was deliberately inclusive.

The Proclamation addresses both Irishmen and Irishwomen. Its second paragraph calls on "our exiled children in America". We might linger a moment on that language: not "our exiled sons" as would have been in no way unusual at the time, but "our exiled children", to include both daughters and sons.

The Proclamation's most sacred promise is the new Republic's guarantee of "religious and civil liberty, equal rights and equal opportunities to all its citizens".

Women were at the heart of the Easter Rising. They helped to forge its cultural underpinning; among their many roles during Easter week, women from *Cumann na mBan* did vital duty as nurses and dispatch carriers; and women from the Citizen Army participated as combatants.

In the vision of many of these women, shared by some of the male leaders, there was a sense of a forthcoming Ireland that would be not just free but feminist, not just feminist but free.

Alongside all our pride in the visionaries of 1916, we know that proclaiming a vision does not guarantee it will come to pass.

This centenary year is time for stock-taking by all of us in

Ireland. We are invited to examine the balance sheet of the past one hundred years, the paths we have taken and the priorities we have chosen. We look back with deep and genuine pride on all the many achievements, but we acknowledge also where we have fallen short, where the rhetoric of the Proclamation did not translate into the reality of people's lives.

As we carry out this stocktaking, we recognise that for Irish women for much of the past century, the promise of the Proclamation rang hollow. The feminist Ireland that many of the protagonists of 1916 envisaged was lost to sight over subsequent decades.

Our history in this regard is in no way unique. What happened to women in Ireland in the aftermath of 1916 is part of a larger pattern – a global pattern – that continues in our day.

In 2011, as Ireland's Ambassador to the UN, I addressed a Security Council debate on Women, Peace and Security. I spoke about the Arab Spring, which had not then so tragically unravelled as it has in the intervening years. But it was already clear that, despite their inspirational roles in Tahrir Square and elsewhere, women were at risk of being sidelined. I said in that debate:

"The risks for women are obvious: revolutions begin in the street, but at a later stage key decisions may be taken in smoke-filled rooms. In that transition, women all too easily lose out: their courage helped to make the revolution, but their inexperience of power can allow others to shape the outcomes."

That is what happened – or at least part of what happened – in Ireland as the new State came into being.

Building on an honest reckoning of the past, our task now is to go forward with purpose and conviction. In this centenary year, we recommit ourselves to finally redeeming the promise of the Proclamation. As President Michael D. Higgins said in his eloquent address earlier this week on the Role of Women in the Rising:

"Taking stock of what we have achieved, we must relentlessly seek to complete our collective journey towards the full enjoyment of women's rights."

Especially against this backdrop, the step you have taken here in Philadelphia could not be more fitting, and will stand as a proud moment in our centenary celebrations.

It is heartening, and moving, that Irish America should be marking this centenary year with new steps toward inclusivity. Five days hence, we will cheer a very different St. Patrick's Day parade as it proudly marches down Fifth Avenue – a parade that for the first time includes Irish LGBT groups. Tonight the Friendly Sons have broken down barriers of 245 years; on 17 March in New York, we will see another barrier of very long standing dismantled.

In both instances, Irish America is making a statement: there are no second class citizens; no children of a lesser God.

Two hundred and forty five years ago, in choosing to become a non-sectarian organisation, the Friendly Sons grasped something essential: that inclusivity enriches us all. It is not just a gift bestowed or a right recognised. It is something which carries its own reward: binding us together, making our communities stronger and more resilient.

And so let us celebrate the more inclusive Irish America that is emerging in Philadelphia tonight and in New York next week – an invigorated Irish America, more ready to take on new challenges, better equipped to embrace the future.

As I conclude, let me emphasise again how meaningful this night is. In this hallowed city, in this centenary year, your Society has shown true leadership, decisively embracing renewal and modernity. As so often before, history is being written in Philadelphia. It is a privilege and a joy to be part of it.

Annual Ambassador's Reception,
Society of the Friendly Sons of St. Patrick, Washington DC
18th October 2016

I have had the pleasure of joining you for your annual Ambassador's reception over each of the last three years. This is my fourth time to share this special evening with you, and – since I will complete my posting next summer – it will also be my final time.

My thanks to all of you, together with your spouses and partners, for the welcome you have extended to me at these annual receptions. And my appreciation to your President and Secretary for their work to ensure the success of our gatherings.

This evening is special to me in a very particular way: it is the first time I join you as a member of your Society. Tonight, I am proud to wear the blazer that was presented to me by the Friendly Sons of St. Patrick in Philadelphia when I was admitted as their first woman member in February this year.

In a memorable and moving ceremony, I was joined by more than twenty other women also being welcomed into full membership. From now on, in Philadelphia, the doors of the Friendly Sons are equally open to men and women.

Perhaps the most affirming aspect of the ceremony was the spirit in which this step was taken. The admission of women was not something wrested from a begrudging membership. On the contrary: it came after an overwhelmingly positive vote, with a shared sense of the appropriateness of taking this step at this time.

The Friendly Sons rightly see themselves as heirs to, and custodians of, a long and proud tradition.

In my annual addresses, I have made clear my respect for the legacy and work of your Society. Your pride in your Irish heritage resonates with us all; you foster a great sense of community among your members, and your Scholarship Foundation has changed many lives.

But perhaps the defining characteristic of the Friendly Sons is the non-sectarianism which your Society embraced from the very outset. Two hundred and forty five years ago, when the founders came together in Philadelphia, they consciously saw themselves as progressives, as trailblazers, in this respect.

For each succeeding generation, there is need to reflect on what it means to be a responsible custodian. Is it to keep things as they always were, or to preserve the essence of the founding vision while adapting and interpreting it for contemporary times?

That debate is of course for you to conduct. But I would just say this. In Philadelphia last February, the cradle of your Society, there was a proud sense of continuity – of keeping faith with the founding vision, being true to the progressive thinking of 1771, but replenishing and renewing that vision for the 21st century.

Especially in this centenary year, it is appropriate to reflect more broadly on the themes of renewal and re-imagining.

In addressing you last year, I spoke about the plans for commemorating the centenary of that iconic year of Irish history: 1916. It was clear from the outset that these commemorations would be especially meaningful in the United States. Were it not for the inspiration and practical support from the US, the Easter Rising could not have happened when and how it did. And, as we all know, the ties have deepened further over the intervening century.

It was important that the centenary commemorations in the US be fully commensurate with the strength of those ties.

As we approach the end of the centenary year, I think we can take pride in what we all achieved together. Across the United States, more than 200 commemorative events were held. Here in DC, the three-week festival at the Kennedy Center – "Ireland 100" – was the largest Irish cultural festival ever held outside Ireland, attracting over 65,000 visitors to hundreds of performances.

And, together, we have done so much more in the nation's capital: a number of lecture series, a range of cultural offerings, the rededication of the Robert Emmett statue on Massachusetts Avenue, resolutions passed in both Houses of Congress.

What was especially uplifting about the events at home and abroad was the spirit which imbued them. There was a clear and conscious commitment to a commemoration that would be inclusive and broadly based, honouring the past but not allowing ourselves to be straitjacketed by it. As well as celebrating the legacy, we would interrogate it.

We did not shrink from asking ourselves some truly searching questions. What kind of country have we become? To what extent have we fulfilled the ideals of the women and men of 1916?

I believe this year-long reflection has helped to re-energise us as a nation, jolt us out of any complacency, and redouble our commitment to a society that is more inclusive, more fair, more reflective of the founding values.

There is no doubt that Ireland faces extraordinary challenges over the next few years – sustaining the economic recovery and ensuring that its benefits are more fully shared, while at the same time dealing with the profound implications of Brexit for our island. To the extent that we can hold on to the spirit of our commemorations, I believe we will be stronger and better equipped to deal with these challenges.

In Irish America too, I sense that feeling of renewal, expressed through so many of the commemorative events. Accompanying all the legitimate pride in the past achievements, there has been a thoughtful reflection on how Irish America redefines its role in 21st century America.

Just as back at home, I see a new energy and sense of purpose in Irish America. A determination to connect even more closely with contemporary Ireland; and to ensure that Irish America remains potent and relevant at a time of rapid demographic and social change in this country.

I believe that this is a reflection that will outlive our centenary year, and that will continue to gather pace. And I am optimistic as to where it will lead, because I truly believe in the creativity, the resilience, and the generosity of spirit of Irish America.

I wish all the very best to the Friendly Sons. I hope that your continued deliberations will lead to an opening of doors in DC in the way that the doors of Philadelphia have already opened. And I know there will be many who will walk through those doors with joy and pride.

Once again, my appreciation to your Society for all you have done, for what you continue to do, and for what you will go on to achieve and contribute in the years ahead.

CAMPAIGNING FOR IMMIGRATION REFORM

"My time as Ambassador to the US had many highlights, and there are memories that I will forever cherish. But of course there were disappointments too. And let me say quite bluntly that there was no sharper or keener disappointment than the failure to achieve progress on Immigration Reform."

That is an extract from a fairly lengthy speech I gave in Boston on St Patrick's Day 2019, where I was honoured to receive a Lifetime Achievement Award from the Charitable Irish Society - almost three hundred years in existence, the CIS has the distinction of being the oldest of the Irish-American societies. I availed of the opportunity to tell a story: to describe our sustained efforts to achieve immigration reform throughout my years in Washington. It seemed important to capture the chronology in some detail. Part of it is the historian's attempt to document; part of it is the hope that future campaigners might learn something from our story.

Throughout those Washington years, the purpose of our efforts was twofold: to try to secure legislative reform that would allow the undocumented Irish immigrants to come out of the shadows, and to improve the prospects for legal immigration from Ireland, which over the years had slowed to a pitiful trickle. We knew that the first would have to be part of a much broader effort to secure status for the undocumented of all nationalities; the second was a challenge we had to navigate by ourselves. We were not naive as to the scope of that challenge, but there were moments when a breakthrough seemed within our grasp. I hope the 2019 speech, looking back on it all, provides context and narrative for the efforts of those years.

The push for legislative change inevitably found its way into very many speeches I gave during my time in Washington, and it surfaces in a number of speeches in other chapters. I have chosen just two for this section: the first, from April 2014, still imbued with the optimism of my first year in DC, and the second from December 2016, in the early aftermath of President Trump's election when I was trying to keep alive some hope that all might not be lost on the immigration reform front.

In April 2014 Xavier Becerra, a Democrat from California - who is now the Attorney General of California but was Chair of the House Democratic Caucus during my DC years - invited me to address an annual gathering he hosted for Democratic spouses and guests. The theme chosen for that year was "America the Beautiful" and the audience included a cross-section of Democratic members of Congress. I was happy to have an opportunity to reach beyond the Irish-American circles in Congress who were our regular and most ready audience. And at the end of what had been a moving week for me (first in Dublin with a delegation accompanying Congressman John Lewis, and later in Connecticut visiting the Great Hunger Museum) I was emotionally attuned to the theme.

Over two and a half years later, when I spoke to the Irish International Immigrant Center in Boston in December 2016, it was hard not to feel that America had become less beautiful. As the speech acknowledged, it was an unsettled and anxious time, but it was still possible to hope that the immigration policies of the new Administration might be somewhat more benign than the campaign rhetoric.

Separate from the wider question of legislative reform, another dimension of the immigration agenda also preoccupied me during my time in Washington. Over many decades, the J1 visa programme - both the twelve-month version "Ireland Work and Travel Programme" and the seasonal J1 Summer Programme - has brought opportunity and discovery for thousands of young Irish people, and created lifelong memories and attachments. I have heard Irish people in all walks of life reminisce about those never-to-be-forgotten summers that combined hard work with carefree adventure.

Maybe that was why the balcony collapse in Berkeley in June 2015 seemed so unspeakably cruel: five of our J1 students dead together with another young Irish-American and seven seriously injured, just as these golden young people were reaching for the promise and adventure of a luminous J1 summer.

Against such a background, the article that appeared in the *New York Times* on 17th June 2015, the second day after the tragedy, felt like a slap in the face. The article "Six Deaths in Berkeley Cast Pall on Program" alleged pervasive misbehaviour by Irish J1 students and claimed the programme was an embarrassment to the Irish government.Combining gross insensitivity with factual error, the article was deeply unworthy of a newspaper like the *New York Times* that prides itself on serious journalism.

I remember the outrage of the Embassy Press Officer as she showed me the article, just as I was rushing to catch a train to attend an event in Philadelphia. I sat down straightaway to write a letter of response and we dispatched it immediately. The *New York Times* chose not to publish my letter but that hardly mattered: we posted it on the Embassy website and it reached a very wide audience. In the months afterwards, young Irish people would tell me that it helped assuage their anger at that sloppy and ill-judged piece of *NYT* journalism.

Apart altogether from the Berkeley tragedy, these were rocky times for the J1 programme. As the whole mood towards immigration darkened, the State Department kept telling us about Congressional pressure to constrain or abolish both the 12-month and summer programmes. We were fighting a rearguard action to protect both programmes, always emphasising the mutuality of benefit for both countries. In the interregnum between President Trump's election and his assumption of office, we accelerated the negotiations to extend the 12-month programme. It was with a real sense of relief that I signed the Memorandum of Understanding at the State Department on 5th December 2016 which extended the programme for a further three years.

Acceptance of Lifetime Achievement Award
The Charitable Irish Society, Boston
17th March 2019

I am deeply honoured to be here tonight and to be the recipient of your Lifetime Achievement Award for 2019.

Everything that your Society stands for resonates with me: your history, your values, the words you have lived by for over 280 years: "With good will doing service". You epitomise openness and inclusivity: beginning as a Society for Protestant men, over time you became became free from restrictions of religion or gender. For most of your history you were focussed exclusively on Irish immigrants; today you look to all immigrants in need, irrespective of their country of origin.

I vividly recall my visit to the Society early in my time as Ambassador in Washington, and it a genuine pleasure to be back some twenty months after the end of my tenure. The pleasure is all the greater because the invitation was conveyed by your Dinner Chair Catherine Shannon. Catherine is a towering figure in Irish America and one of its foremost academics. She is a woman of intellect, of heart, of commitment and determination.

Life has definitely not lacked interest since I retired as Ambassador. I am privileged to serve on various Boards which continue my engagement with business, education and the arts. I am also a member of the UN Secretary General's Advisory Group on Peacebuilding, which keeps me ever mindful both of the fragilities and cruelties of our world, as well as of the extraordinary resilience of the human spirit.

Drawing on the work I am currently doing, and with so much that is momentous unfolding on the European and international stage, there is certainly no shortage of choice when it comes to topics to speak about this evening. In particular, there is the all consuming Brexit, especially with this week's dramatic developments and the important role of Irish America in safeguarding the Good Friday Agreement. But given the role and history of your Society, I want to focus in particular on immigration issues; in any event, maybe on St Patrick's Day we all deserve a one-day break from the Brexit overload!

As I talk about immigration, one of the things I would like to do is to give some chapter and verse about my personal experience during my Washington years. Alongside the big ambitions and aspirations, I think it is important to share some of the experiences in a more granular way. If I relive some of the key moments with you, it is not just for the sake of excavating history but in the hope that something can be learned - because the needs remain as great as ever and the challenges as daunting.

My time as Ambassador to the US had many highlights, and there are memories that I will forever cherish. But of course there were disappointments too. And let me say quite bluntly that there was no sharper or keener disappointment than the failure to achieve progress on immigration reform. It was all the more heartbreaking because on occasion we came tantalisingly close - times when we felt the roadblocks had been painstakingly cleared and an outcome was within our grasp, only to have unforeseen difficulties throw everything off course.

Before reliving the history, first perhaps a few ground-clearing points. When we talk about immigration challenges, none of us denies the inherent complexity of those challenges. Every nation must look to the security of its borders, and every country needs to fashion and implement a rules-based immigration system. But there is a balancing truth: we do not live in a world of absolutes. Especially in this globalised 21st century, no enlightened country can turn itself into a fortress; no country of conscience can be blind and deaf to human misery at its borders.

If we try to close our eyes and our hearts, what price is to be paid in terms of a country's self-esteem and standing in the world? And even if all claims of morality and conscience are discounted, there are the arguments of economic self interest - the unchallengeable data as to what immigrants bring to a country by way of revitalisation and reinvigoration.

A second ground-clearing point. Whenever I speak in an American context about the challenges and complexities of immigration, I am conscious of our struggles with this issue in Europe. The classic push-pull factors have been fully and painfully in evidence over recent years. The conflict on the southern shores of the Mediterranean and the poverty across so many parts of Africa, have driven desperate people to take unimaginable risks in trying to reach European shores. I often think of James Joyce's description of the Atlantic as a "bowl of bitter tears". In recent years, it is another sea - the Mediterranean - which has become that bitter broth.

And sadly we have seen the backlash in some European countries: how, for example, the selfishness of a Viktor Orban has been rewarded electorally in Hungary, while the generosity of an Angela Merkel has been penalised in elections in Germany. And we in Ireland have seen up close what the forces of nationalism and populism have unleashed in our nearest neighbour.

So we Europeans come to this debate with no complacency: our own responses have been unsteady and inadequate. But despite all the necessary soul-searching, I think it is fair to say that there has been a majority and mainstream rejection of those who would try to construct a fortress Europe. The battle over the EU's immigration policies will continue, and as we engage in this debate, there is a particular obligation on a country like Ireland whose identity and historical experience is so shaped by the harsh realities of emigration.

While it is important to establish that context, I do not believe that acknowledging the shortcomings in Europe or elsewhere provides an answer or an excuse for America. This country must judge itself by its own history and its own standards.

That history has certainly not seen a linear progression on tolerance or acceptance of immigrants: one has only to look to the history of this great city of Boston, and limit oneself to the history of Irish immigration here, to be conscious of the stains and setbacks as well as the the extraordinary triumphs.

And yet America is a country like no other - a country whose very essence and identity is defined by immigration. That identity as refuge and melting pot finds expression in so many ways, far too many for me to consider this evening. But I would suggest that the soul of a country is best captured in its most hallowed songs and stories, in lines and language that over time become known to every schoolchild. More so than almost anything else, they form the mirror that a people holds up to itself.

One of my prouder moments as Ambassador was exactly two years ago, my final St Patrick's Day in Washington, at the lunch on Capitol Hill, when our then Taoiseach Enda Kenny addressed the assembled guests, including the newly elected President Trump. In a speech that was gracious in tone but unmistakably clear in its message, the Taoiseach quoted the immortal lines inscribed on the Statue of Liberty: "Give me your tired, your poor, your huddled masses yearning to breathe free......" He reminded his powerful audience - and he returned to the same theme at the White House reception later that day - that this is the America which has acted as a beacon to the world; this is the America which has commanded the love and loyalty of millions who have come from all over the world and given their all to their country of adoption.

And I often myself quoted from that other magnificent hymn that expresses the soul of this nation: "America the Beautiful". It is, as you all know, a song of pilgrims and their heroic journey:

"Who more than self their country loved,

And mercy more than life......."

And so this idea of mercy, of tempering justice with mercy, has always seemed to me to be part of the grace of America, part of its founding reality, fundamental to how America sees itself.

Let me take you back to summer of 2013 when I arrived in Washington as Ambassador. It was a time of optimism on the immigration front. After years of effort, the Democratic-controlled Senate had finally passed a comprehensive immigration reform bill: 63 votes to 32, with 14 Republicans crossing the aisle to join the unanimous Democratic vote. No-one underestimated the difficulties of getting a similar Bill through the Republican controlled House, but the degree of bipartisan support allowed a reasonable basis for hope.

That 2013 Bill was a great Bill for Ireland. As well as comprehensive measures to address the situation of the undocumented from all countries, there was a specific add-on provision - inserted through the efforts of Senators Schumer and Leahy and others - that would provide 10,500 E3 visas annually for Irish people wishing to come and live and work in America.

From summer 2013 onwards, we had a single-minded focus on trying to get corresponding legislation through the House. Visiting Government Ministers spared no effort and it was a top priority for the entire Embassy team. Throughout my early months in Washington, stretching through Autumn 2013 and Spring 2014, I wore out a great deal of shoe leather up and down the halls of Congress, knocking on the doors of House Republicans in particular, since theirs were the votes we needed.

John Boehner, the then Speaker of the House, did us no favours. The Speaker was always personally affable, and I accompanied the Taoiseach to a number of genial meetings. But Mr. Boehner refused to depart from the so-called Hastert rule: which meant he would not bring an immigration Bill to the House floor unless it had the support of the "majority of the majority". And so, although a cross-Party majority would almost certainly have been available to pass a Bill, the Speaker would not act until he was confident of a majority of Republican votes.

Although Mr. Boehner temporised, he was tolerant and even encouraging of efforts behind the scenes to assemble the necessary Republican votes. A number of our Republican friends, including ones as influential as Paul Ryan, were involved in such efforts. By early summer of 2014 we were quietly being briefed that the threshold had been reached and the Speaker was about to receive the necessary reassurance. And then a bombshell. Eric Cantor, a conservative Republican from Virginia and the House Majority Leader, suffered a shock defeat in his primaries by an anti-immigrant Tea Party candidate.

Cantor's defeat was attributable to a variety of factors, principally what was a perceived neglect of his constituency. But it was touted as related in part to a softening of his position on immigration. His fate triggered a kind of panic among other Republican members of Congress, who feared they too might become vulnerable to Tea Party challenges in their primaries. Many of them became newly nervous of anything that might be viewed as soft on immigration. Within days of the Cantor upset, we were told that the arithmetic no longer worked; that there was no Republican majority for a House attempt at immigration reform. Once again, Speaker Boehner was sitting on his hands and hopes died for the 113th Congress.

The next Congress, the 114th, presented an even tougher challenge. The elections of November 2014 brought the largest Republican majority in over eighty years, and put the Republicans in charge of both the House and Senate. It was the near universal view that comprehensive immigration reform was close to a non-starter in this Congress.

At this point, it is important to clarify one key element which has shaped our approach throughout, and certainly has conditioned my own thinking. And that is the distinction we have made in trying to address the two separate if inter-related aspects of the immigration challenge: finding a solution for the undocumented, and identifying new pathways for legal immigration.

I have never believed that relief for the Irish undocumented could come separately or apart from a comprehensive approach that embraced the undocumented from all parts of the world. This is not just unachievable from a political perspective, it is also morally unsustainable.

Our hearts go out to the Irish undocumented; they are the ones we have met, whose stories we know, and whom we can most readily identify with. Indeed, if our lives had taken a slightly different turn, you or I might be walking in their shoes today. But when it comes to the loneliness and human cost of life in the shadows, and the ever-present fear of a knock on the door, there is no monopoly of pain - the experience is shared whether one's skin is white, or black, or brown. In fact, based on some of the stories and statistics, the vulnerability may be even greater for people of colour.

And so in all our efforts to support solutions for the undocumented, we have worked as part of a broader coalition. I would like to pay special tribute in this regard to Senator Billy Lawless, who represents diaspora interests in the Irish Seanad. Over many years, Billy has helped build a strong friendship and working relationship with the Hispanic community in particular. I recall a number of very positive meetings in Billy's company with Congressman Luis Guterres, a seasoned warrior on behalf of

Hispanic and other immigrants.

But side by side with this position of principle in relation to the undocumented, there are very different considerations in my view when it comes to new quotas for legal immigration to the United States. I have never felt in any way hesitant about making a special and separate pitch for a dedicated Irish quota. And why? Because of the imbalance that exists at present.

In the sweeping reforms of the US immigration system that took place in the mid 1960s, there was a strong sense that immigration to this country was too Eurocentric and had to become more open to the rest of the world. But the authors of that needed change - Senator Kennedy among them - did not anticipate that there would be so much collateral damage to immigration from Ireland.

We have now arrived at a stage where legal immigration from Ireland has dwindled to not much more than a trickle. Take one statistic: Green Cards. People born in Ireland account for just under 1500 of almost 1.3 million Green Cards issued in 2017: a little over one tenth of one percent. This flies in the face of historical and contemporary realities. How can it make sense in a country which Irish immigrants did so much to build, where over 30 million of its citizens claim Irish descent, and where the two countries are bound today by increasingly deep two way economic ties?

In arguing our case for a specific visa allocation for Ireland, we relied on a rationale that was simple and straightforward: there is no country with a greater mismatch between historical connection and contemporary business ties, and the current levels of legal access.

Back to January 2015 when we faced the conundrum of a new Congress where the prospects of comprehensive immigration reform seemed such a very long shot. Our resolve was to continue to do everything we could to help our undocumented, but at the same time try to spotlight the one area where there was perhaps a better chance of achieving some success - the fact that Ireland was so shortchanged when it came to legal access for new immigrants.

We consulted widely: where should we start: Senate or House? Was there any chance of bringing something directly to the floor, or would we be obliged to go the Committee route? If the latter, which member of the Senate or House might prove the most effective champion or advocate?

With Mitch McConnell as Senate Majority Leader, and Chuck Grassley Chair of the Senate Judiciary Committee - neither of them in any way sympathetic to immigration reform - our better option was the House. So we sought a Republican member of the House Judiciary Committee who might be willing and able to shepherd a Bill through the Committee. Our contacts and conversations brought us to Jim Sensenbrenner, a veteran Republican member of the Committee and former Chair, who had been intimately involved some years earlier in securing the annual allocation of 10,500 E3 visas for Australia. Congressman Sensenbrenner was ready to table a Bill that would give Ireland equivalent treatment to Australia, but he needed to navigate his way forward with Judiciary Committee Chair Bob Goodlatte.

Chairman Goodlatte had some familiarity with Ireland: his wife was Irish American; he had visited Ireland; and our conversations were cordial. But nothing would soften his opposition to issuance of new visas. After some soundings, Mr. Sensenbrenner brought word back: Goodlatte would not budge: the best we could hope for was the unused portion of the Australian visa allocation - less than we wanted, but still amounting to some thousands of new visas annually for Ireland.

On the basis that half a loaf was better than none, we reluctantly settled for this. And so the re-allocation to Ireland of the unused Australian E3 visas became the basis of the Sensenbrenner

Bill tabled in September 2015. You might imagine our disappointment when the Congressman subsequently reverted to indicate that Chairman Goodlatte had thrown up a new roadblock: he was now insisting that the House Committee would deal with the Sensenbrenner Bill only if a corresponding Bill first passed the Senate Judiciary Committee. Goodlatte's argument was that, even if the House passed an Ireland-specific Bill, there was a danger of it becoming a Christmas tree on its way through the Senate, loaded down with additional provisions that the House would not find acceptable.

We spent the remaining months of the 114th Congress trying to find a way around or through this new roadblock but in the end it proved insuperable. We were encouraged when Paul Ryan, who knew and understood our cause so well, became Speaker in October 2015. But it didn't change the requirement to go the Committee route. In coming to office, the new Speaker had pledged to his Caucus that he would respect and enforce due order - which included all Bills being processed through the relevant Committees before coming to the House floor.

And then came November 2016, with the election of Donald Trump to the White House and the Republicans once again in control of the House and Senate.

So this was the tortuous path that brought us to that memorable day I invoked earlier - St Patrick's Day 2017, with Taoiseach Enda Kenny in the Oval Office seeking to explain to President Trump the issues arising for the Irish undocumented, and later at the Capitol Hill lunch and the White House reception reminding the President and everyone else of the history and promise and true greatness of America.

The story of course has moved on since 2017, and continues to evolve. I am no longer one of the dramatis personae, and others are better placed to bear first hand witness. But what I see is continuity of determination and resolve. The Embassy pursues its unstinting efforts under the leadership of my successor Dan Mulhall, who is supported as I was by an able and immensely committed Embassy team. In Dublin, Taoiseach Leo Varadkar has taken over the baton from Enda Kenny, Tanaiste Simon Coveney leads the effort from Iveagh House, and Special Envoy John Deasy has put his shoulder to the wheel with regular and intensive engagement in Washington.

In the final weeks of last year, in the dying days of the 115th Congress, a breakthrough on the E3 visas seemed agonisingly close. Once again, the sharing of Australia's allocation emerged as the goal. This time a key element had changed: with Speaker Paul Ryan about to retire from Congress, and Bob Goodlatte stepping down as Chair of the Judiciary Committee, there was no longer the same insistence on going the Committee route. A skilful effort by Congressman Richie Neal - well known to everyone in this room and one of Ireland's greatest friends on the Hill - together with Congressman Sensenbrenner, succeeded in having the E3 provision adopted on the House floor. It was then a matter of maintaining momentum and securing the required unanimity in the Senate. Everything possible was done, only to have a single hold-out, Senator Tom Cotton from Arkansas, stand in the way. The clock wound down and once again the goal had proved elusive.

There are many lessons to be taken from this saga of almost six years past, and let me allude to just a couple of them. On the downside, it illustrates just how difficult it is to get any change through Congress, no matter how modest. Time and again, when we seemed to be on the cusp of achieving something, there was a setback, often from an unexpected quarter. That history teaches us how cautious we need to be about raising any hopes, particularly among our undocumented. Their situation is traumatic enough without repeatedly having their hopes raised and dashed.

But coming so close also has an upside lesson. Change is not beyond reach; it is not some impossible dream. With such a broken immigration system, sooner or later the logic of comprehensive reform has to reassert itself. And when it comes to a specific allocation of new work visas for Ireland, we have a well of sympathy and support: future efforts can point to the last days of the last Congress when all but one Member of the combined House and Senate stood ready to approve or acquiesce in such an allocation.

Following last November's election, of course, the kaleidoscope has again shifted, with Democrats now controlling the House and the campaign for the White House in 2020 already well under way. All of the issues confronting America will be threshed out in the course of that campaign. Since President Trump has put immigration and his attempted wall on the Mexican border at the very centre of his engagement with the Republican base, it is guaranteed that immigration issues will remain front and centre in the national discourse over the period ahead.

We don't yet know what opportunities may emerge in the lifetime of this Congress and obviously we don't know what outcome the 2020 elections will bring. Of one thing we can be confident: that the effort will continue at full throttle on the part of the Irish government and diplomatic network and our supportive friends in Congress.

Many of you will have followed this week's proceedings in Washington, when Taoiseach Leo Varadkar visited for the annual St Patrick's Day meetings and festivities. Once again, a visiting Irish Prime Minister spoke in the White House about the true meaning of American greatness. It was also clear from the Taoiseach's remarks that efforts to secure the E3 visas are being revived, and there are some indications that an early breakthrough may prove feasible.

The larger goal of comprehensive reform will also remain fully in our sights. It is easy to despair of change being achieved in today's broken system, when bipartisanship is viewed with such suspicion, compromise has become a pejorative word, and crossing the aisle is castigated in some quarters as little short of treasonous. Our hopes must continue to rest on thoughtful and enlightened and courageous members of both Houses, whatever their political persuasion. And such legislators do exist. I am conscious of speaking tonight in Massachusetts, which continues a proud tradition of being represented by some of the very finest on Capitol Hill - many of whom occupy influential and prestigious positions in the current Congress.

The story does not play out only at the national level. My remarks this evening have focused mostly on experience in Washington, reflecting my four years at the coalface there. But of course we also follow and engage with developments around the country, particularly through the Consulates. While awaiting comprehensive action at national level, steps taken at state and city level can bring a real and tangible measure of relief. I know that Boston is a leader in that regard, including with the 2014 ordinance that in effect makes this a sanctuary city. Without taking our eye off the ball of national action, every further step that can be taken at city and state level is immensely worthwhile.

And a final point I want to come back to is this: as we seek the comprehensive reform that will address the situation of the undocumented, the more narrow goal of achieving a new allocation of working visas for Irish people should not be undervalued. There are larger issues at play here, beyond the creation of opportunities for potential beneficiaries.

In successive reviews of the Irish-US relationship, we have described Irish America as "a resource of incomparable benefit". That it surely is, and by any calculus the role and contribution of

Irish America will continue to be absolutely vital. But there is no denying the demographics: with the radical reduction over recent decades in pathways for legal immigration, Irish America is shrinking in size and the ancestral ties with Ireland are becoming more distant. There is less of the fresh oxygen that is brought by newer immigrants.

No one is advocating a return to past patterns that no longer fit today's relationship. We have outgrown the old paradigm - America giving and Ireland taking; America the benefactor and Ireland the beneficiary. The picture was never quite as simple as that, even at our time of direst need, but that is how it was often presented and portrayed. Thankfully, today's paradigm is entirely different: a mature 21st century relationship with strong mutual benefit. And today's Ireland, confident in its identity and its prosperity, no longer needs to export its people.

But even in this transformed Ireland, our educated and adventurous young people still want to have an opportunity to spread their wings, even if only for a few years. Many of them are bringing their talents and creativity to Australia and Canada as well as to our European partner countries. But their path to America is so much more difficult to navigate.

And this is a loss on many levels. America is losing out on the contribution that highly educated Irish people are making elsewhere. There is a missed opportunity for nurturing the bilateral relationship with two way flows of some of the best and brightest. There is also the broader trans-Atlantic context. In the new landscape emerging over the past couple of years, with tensions and stresses between the US and the European Union, it is unquestionably a time for America to value and grow its friendships in Europe. And we cannot say it often enough: nowhere will America find a warmer and readier friendship than among Irish people.

Perhaps that is an appropriate note on which to conclude tonight - reminding ourselves of the extraordinary friendship that binds and braids our two countries together. It is a friendship for all days and all seasons, but St Patrick's Day provides us with a special opportunity for stocktaking. This is a day which fortifies us all. We feel the sentiment and pride of the past, and the fundamental confidence in today's rich and multi-faceted relationship, but without allowing ourselves any complacency about the future. It is a day to renew our determination - to remind ourselves that the future is not something that just happens, but something we must shape and build.

Your own Society, as I said at the outset, teaches us important lessons about how to endure and evolve. Throughout your long and distinguished history, as you have extended your membership and your mission, you have remained true to the essence of who and what you set out to be. I know you will continue to work for your vision of America: an America that continues to hold the torch aloft, an America that continues to temper justice with mercy.

And I know too that you will remain equally committed to promoting the deep and special bonds between our two countries. When your Society celebrates new milestones in the years ahead, when you mark your 300th anniversary and beyond, we want to be able to raise our glasses to a relationship that remains rich and vibrant, that is replenished by a generous flow of people in both directions, and where our two countries remain united in common purpose - to create a better, more just and more equal world.

America the Beautiful
Reception for Democratic Spouses and Guests,
US House of Representatives, Washington DC
30ᵗʰ April 2014

It is a great honour for me to join you this evening to speak with such an audience on such a theme.

Although I am less than a year in my current post as Irish Ambassador in DC, it is my ninth year to live in the United States. Throughout those years, the physical beauty of America has always enraptured me: the scale, the grandeur, the awe-inspiring vistas.

But it is a different and deeper sort of beauty I want to speak about this evening – what it is that represents the soul of America.

As it happens, today is a day when my head is full of these thoughts. And let me tell you why.

During this past week, I had two experiences that left a deep impression on me. This day last week, I was in Dublin accompanying a US delegation – a Faith and Politics delegation – let by Congressman John Lewis of Atlanta. Yesterday, I was at Quinnipiac University in Connecticut, opening an exhibition at their Great Hunger Museum relating to the devastating Irish Famine of the 1840s.

I want to take a moment to tell you something about these experiences: how they resonate and how they thread together.

Congressman Lewis is of course an iconic figure in the American civil rights movement. As well as being a leader and activist, he has written beautifully and eloquently about the movement and its lessons and legacy.

In welcoming the Congressman to Dublin, our Foreign Minister quoted from "Walking with the Wind" – John's memoir of the movement. Here is that quotation:

"Children holding hands. Walking with the wind. That is

America to me – not just the movement for civil rights but the endless struggle to respond with decency, dignity and a sense of brotherhood to all the challenges that face us as a nation, as a whole."

As we consider John's words, let me say something about yesterday's experience in the Great Hunger Museum.

Any of you with Irish ancestry, or with an interest in Irish history, will know something of the Great Famine that ravaged our country in the 1840s. Out of our population of eight million at the time, one million died and two million emigrated – almost all of them to America.

Our people came in conditions of utter devastation. The choice, for those who had a choice, was an existential one: starve to death in Ireland or grasp at the chance of survival in America.

And so our people came. And they didn't just survive here; they gave heart and soul to help build this country that had given them shelter.

They built the physical infrastructure – the railroads, the canals, the skyscrapers. They built the communities – as teachers, police, fire fighters, union leaders. And as the roll call of Irish names in Congress attests, they found their place in the political institutions of this country.

Today, reflecting on the theme of America the Beautiful, these two experiences of the past week intertwine for me. John Lewis' call for decency, dignity, brotherhood. And yesterday's reminder of how America opened its arms to the Irish at their time of need, and how the Irish have never stopped giving back.

I am left with many thoughts and emotions. But among the clearest is the need for immigration reform – one of the great causes of this Congress – to move forward.

I am conscious of all the dedicated crusaders who are advancing this cause. The voices of many groups and many ethnicities are joining together and powerfully reinforcing each other.

The Irish voice is among them. For us, there is a two-fold interest. With an estimated 50,000 undocumented Irish in the US, we want to help them find a way out of the shadows. And – given the current near impossibility for Irish people to come and live and work legally in this country – we ardently hope to see an avenue created for legal immigration from Ireland in the future.

These two great countries of ours are bound by the closest ties: of blood, of toil, of language and culture, and – today – of business. There is such openness in almost every respect. How can it make sense, when it comes to immigration, that your doors should remain largely closed to us?

The economic and business case for immigration is clear. Study after study has demonstrated the increment in entrepreneurialism, in innovation, and the other benefits.

Today's emigrants from Ireland are educated, confident, cosmopolitan – in most ways, almost unrecognisable from the Irish emigrants of the last century. But they share this with the generations who went before: like their forebears, they too want to roll up their sleeves and contribute. The US would be enriched, in every sense, by their presence.

But tonight I am not making the economic case for immigration. It is not an occasion for pocketbook arguments. Tonight's theme is *America the Beautiful*. It is about the fundamental things that have always defined America: dignity, decency, opportunity. It is about the identity and soul of this country.

No one denies the complexity of immigration reform. We know that getting it right is a matter of negotiation and compromise – addressing legitimate concerns, finding appropriate balances.

That can happen; that is the normal business and challenge of legislators.

But the first and most important step is surely to frame the debate in the right way.

I believe that tonight's theme – *America the Beautiful* – establishes the right starting point. That great patriotic hymn has stood the test of time. It sings of a country of strength and self-control, but also a country of grace and mercy.

That indeed is the enduring America, the beautiful America.

Solas Awards
Irish International Immigrant Centre, Boston, Massachusetts
1st December 2016

I thank you from the bottom of my heart for this beautiful award. I will cherish it as a symbol of the deep ties of kinship and friendship between Ireland and Boston, this city that for so long has opened its arms to Irish people, and has become home to hundreds of thousands of Irish emigrants.

You already know, but it bears repeating tonight, the IIIC has the strong support of the Irish government – not just our moral support but also our practical and financial support.

Over the last 48 hours or so in Boston, I have had the opportunity to speak to different audiences on a range of issues – about our centenary commemorations; about the solid and broad-based economic recovery that is taking hold in Ireland; and also about the challenges we face, including Brexit and the refashioning of EU-US relations that may be underway as we deal with new political realities on both sides of the Atlantic.

But tonight, I want to speak specifically about immigration, and the issues we face. We are all conscious what an unsettled and anxious time this is for immigrants, especially undocumented immigrants, and the need to engage in calm and considered reflection.

In the almost three and a half years since I became Ambassador, perhaps the most frustrating aspect of my work has been the failure to advance on immigration reform. It is something which our Government cares deeply about, and something I personally feel passionate about.

I have spoken on other occasions about the family stories that helped to shape my own childhood, my mother's account of her oldest brother departing for America on the liner from Cobh, her mother's weeping that she would never see her son again, and indeed she never did. That is the Ireland of the past, and we have very largely moved on. Today, we see the Atlantic as a bridge of opportunity and not, as James Joyce described it, a bowl of bitter tears. But as we watched the awful scenes in the Mediterranean unfold over the past few summers, one thinks of the many bereft African families for whom the Mediterranean – that cradle of civilisation – has become the new bowl of tears.

Most of us in this room are not generationally distant from the experience of immigration, some of us perhaps very close to it. It resonates therefore when Pope Francis recently spoke movingly about the plight of the outsider, the refugee, the immigrant. "Little by little, our differences turn into symptoms of hostility, threats and violence...Their voice is weak and silenced by this pathology of indifference." Above all, let us fight that pathology of indifference – as the IIIC does every single day, and as all of you do by your presence here tonight.

But let me return more specifically to the experience of the past few years. When I arrived in DC in summer 2013, comprehensive Immigration Reform legislation had been adopted by the Senate and action in the House was awaited. We were part of a coalition of activists who did everything possible to secure movement in the House – the Taoiseach and other Government Ministers pressed the issue at every opportunity, and I wore out much shoe leather on Capitol Hill.

At times, we felt ourselves on the verge of a breakthrough, particularly at one point in the summer of 2015 when it seemed a coalition of Republican Members of Congress was genuinely ready to act. Then came another setback, the moment passed, and the 2016 elections began to cast their long shadow in advance.

We have all see how immigration became an issue in the Presidential   election   campaign;   and   we   all   heard   the anti-immigration rhetoric. It is entirely understandable that, in the aftermath of the election, there are unprecedented levels of fear and anxiety in immigrant communities.

But what we do not yet know is what **policies** the new Administration will follow. The heat of the campaign may be different from the realities of government. And there are checks and balances in the system: there are roles for Congress, for the judicial system, for Mayors of cities (and I note Mayor Marty Walsh has been very clear in what he has said). So, without offering any facile reassurance, which we are in no position to do, there is every reason to urge calm and wait and see.

And let's remember how multi-faceted the whole immigration issue is. There is the emotional response, whether one's instincts are ones of sympathy or hostility. But there are arguments of logic, of common sense, of economic self-interest. Once in office, an Administration will find itself confronting these complexities.

One thing I can promise – the Irish political establishment, and the Irish diplomatic network, will not cease in their lobbying efforts. We will continue to reach out across both sides of the aisle, and the Taoiseach and Ministers will engage at every opportunity. As we live our safe and secure lives, we will not forget the undocumented, living in the shadows, afraid of a knock on the door.

The motto of your centre is the old Irish proverb: "Ní neart go cur le chéile", "There is no strength until we come together". That togetherness is something which your Centre stands for and embodies. It will inspire all of us as we navigate these challenging times ahead.

AMBASÁID NA HÉIREANN

TELEPHONE: (202) 462-3939

FAX: (202) 232-5993

EMBASSY OF IRELAND

2234 MASSACHUSETTS AVE., N.W.

WASHINGTON, D.C. 20008

17 June 2015

To: The Editor, New York Times

In the aftermath of the tragic accident in Berkeley, resulting in the deaths of six young Irish people and the serious injury of seven others, there has been an outpouring of sympathy across the United States. All the messages we receive strike the same note: deep sadness at these bright young lives cut short, or profoundly affected by injury, and hearts going out to the grieving families.

At such a time, we found some of the language in your article today ("Six Deaths in Berkeley Cast Pall on Program") both insensitive and inaccurate. No one yet knows what caused the collapse of the fourth-floor balcony; the matter is under urgent investigation by structural engineers. The implication of your article - that the behaviour of the students was in some way a factor in the collapse - has caused deep offence.

It is quite simply wrong to say that the J1 visa programme is "a source of embarrassment for Ireland". On the contrary, we are fully supportive of this programme and we know that it brings enormous mutual benefit. Some of our best and brightest young people participate; they come for a summer in the US on the threshold of their adult lives, and take back experiences and memories that establish life-long bonds. And they make a real contribution here; one of the messages of condolence we received yesterday put it simply: "We welcome their energy and joy".

Yes, there have been isolated incidents of the type to which your article refers. But they are wholly unrepresentative: bear in mind that 150,000 young Irish people have participated in the J1 program over the past 50 years, and some 7,000 are here for Summer 2015. From all the feedback we receive, we know that the overwhelming majority of our J1 participants behave in a way that does Ireland proud.

At this time of searing grief, the messages of condolence and offers of support which are flooding in to the Embassy and our Consulates are balm to the soul. They reflect far more accurately the feelings of the American people than does your article.

Anne Anderson

Anne Anderson
Ambassador

Signing Ceremony for Extension of Memorandum of Understanding for *Ireland Work and Travel Programme* US State Department, Washington DC 5th December 2016

As 2016 draws to a close, we can look back on a landmark year in Irish US relations.

The 1916 centenary has had a particularly deep resonance in the United States. Taoiseach Enda Kenny was here in May to launch the Ireland 100 Festival at the Kennedy Center, and to plant an Irish oak tree on the grounds of the Capitol. Across the country, we worked with community organisations to organise more than 300 commemorative events – all honouring and interrogating the 1916 legacy, reminding us of how America travelled with us on the road to the Rising, and has remained at our side throughout the subsequent 100-year journey.

Again and again throughout the year, we were reminded of those immortal words of President John F. Kennedy when he addressed the Irish Parliament in 1963: "No people ever believed more deeply in the cause of Irish freedom than the people of the United States. And no country contributed more to building my own than your sons and daughters". These words will undoubtedly echo and re-echo in the course of next year, when we commemorate the centenary of President Kennedy's birth.

The contemporary relationship between the two countries remains extraordinarily vibrant. One simply has to look at the rhythm of high level visits – the Taoiseach has just completed his third visit to the US within twelve months. The centrepiece each year is the St. Patrick's Day programme, now well-established through successive Presidencies, and which we so greatly cherish.

And we have been delighted to welcome so many high level visits in the other direction: Vice President Biden, together with his family in June; Secretary of State Kerry at the end of October to accept the Tipperary Peach Prize; a Congressional delegation in March to attend the Easter Rising commemorations; a delegation from the House Appropriations Committee in August. And so many others came: Governors, Mayors, and of course those thousands that showed up for the wonderful Boston College-Georgia Tech football game in Dublin in September.

As we experience the warmth and vitality of the relationship – constantly renewed and reinvigorated from decade to decade – one thing is clear: the people to people contacts are the very lifeblood of this relationship.

Over so many years, the J1 Programmes – including both the summer programme and the 12 month programme – have made a contribution which is hard to overstate. When our young people spend time in each other's countries at a formative period in their lives, the experience stays with them long into the future.

Time and again, throughout my years here as Ambassador, I have heard from Irish political leaders and decision-makers in every walk of life, about their J1 experience in the US and the positive imprint it has left on them. The comments are almost always along the same lines: the experience has challenged them, helped them grow, left them with an enduring sense of warmth about this country. It is not that they will always necessarily agree with every aspect of American policy, but they will have a context in which to make an assessment, and a level of understanding they would not otherwise have.

And of course this is not a one-way street: just as the participants in the programme benefit greatly, so too do the businesses or institutions who hire them and host them, and who highly value their enthusiasm and hard work.

And so I am extremely pleased to be signing today the extension of the Twelve Month Work and Travel Programme for a further three years. The current Memorandum of Understanding has worked well from our perspective; in particular, the flexibility of the programme has been a key factor in making it attractive to Irish participants and we are very pleased that this can continue.

We are also happy to work with our US counterparts to identify how US participation rates in the J1 programmes might be improved. As I said, these are win-win experiences, benefitting both the young people who participate and those who host and employ them. Especially with Ireland's economy now in recovery, we look forward to seeing the numbers of US participants increase.

Let me say a word about the J1 Summer Programme, which is not affected by the Memorandum we are about to sign, but which will be the subject of discussion at a meeting this afternoon with our State Department colleagues.

The J1 Summer Programme for fifty years has been a cherished rite of passage for so many young Irish people, and there can be few better examples of public diplomacy in action. The programme attracts some of our best and brightest. Before they leave, we remind them that they are ambassadors for Ireland; after they return, we see them develop a dual mandate - as well as being the face of Ireland in America, they help communicate America to Ireland.

And so we have no doubt that it is in the interest of both countries to nurture and develop this programme. We had concerns that changes to the summer programme introduced last year would have the unintended effect of reducing numbers, and this in fact proved to be the case. As we continue our discussions with the State Department, we want to do everything possible to restore numbers to the 2015 level. Our objective is clear: to have the best quality programme with the highest possible level of participation.

Just one final comment. We are on the threshold of a new

Administration taking office in the United States, and we can anticipate that there will be a strong focus on immigration issues. As part of that debate, there is likely to be some consideration of exchange programmes and the role they play. Ireland will of course be making its case on the wider issues of immigration reform, but we will also be happy to share our tremendously positive experience of J1 programmes.

And our central message will be this: these J1 programmes are not just an act of generosity towards young people, although they certainly offer life changing experiences and opportunities. But they are about so much more than that – conferring mutual benefit, projecting soft power, and building enduring relationships.

Especially as we round out this special year, which has helped to fortify and re-energise the extraordinary relationship between our two countries, I am delighted to sign this agreement.

MARKING THE CENTENARY OF 1916

The evening of 17 May 2016 remains vividly in my memory - a definite high point of my term in Washington DC. It was the Gala opening night of the "Ireland 100" festival at the Kennedy Center. A wonderful event, with the presence of the Taoiseach, Vice President Joe Biden, members of Congress, the Chief Justice, members of the Kennedy family, and a "who's who" of Washington. A night of undiluted joy for myself and the entire Embassy team.

The 1916 centenary programme in the US was the fruit of long and painstaking planning on the part of many people. It certainly loomed very large for me. Even before taking up my DC posting, I was thinking about the shape and tone of the programme and soliciting advice from people I respected. I recall a sunny day in early 2013, still in New York, walking around Central Park with Irish writer Colum McCann and listening to his urgings that we avoid complacency and nostalgia.

The programme clearly had to be impactful, ambitious, something special. In any circumstances, the centenary deserved a high-profile marking in the US. This was the country with the highest concentration of our diaspora, the only foreign country specifically mentioned in the 1916 Proclamation, and five of the seven signatories of the Proclamation had spent formative periods in the US.

But there was also the concern to occupy the ground - the importance of getting out early enough, and with sufficient scale of ambition, to shape the narrative. If there was a perceived vacuum, there were elements in Irish America who would want to claim the commemoration in a narrow, backward-looking way - more reminiscent of 1966 than something that fitted with the confident, mature, multifaceted country Ireland had become.

As so often, culture helped us to rise to the occasion, and bring it all together. The festival at the Kennedy Center - "Ireland 100": Celebrating a Century of Irish Arts and Culture" - was the centre piece of our US celebrations. It was the biggest festival of Irish culture ever held outside Ireland, with over 65,000 people attending the events. And it proved to be a phenomenal showcase for Irish talent, featuring the very best of traditional and contemporary Irish culture across the full range of the arts: theatre, literature, music and dance.

The main speeches on that triumphant opening night of the festival were given by the Taoiseach and Vice President Biden from the Kennedy Center stage. My remarks at the gala dinner following the concert were very brief, but I decided to include them because the chapter would have seemed incomplete without some record of such a magnificent evening.

The whole year of commemoration involved a huge collaborative effort between the Embassy, the Consulates and Irish America. Throughout the year, I attended moving and memorable events across the country (more than three hundred events were held in all). We were in close contact throughout with planners in Dublin, and I accompanied a US Congressional delegation to the beautifully organised ceremonies in Dublin over the Easter weekend.

In the procession of events in DC during that year, one that was especially meaningful to me was the refurbishment and re-dedication of the statue of Robert Emmet, and I am including the short speech that I gave at the re-dedication ceremony. This statue is on Massachusetts Avenue, and I passed it every day on my walk from the Residence to our Embassy. It is an important statue - the first statue of Emmet created anywhere in the world. I wanted to honour him as an Irish patriot but also to reach beyond the particulars of Irish history. I quoted his response to the trial judge, words which I felt "might be emblazoned in courtrooms everywhere, or indeed in any place where people wield power over other human beings".

I am also including another brief speech I made at an evening of Music and Poetry at the Catholic University of America in April 2016. Much more low-key than the Kennedy Center programme, the evening was representative of so many events around the country that were organised with huge commitment and enormous attention to detail and to quality. My remarks that evening also speak to our determination to include women's voices in the commemoration: I consciously chose two short poems by women: Eva Gore-Booth and Paula Meehan. (Irish diplomats everywhere will identify with that line in Paula's poem… "I've lived for Ireland with every breath of my being…").

Our final commemorative event at the Embassy that year was a "Women Rising Symposium" in December. We linked past and present, Ireland and the world, with a first panel on women in 1916 and a second that looked at how, within the framework of UN Security Council Resolution 1325, women are increasingly central to the Peace and Security agenda in the world today. (Colum McCann was one of our panelists at the Symposium and I hoped that he felt his advice from more than three years earlier had been heeded.)

About six weeks after the centenary year wrapped up, I gave a speech at Glucksman Ireland House in New York:"1916 to 2016: Reflections". I used the occasion, and the overall themes of the commemoration, to frame a wide-ranging talk about some of the significant issues in Irish-US relations.Towards the conclusion of the speech, I inject a personal note, looking back to how I experienced the 1966 commemorations at a "pinched and joyless time in our country". I felt that what had been achieved in 2016 was the very opposite of that.

Launch of Ireland 100 Festival: Remarks at Gala Dinner
Kennedy Centre, Washington DC
17th May 2016

This is truly an evening to cherish, an evening that will live in all our memories - to be here in this iconic setting, to have had such a wonderful experience in the Concert Hall, to have the promise of all that is to come over the next three weeks.

I will be very brief, as we have already heard wonderful speeches in the Concert Hall this evening. Just a couple of things I want to say.

It took the faith and vision and hard work of a lot of people to get us here. First and foremost the wonderful Kennedy Center team. President Deborah Rutter is a star in this town, and I came to see why. Vice President Alicia Adams is something close to a saint - she has steadfastly believed in this project from the outset, and worked with skill and passion to turn the vision into reality.

My own Embassy team were wonderful - all if them, but everyone will understand if I single out Claire Fitzgibbon who has worked with such great commitment on this project from the outset.

The whole effort was characterised by team work: we had unstinting support from Dublin; top down and bottom up. The Taoiseach championed this project throughout, as did Minister Flanagan and Minister of State Deenihan. Culture Ireland gave their invaluable advice and expertise, and we had the full support of the 2016 centenary team.

And of course the artists are the heart and soul of it all. As a nation, we are extraordinarily rich in our artistic talent. When all these immensely distinguished musicians and writers and actors were approached, what struck me was the sense of pride and privilege they all felt in being part of the festival. They wanted to do this for Ireland; they wanted to celebrate our extraordinary 100-year journey and where we have arrived; and they wanted to perform in the Kennedy Centre.

And this is my key point. In identifying the centrepiece for our centenary celebrations outside Ireland, all roads led to the Kennedy Center. It had to be America, for reasons the Taoiseach outlined earlier. And we wanted it to be this special place in the nation's capital, because it is America's premier arts centre and because of everything its name and legacy evoke for Irish people. We feel at home here.

The event on 29 May that will launch the celebration for President Kennedy's centennial has a perfect title: "Celebrating the Past to Awaken the Future". That is what this whole festival is all about. There is so much to celebrate - so much in this relationship over the past one hundred years which inspires us with pride and joy - and tonight let us hope and believe and pledge that the best is yet to come.

Robert Emmet Statue Re-dedication, Washington DC
27th April 2016

I want to thank all those who have worked so tirelessly to make today's event a reality. It is a wonderful coming together of three centenaries – of the Easter Rising, of the casting of this statue, of the foundation of the national Park Service.

The connection between the Robert Emmet statue and the commemoration of 1916 is not merely symbolic or circumstantial. The men and women of 1916 were heirs to a long tradition of which Emmet's story formed an important part. Patrick Pearse, in particular, venerated Robert Emmet and gave expression to his admiration in stirring speeches he made in New York City and Brooklyn during his US visit in 1914.

The parallels between the two men are striking: both understood heroic failure; both faced execution with stoicism and dignity; in both cases, their voices resonated more powerfully from the grave than they did in life.

This statue we rededicate today is uniquely important. Although over 100 years had passed since his death, this was the first statue of Robert Emmet created anywhere. And the history of the statue speaks powerfully to the Irish-American connection: commissioned by the Smithsonian, cast by Irish sculptor Jerome Connor, funded by a group of Irish Americans, and unveiled in the U.S. National Museum in the presence of President Woodrow Wilson.

In April 1966, in an imaginative gesture to commemorate the 50th anniversary of the Easter Rising – and a generous gesture on the part of the Smithsonian – the statue was moved to this site.

It was a carefully chosen location. This small and intimate space forms part of a triangle, the other points being the Irish residence on S Street and the Irish Embassy on Sheridan Circle. Appropriately, Woodrow Wilson's home is just a stone's throw away.

The site, as we see, has been renovated to mark the centenary anniversaries. The statue is now more visible, more open to the gaze of passers-by, with a new planting of Irish yew trees and a new wayside marker.

Among those who will pass by, I have no doubt that Irish Americans will pause here, and reflect, and acknowledge Robert Emmet's place in the pantheon of Irish heroes.

But I hope that many others who do not share our Irish ancestry, might pause for a moment too, and be led to explore who Robert Emmet was and what he stood for.

And what they find will hold their attention. Beyond the mantle of romantic hero, Robert Emmet was a man of intelligence and eloquence, a man of principle and passion.

Anyone in search of who Robert Emmet was inevitably will be led to that defining speech from the dock. It is a speech which takes us beyond the particulars of the 1803 uprising, or even the particulars of Irish history. Consider, for example, Emmet's response to the trial judge, Lord Norbury, who repeatedly interrupted him as he spoke... "I am a man, you are a man also; by a revolution of power, we might change places... As men, my lord, we must appear at the great day at one common tribunal".

These are words which might be emblazoned in court rooms everywhere, or indeed in any place where people wield power over other human beings.

In all of that eloquent speech, there are no more powerful lines than the final ones. Robert Emmet insisted that he be allowed "repose in obscurity and peace" until such time as "my country takes its place among the nations of the earth, then and not until then let my epitaph be written".

These lines help to explain the delay in casting the first statue of Robert Emmet. If a statue is a form of epitaph, who dared to create one during that long and sad century succeeding his death – when Ireland was not only unfree, but tragically scarred by poverty, hunger, and the million dead in the Great Famine.

But change came, shaped in significant part by the 1916 uprising. The milestones of the twentieth century saw Ireland definitively take its place among the nations of the earth – independence in 1922, the final break with the Commonwealth in 1949, joining the United Nations in 1955, becoming a European Union member in 1973.

Our present-day security in our identity, fully at home within the family of nations, has brought maturity and perspective to our commemoration of the 1916 centenary. Our homage to our patriot dead is heartfelt, but it is not hagiography. Our legitimate pride in all the achievements of the past 100 years is tempered by recognition of where we have fallen short. Looking to the future with optimism and confidence, we do not underestimate the challenges that lie ahead.

Today, as we rededicate the Robert Emmet statue and this park, there is an opportunity for rededication in a larger sense.

Ours has been a long and hard-won struggle for a place among the nations of the earth. Robert Emmet, along with many who went before and came after, paid with his life. It is our task, in our time, to safeguard and give substance to what was so dearly won.

As we re-familiarise ourselves with the Proclamation, we are strengthened in our resolve to be true to its vision and ideals. And as we remind ourselves of those powerful final words of Emmet's speech, we are more than ever determined that our foreign policy – our mark on the world – will be purposeful and values-driven.

At this time of remembrance and renewal, today's gathering in this spot is especially meaningful. With its statue of an Irish patriot who drew deeply on the American Revolution for his inspiration, this park honours the ties of our shared past. Even more importantly, today's ceremony helps to fortify us for the future, confident that the precious friendship between our two countries will be renewed and replenished by the events of this centenary year.

Irish Studies and Comhaltas Ceóltoiri Éireann
Evening of Music and Poetry
Catholic University of America
20th April 2016

I am delighted to be here with you this evening for this special concert. It is a kind of curtain raiser for the weekend ahead: the weekend of 23/24 April, which of course is the centenary of the actual date of the Easter Rising.

I was very proud and happy to be in Dublin a few weeks ago, with an American Congressional delegation, to attend the commemorative ceremonies over Easter weekend. It was a very dignified and moving parade and series of ceremonies on Easter Sunday: pride without triumphalism, homage without hagiography, and – for the future – optimism without naivety.

As Irish Ambassador, I am deeply impressed and heartened by how Irish America has embraced the centenary. There are so many wonderful events, here in DC, in New York, and right across the country. It is a reminder not just of the ties of the past – how Irish America was by our side on the road to the Rising and thereafter – but how strong and enduring and unbreakable these ties continue to be.

My deepest appreciation to Comhaltas, to all of our performers tonight, and to everyone in the audience who has come along to be part of the celebration.

Both in Ireland and in America, it is remarkable just how central our cultural celebrations are to the centenary commemorations. It is part of who we are as a people – part of the human condition but very pronounced in the Irish – that we turn to music and song and poetry to give voice to our deepest emotions.

It also reflects the particular circumstances of the 1916 Rising. It was a movement born out of the Irish cultural revival which began in the early 1890s; five of the seven signatories of the Proclamation were published poets, and the Rising was immortalised in so many iconic and beautiful poems and songs.

I wanted to read some poetry, just very briefly, to launch this evening. There are majestic poems of the period – none more so than Yeats' "Easter 1916" – and a wealth of new poems being published in Ireland to mark the centenary. Rather than quoting from the more established canon, I decided to share two very short and little known poems – 15 lines between them – both by women, one of the period and one contemporary.

The first is by Eva Gore Booth, entitled "Easter Week".

> Grief for the noble dead
> Of one who did not share their strife,
> And mourned that any blood was shed,
> Yet felt the broken glory of their state,
> Their strange heroic questioning of Fate
> Ribbon with gold the rags of this our life.

Eva Gore Booth was a sister of the rebel Constance Markiewicz – but unlike her sister, she was a life-long pacifist. I like the poem's ambiguity; she mourned the bloodshed but recognised what was heroic about the Rising.

The second is by contemporary poet Paula Meehan, whom I have known over many years. Last year, she wrote a suite of poems about 1916, and one of them is entitled "The Graves at Arbour Hill".

> We all die for Ireland in the end,
> Whether sooner or later, I'll die
> Myself for Ireland one of the days.
> And even though I've lived for Ireland

With every breath of my being,
With each and every beat of my heart
There'll come a day I'll be dust in the wind,
Irish dust in Irish wind, a hundred
And a hundred million years from now.

There is something both humbling and comforting about that thought – "Irish dust in Irish wind" – and the musing about what links us all to the patriot dead in Arbour Hill.

Once again, thank you all for joining with us in this year of pride and reflection.

1916 to 2016: Reflections
Glucksman Ireland House, NYU, New York
16th February 2017

Introduction

Just about six weeks ago, our centenary year came to an end. At home and abroad, the commemorations resonated beyond our greatest expectations. The impact in the United States was truly extraordinary – with more than 300 events, spanning every part of this country. I was privileged to participate in very many of them, across large cities and small towns, and so many scenes are etched on my mind. These include some glorious New York memories. Who among us will forget, for example, that beautiful blue sky day when we gathered in Battery Park and heard an Irish Army officer read the 1916 Proclamation against the backdrop of Ellis Island and the Statue of Liberty?

I would especially like this evening to pay tribute to the part played by Glucksman Ireland House in the New York centenary programme. I know that you had a rich cornucopia of events: symposia, screenings, panel discussions, musical programmes, lectures, and so much more besides. Our warmest appreciation to everyone involved.

While the calendar year 2016 came to an end on 31 December, we never envisaged it as a year to be packed up and put behind us. The legacy was intended to live on. We said from the beginning that the centenary was not just about commemorating the events of 100 years ago, but also about stocktaking where we have arrived as a nation and setting our compass for the years ahead.

The themes of the centenary year were threefold: *remember, reflect, reimagine*. And these are the themes around which I would like to frame my talk this evening. At a time of immense challenge in Ireland, in Europe, and in the United States, it is important that we draw on the perspective of memory, steady ourselves with reflection, and think boldly about the future.

Remember

We recalled and remembered so much in the course of 2016, but for me one of the most powerful messages was the reminder of the importance of America's engagement in Ireland at critical moments over the past century.

The book produced by Glucksman House, "Ireland's Allies: America and the 1916 Easter Rising" – conceived and brilliantly edited by Miriam Nyhan Grey – documents the layers of connection around the Rising. And the quotation from Professor Joe Lee, emblazoned on the back cover of that book, sums it up succinctly and powerfully: "No America, No New York, No Easter Rising: Simple as That".

The 1916 connections of course were not the beginning; they continued a long-established pattern of engagement. The story of Irish American involvement in political movements in Ireland stretched back a century earlier: in the 1820s, Irish Americans were already sending back dollars to support Daniel O'Connell's drive for Catholic emancipation, and later in the nineteenth century Irish American money supported the Home Rule campaign of Charles Stuart Parnell and Michael Davitt's agrarian movement. And the engagement extended on beyond the Rising; already in the few years after 1916, Eamon de Valera came to the US to launch an Irish bond drive to fund the Irish Republican Army in the War of Independence. And on the story went.

One key point: it was never just about fund-raising. In the long and tangled history of Ireland's relationship with Britain, Irish America always hoped and sought to get the American government involved on the Irish side, so as to help balance the scales as a small country sought to work out its relationship with a larger neighbour. Sometimes the attempt failed, as when President

Woodrow Wilson refused all entreaties to bring the Irish case to the table at the Versailles Peace Conference. Sometimes there was a degree of success, as in 1940 when the US warned the British not to seize Irish ports as part of the war with Germany.

Fast forward from 1940 to some thirty years later. The dialogue with America became more complicated when the Troubles erupted in Northern Ireland in the late '60s, and Irish America was deeply divided about how best to interpret what was happening and how best to engage. The subsequent fifteen years or so, culminating in signature of the Anglo-Irish Agreement in 1985, were long and agonising ones, played out against a backdrop of violence and terrible atrocities in Northern Ireland, perpetrated on both sides of the divide. For much of this period, the British and Irish governments battled for the ear of the US Administration, until the two governments finally came to a sense of partnership in dealing with Northern Ireland, with important concessions on both sides.

This partnership between the Irish and British governments has largely held over the past thirty years – not without differences of judgement and perspective, but with a broad sense of shared purpose and with evolving structures and institutions within which these differences could be addressed. The existence of such a partnership has freed the US Administration from trying to adjudicate between two friends and allowed it to throw its weight solidly and consistently behind the peace process. Through the involvement of successive US Presidents, and the role of successive envoys – most notably Senator George Mitchell, who brokered the Good Friday Agreement – as well as through America's financial contribution to the International Fund for Ireland, America has established a critical stake in the Northern Ireland peace process.

It is imperative that this active American involvement should continue. For all the extraordinary progress that has been made, there is significant unfinished business in Northern Ireland. The fragilities continue; currently, the outcome of the Assembly elections on 2 March is awaited with some anxiety. As we look back at the long sweep of the past 100 years and more, and particularly at developments over the past decades, our message to the US government and to Irish America is clear: your involvement in the peace process on our island is still needed, still vitally important, and still capable of making a real difference.

Reflect

The second theme is reflect. Here too, we have covered a great deal of ground in so many centenary discussions and get-togethers, and time permits me to draw out just a few threads. I will focus on three areas which have significantly shaped Irish-US relations over much of the past century: immigration reform; our European Union membership; and the evolving economic relationship. In each area, I would like to touch on the historical context and link it to the contemporary challenge.

Immigration Reform

We all know the foundation stories of Irish America: the Irish who poured into American cities before and after the Great Famine, until the middle of the 20th century. This narrative changed some fifty years ago. The immigration reforms in the US in the mid-'60s were intended by the authors, and Senator Kennedy was principal among them, to end pro-European bias in immigration to the US and to bring greater diversity to the immigrant pool. It was a perfectly worthy and understandable objective, and succeeded possibly even beyond the authors' expectations. Senator Kennedy subsequently admitted that he did not anticipate that the Irish would suffer quite as much collateral damage as they did.

Over the past fifty years, the channels for legal Irish immigration to the US have narrowed considerably. From time to time, there has been some temporary and time-bound relief, such as the Donnelly visas and the Morrison visas, but the trend has been inexorable. Today, we see the results: less than one fifth of one percent of all green cards issued in the US go to Irish people.

As the demographics of this country have shifted, Irish America is shrinking in absolute terms and as a percentage of the overall population. And the generational distance has grown: now we have fewer and fewer first and second generation Irish, and more third and fourth generation. Inevitably, this has consequences in terms of engagement and connectivity, and obliges us to think in new and creative ways as to how we nurture and sustain that connectivity.

This narrowing of the channels for legal immigration over the past decades has had another consequence: the number of undocumented Irish in the US has grown. While it is hard to arrive at a reliable figure, estimates from the Irish community suggest a number of 50,000 or so. It has been a longstanding objective of the Irish government – and one to which as Ambassador I have devoted a great deal of my time – to help bring about immigration reform that would allow our undocumented to emerge from the shadows and to take their place in American society.

Side by side with that, we have been trying for years to open up a better channel for Irish people to enter and work here legally. For a people who did so much to help build this country – its physical fabric of roads and railways and bridges, and its social fabric of teachers and police and firefighters – it is surely reasonable that we should seek to improve our position beyond the current one fifth of one percent of green cards.

We all know the current uncertainties on the immigration front, and we are acutely conscious of the heightened fears and anxieties in the immigrant community in the aftermath of the US elections. I want to reaffirm that the Irish Government will continue to relentlessly press the case, both for the undocumented and for improved legal access, using all our friendships within the Administration and on both sides of the aisle in Congress. We will continue to set out the compelling human case for the undocumented. With regard to improved legal access, our point will remain a simple but cogent one: there is no country which has a greater mismatch between its contribution to the building of America and its current level of immigrant access.

European Union

This past year has provided much scope for reflection on the various interlinked relationships: between Ireland, Britain, the European Union, and the US. As we look back over the past one hundred years, there is a significant point to be noted: for the first fifty years of the Irish state, prior to our joining the European Union, Ireland's relationship with the US was a bilateral one; now it is a relationship that in some important respects is mediated through our EU membership.

Ireland and Britain joined the European Union together, on 1 January 1973. For Ireland and the Irish people, the experience of EU membership over nearly forty five years has been transformative – a subject deserving of a lecture by itself. This evening, I will limit myself to a point about relationships: our joint membership of the European Union has done a great deal to strengthen the British-Irish relationship, and also I would suggest, has conditioned our relationship with the US in a very positive way.

In terms of shared values and a shared world view, there has been no closer alignment than that which has existed between the US and Europe. Together, we helped construct the post-World War II international order; whether at the United Nations, the World Trade Organisation or the Bretton Woods institutions, we have built the scaffolding which supports and underpins that order.

Today, what has been so carefully built over so many decades is at risk. The unequal benefits of globalisation, and the tensions caused by the inexorable advance of technology and the consequent redundancy of some traditional forms of human labour, have been eating away at our societies. Populism is becoming an increasingly potent force, and we are seeing its outworkings on both sides of the Atlantic.

For us in Ireland, although of course we fully accept the democratic outcome of the British referendum, the Brexit decision was deeply unwelcome. Dealing with the implications of that decision – for our economy, for the relationship between North and South on our island, for Europe as a whole – will be one of the biggest challenges we have faced in the history of our state.

Brexit is also impacting the EU-US relationship in ways that are only beginning to be played out. President Trump and members of his Administration have made clear their sympathy for Brexit, and that indeed is their choice and prerogative. But it is crucially important that this is not seen as a zero-sum game: maintaining the US bond with Britain in no way requires or provides a rationale for loosening the US bond with Europe. Too much is at stake to allow that vital relationship to erode or fray.

For Ireland, our history and geography tie us closely both to the US and to Europe. In a well-known speech delivered seventeen years ago, our then Deputy Prime Minister Mary Harney mused as to whether Ireland was closer to Boston or Berlin. In truth, we would never wish to be put in a position of choosing between the two. We want to see the continuation of a robust and firm friendship between Europe and the US, built on shared values of respect for human rights, rule of law, and working together towards a more peaceful and just world.

As the new Administration beds down here, as Europe prepares for key elections in France and Germany over the coming months, and as Britain and Europe work their way through the divorce proceedings which lie ahead, all of these relationships have the potential to become more brittle. Ireland has an important role to play, and multiple interests to protect. Britain is our nearest neighbour, with whom we share unique ties. At the same time, we are a deeply committed member of the European family, and we enjoy an exceptionally close friendship with the US. At this time of fluidity and shift, we will be working to protect and strengthen these various relationships and to try to ensure they do not come into tension with one another.

Vibrancy of the Economic Relationship

How things have evolved and changed over the past century. I mentioned earlier the fundraising for Irish political causes that was so much part of the Irish-American tradition in the 19th and first half of the 20th centuries. Today, we still have a thriving philanthropy on the part of Irish Americans – through the Ireland Funds and other organisations – which support a tremendous range of worthwhile projects in both parts of our island.

We are gratified that Irish Americans are still, with great generosity, ready to offer such philanthropic support to their ancestral homeland. But I am also glad to say that the scales have evened up somewhat over recent years, with the Irish Government providing substantial financial assistance to our diaspora through the Emigrant Support Programme and other programmes.

In the classic area of economic relationships – investment and trade – the changes have been truly striking.

The first half of the twentieth century saw a succession of bleak economic decades for Ireland; the post-war economic recovery which much of the rest of Europe enjoyed passed Ireland by. By the '50s, emigration was sky high and emigrants' remittances from Britain and the US kept many families afloat.

From 1958, there was a radical reframing of economic policy in Ireland, when the then Finance Minister, later Taoiseach, Sean Lemass, launched the First Programme for Economic Development.

Over the subsequent years, during the '60s and especially following our EU membership in 1973, we were transformed from an economic backwater, with domestic markets protected behind high tariff walls, to one of the most open and globalised economies in the world.

Throughout the past decades, foreign investment in Ireland has thrived on the back of a low corporate tax rate, investment in free education which gave us one of the best educated and most highly rated workforces in the world, and access from 1973 onwards to a European wide free market in goods and services. FDI, especially from the US, became a key driving force in our economy.

Ireland's economic story since the '60s is certainly not one of uninterrupted success, and the experience of the post 2008 crash is still raw and recent. But though the pain of the austerity years has not been erased, Irish people have shown extraordinary determination and resilience in reaching for recovery. That recovery has now fully taken hold and our economic growth over the past few years has been healthy and broad-based.

Looking back over the past couple of decades, one of the critical points to underline is that the economic relationship between Ireland and the US has become a two-way street. In the earlier years, FDI was almost exclusively one-way traffic; the US was sending and Ireland was receiving. Now, with some of the more traditional Irish companies – such as Oldcastle – very active in the US, but also many young Irish-based companies – whose founders often got their start in US multinationals in Ireland – seeking to spread their wings in the US market, we have a very different equation.

Today, US multinationals in Ireland directly employ some 140,000 Irish people, and Irish companies in the US have tens of thousands of American employees across all 50 states. Trade too has evened up; we are still a big exporter of goods to the US but now also a major importer of US services. In other words, mirroring many other aspects of the relationship, there has been a coming of age in economic relations.

This is another area where we will need to stay vigilant and engaged. With the current fierce questioning of globalisation, it is important that Ireland be a voice for the kind of "good globalisation" we have experienced. Not an unthinking cheerleader for every aspect of globalisation, but a strong advocate for the shared benefits that flow from rules-based international investment and trade. We know from our own history the dead ends of protectionism, and we know that openness is the only viable choice for the 21st century. We will continue to make that case clearly and vocally.

Re-imagine the Future

I want to turn briefly to the third strand of our commemorative year: re-imagining the future.

Back in Ireland, the centenary commemorations have been a catalyst for some serious self-examination. There has been heartfelt and genuine pride in our 100-year journey, and all the undoubted achievements along the way. But we know too that there are areas where we have fallen short of the vision of 1916, and of the principles set forth in the Proclamation.

Again and again, throughout the past year, we have reminded ourselves of that most sacred promise of the Proclamation to cherish "all the children of the nation equally". Great strides have been made, but we have yet to fully deliver on that promise. I believe the honest stocktaking of the centenary year has helped to strengthen our resolve, and our determination to reset our compass for the years ahead.

In Irish America too, the commemorations have given us all a lot of food for thought. Through the hundreds of commemorative events on this side of the Atlantic, there has been a great deal of re-energising of the community, and Irish-American organisations have come together in truly collaborative and innovative ways.

The question for us now is how do we harness that energy and sustain that collaboration? How do we best engage Irish America in the conversation back in Ireland about the direction of our country? And the challenge too of ensuring that Ireland and Irish America understand the contemporary realities and not live with outdated images of each other: that Irish America understands the modern, fast changing, multicultural Ireland; and that Ireland moves beyond stereotypes of Irish America and understands the dynamics that are shaping today's Irish America.

Here in the US, we need to address the demographic challenge I talked about earlier: the shrinking Irish America and the need to maintain connectivity. In particular, there is need to reach young people and to create a meaningful set of 'Next Generation' projects – through cultural and sporting links, through educational and exchange visits to Ireland.

We clearly are not starting from zero – a great deal is already happening – but we need to map the initiatives better and see where we can reinforce them.

Creative Ireland

As we speak about re-imagining Ireland, I want to particularly highlight the Government's decision to make "Creative Ireland" an enduring legacy of the centenary year. "Creative Ireland" recently had its international launch here in New York; it is a five-year, multi-stranded, whole of Government initiative, designed to have a real impact both at home and abroad.

The Taoiseach summed it up: "Creative Ireland is about placing culture at the centre of our lives, for the betterment of our people and for the strengthening of our society... we can make an important statement to ourselves and to the world about the interdependency of culture, identity and citizenship."

In this area too, I believe our centenary commemorations helped to remind us of something we were at risk of forgetting. The 1916 Rising was rooted in cultural nationalism; indeed, it has sometimes been dubbed the "Poet's Rising", given the number of signatories of the Proclamation who were published poets. And there is no doubt that the power and impact of the Rising was amplified through iconic poems such as Yeats' "Easter 1916".

This centrality of culture – its place at the heart of our identity – was obscured over much of the intervening century. In the grim economic times of the '30s and '40s and '50s, culture seemed a luxury; sadly, in the high-rolling '90s and early 2000s, we fed our materialism but not our souls. While there was the beginning of a rebalancing in the aftermath of 2008, the cutbacks of the austerity years fell everywhere, and the pitch for the prioritisation of culture was not an easy one.

I hope we will look back on 2016 as the year when culture reclaimed its rightful place in the life of our nation. At home and abroad, so many of the commemorative events were cultural in nature. We were reminded of the power of culture to interrogate and jolt, and strip away complacency, as well as its power to nurture and console and sometimes bring a smile to our lips.

Across the world, we saw the unifying and convening power of our culture. Here in the United States, one of the most exhilarating experiences of 2016 was the flagship three-week festival at the Kennedy Centre – "Ireland 100" – which was the largest festival of Irish culture ever held outside Ireland.

Overall, I find a wonderful fittingness and symmetry in this decision to make "Creative Ireland" one of the most tangible legacies of 2016, and I am greatly looking forward to helping take the initiative forward in the U.S.

1966 and 2016, A Comparison

Among the most telling ways of tracing our one hundred year

journey is to contrast the fiftieth anniversary commemorations in 1966 with the centenary events of last year.

I was fourteen years old in 1966, living through those impressionable years of early adolescence. Looking back, I recall it is a pinched and joyless time in our country. Ireland was a much more claustrophobic and less generous place. We had yet to experience that opening wide our windows to the world which came with EU membership. The multi-ethnicity that characterises today's Ireland was far in the future. Women were marginalised; contraception was banned; homosexuality was outlawed under laws dating from the Victorian era.

And so the pinched and joyless commemorations in 1966 were probably an accurate reflection of the country we then were.

As the planning unfolded for 2016, the limitations of the fiftieth anniversary commemorations were very much in people's minds, and especially the lack of openness towards other traditions on our island. In the years since 1966, the grief and loss of the decades of the Troubles had burnt themselves on our consciousness, conditioning and tempering the way we approached the centenary commemorations. And so there was a much heightened sensitivity, and a strong emphasis on outreach to the Unionist tradition, including the careful embedding of the 1916 centenary within a decade of Commemorations.

Beyond that aspect, however, the approach to the centenary commemorations was different in almost every way, reflecting the different country we had become. We took full ownership of our history, and examined both light and shade. There was a constant mode of interrogation, rather than self-satisfaction or complacency. Women were back from the margins, definitively bringing to an end that "pervasive invisibility" which had been their fate in earlier narratives of 1916. Young people were much more to the fore, and the "new Irish" were properly recognised as part of our story.

The commemorations were also more confident and outward looking in so many ways. We embraced the role that Easter 1916 had played in inspiring anti-colonial movements across the world throughout the twentieth century. And, as we saw in that moving and memorable Parade in Dublin on Easter Sunday, Irish people also came to a greater consciousness of, and took immense pride in, the role our Defence Forces have played in global peacekeeping over many decades past.

One final point. History has its coincidences: it has not escaped us that, just at the time we were commemorating the events of 1916 – the beginning of the end of British rule in Ireland – we found ourselves facing another radical adjustment in the British-Irish relations: for the first time ever, one of us will be inside the European Union and the other outside.

There is no minimising the Brexit challenge that lies ahead, which will test us in very many ways. But I believe that all of our centenary experience – this process we have lived through of remembering, reflecting and re-imagining – will have helped to fortify us to meet that challenge. We certainly do not have all the answers, but we are better grounded, with a surer sense of who we are, as we seek those answers. And so, in that very real sense, the centenary commemorations will have achieved one of their key objectives: looking back has also helped us to face forward.

TALKING TO YOUNG PEOPLE

There is a special stimulation that comes from engaging with young people. I find it bracing and invigorating to encounter their enquiring minds, the freshness of their perspectives, and the directness with which their opinions are expressed. I try to pass on something from my own experience, but I know I am learning as much as I am teaching.

That is why I continue in retirement to devote some of my time to work in the educational area. I currently serve on a couple of boards at US universities and have given talks over the past few years in third-level institutions both in Ireland and the US. Last summer, I was especially happy to address students at a summer course in Princeton University aimed at young people from less privileged backgrounds who are targeting a career in diplomacy.

Among the many speeches for whom young people were the primary audience, I have chosen three for this section that resonate with me for different reasons.

The first dates from 2005, a Graduation address for high school students at St John's International School in Brussels. My daughter had been a pupil at this school from 2001-2003, before going on to attend university in Dublin. I respected the culture of the school and there were a few of the teachers I particularly admired. So I felt I owed them something when the invitation came to deliver the Graduation address.

I was also conscious that we were all at a moment of transition - the pupils on the threshold of adulthood and the rest of their lives, and in my case within a few weeks of leaving Brussels to take up my new posting in Paris. Transitions are the milestones that mark out a life's journey and are always conducive to reflection. And so standing in the school's sports arena, as I looked out at that sea of eighteen-year-old faces and felt the brightness reflecting back at me, I was probably talking to myself as much as to them. Certainly the questions I put to them were ones I have never stopped trying to answer: "How do we know who we are unless we engage with issues? What do I believe in? What am I prepared to fight for? When I look at myself in the mirror, what sort of person is looking back at me?"

Ten years later, in Summer 2015, I was addressing another open-air gathering of young people. This time, I was on the garden terrace of the Residence in DC and the young people of the Washington-Ireland Programme (WIP) were assembled on the lawn. WIP is a wonderful programme, bringing a group of thirty or so young Irish people to Washington each summer, potential leaders drawn from both parts of the island and of diverse backgrounds. One of the rituals towards the end of their summer programme is that they gather for a celebratory evening in the Irish Ambassador's Residence. I loved meeting the group each year and the calibre of the young people always made my heart soar.

The address I include here is one I remember with utter clarity. I describe 2015 as "a summer of sorrow, but also a summer of grace". All our emotions were heightened that summer. The Berkeley tragedy had ended or forever changed the lives of a group of young Irish students - so similar in age and life experience and expectations to the young people gathered before me on the Residence lawn. But I had also just been to Alaska to witness the work of dedicated young Irish people with the Hope Irish Partnership, and in the few days before I addressed the WIP I had attended the Special Olympics in Los Angeles and seen the incredible talent and spirit of the Irish athletes - many of them around the same age as the WIP participants.

And so, when I spoke to the WIP group that evening, I remember struggling with competing emotions almost to the point of tears. The brilliance and sheer goodness of the young people I had encountered that summer threw the random cruelty of Berkeley into even sharper relief.

The final speech is one that I chose to end this section and the collection as a whole. In the months following my retirement, I received an invitation from the Trinity College Historical Society (the Hist) to accept the Society's Gold Medal. The format of the invitation was quite elaborate and the list of previous recipients was impressive. So I thought I had better prepare an address of some substance for the evening.

The subject I chose was "The Conduct of Public Discourse: A Test for Democracies". I availed of the occasion to sound notes of concern about current developments in the US (though still somewhat muffled by my sense of being "former Ambassador"), and also to interrogate the state of public discourse in Europe and in Ireland. None of what I reviewed provided any grounds for complacency.

A speech of this title seems to me a fitting note on which to round off the collection. After all, the crafting and delivering of speeches is in itself a way of conducting public discourse. The speeches we deliver are designed to examine and elucidate issues of the day, and to present a viewpoint in the hope that the audience will be persuaded to share it.

Speeches are words come to life, allowed to echo and gain impact in shared spaces. They dance between speaker and audience, and on rare and special occasions you feel the immediacy of the reaction: the energy level in the room rises and you know a spark has been ignited.

For most of us, the sparks we may have struck with young people are those we value the most. They are the people who will carry the torch forward, and fashion our future. And in my case at least, there is always the hope that some young women and young men out there in the audience, as they ponder their career choices, may want to consider that old and honourable profession of diplomacy.

Graduation Address
St. John's International School, Brussels
4th June 2005

I hope I don't shock you if I say that my first instinct, on being invited to address you as graduation speaker today, was to say how honoured I was by the invitation but to politely express regrets. I'll tell you why I was tempted to say no, and then I'll tell you at the end of my address why I said yes.

I hesitated because I am extremely doubtful about taking on the role of sage – someone who has worked out the answers to life's dilemmas, who has cracked the formula and is now in a position to pass it on. Perhaps there are a few wise, experienced people out there who really have found the answers. But most of us, most of the time, are figuring it out as we go along – trying to find decent compromises, to balance the competing demands made of us, to live with honour while having some fun in our lives.

The title of a book I read some time ago was "Composing a Life". It seemed to me to sum it up well: the challenge of weaving all the disparate elements together so that over time some kind of pattern emerges, apparent to ourselves and others, as to how we have chosen to live.

You young adults graduating today are well into the composition of your lives. The themes have already been struck that will echo and resonate, with variations, throughout the years ahead. Schooldays were the overture, and now the rest begins.

Each of you will approach the composition in your own way, following your own inspiration and shaped by the particular influences and circumstances of your own lives. The music will be distinctively yours; all I can counsel is that you bring the maximum passion and commitment to the task.

What do I mean by living life with passion? I mean a zest for life, a creativity, an engagement with life – the opposite of passivity and detachment and settling for second best. There is a couple of lines at the end of Andrew Marvell's poem "To his Coy Mistress" – a poem whose sentiments your parents or teachers might not otherwise approve of but whose last lines are glorious:

"Though we cannot make our sun stand still
Yet we will make him run."

Adapting those words to a larger context than Marvell intended, I cannot think of a better summing up of what it means to live life with passion.

But I particularly want to speak today about living life with commitment and values. I'm not going to dwell on commitment in your friendships and personal relationships and family – not because these are not hugely important, but because love and loyalty are already a deep part of your lives and I doubt I have much to teach you that you do not already know.

Instead, I want to emphasise engagement in public policy issues and public policy choices – responsibility for the wider society: standing for fairness, justice and a value driven society.

Most of us can come up with convincing-sounding reasons to stand back: "I'm too busy; "life's too short"; "my voice won't count anyway".

But if you don't get involved, there are consequences – not vague and long term but direct and personal. You are acquiescing in a situation where your society is being shaped by others whose values and priorities you may not share. If you're on the beach while others are joining, lobbying, writing, speaking – whatever it takes to get their voices heard – then the outcome is obvious: you have the sun-tan; they have the influence.

Perhaps I might say a special word to the young women in the class of 2005. You have grown up in a home and school environment that is free from sex discrimination. Your results today speak to your abilities and achievements. But take a look at the statistics – the leading politicians, the captains of industry, the judges, almost any sphere you want to name – and you will see the relative disempowerment of women in our society.

If we are to make space for women at the top, then society will have to be restructured in a way that secures a better work/life balance for us all. But women too must rise to the challenge. Of course it's our right to prioritise, and our priorities will probably shift in different phases of our lives. For myself, I would say unhesitatingly that my role as mother is absolutely central to my life. But I also know this: if we women consistently prioritise the personal over the professional, and the personal over the political, then we cannot legitimately complain if the hands on the levers of power are male hands.

And even if I have particularly addressed the young women here today, the implications for the young men are equally profound. To quote Ireland's former President Mary Robinson: "A society that is without the voice and vision of women is not less feminine, it is less human."

The global challenges of course go way beyond sexism. None of us should be lulled by the catch phrases that were fashionable a few years ago: "the end of ideology"; or "the end of history". It's true that the university life many of you are about to enter will be different from that of your parents' generation. Our days at college were dominated by big debates of left and right: most of us saw ourselves as standing squarely against the bourgeois values of our parents' generation. The political landscape has changed utterly since the fall of the Berlin Wall. But the big issues are still out there.

I have spent much of my career dealing with human rights and development issues, and in the last four years I have been immersed in EU issues. And the question has lost none of its urgency: what kind of world do we want?

No matter what part of the globe we call home, none of us has grounds for complacency. In Europe, we have been jolted by the votes on the EU Constitution in France and the Netherlands over recent days. Unless we find a new sense of direction and a new way of connecting to the public, our Union – that has been an instrument of peace and prosperity for fifty years – risks being crippled by fearfulness and introspection. America faces profound questions about how its unprecedented global power is to be exercised responsibly. In many parts of the developing world, issues of good governance and rooting out corruption need to be tackled with far more vigour than we have seen to date.

Beyond issues particular to our regions, there is the global scourge of poverty and underdevelopment. When the UN Millennium Development Goals were agreed with such fanfare five year ago, I thought them insufficiently ambitious. All the more shocking that we rich countries are now falling short of meeting these relatively modest Goals. The radical inequalities in today's world are an affront to our conscience. And even if there were never a moral imperative, enlightened self interest requires us to deal with the deprivation that provides a breeding ground for extremism and fundamentalism.

These are issues not only for those of you interested in studying politics or development economics; they are for all of us. The theme I chose for the year I chaired the UN Commission on Human Rights was "Taking Responsibility". In speaking to you today – some of the best and brightest and most privileged of your generation – my message is the same: take responsibility.

Taking responsibility is about defining your society but it is also about defining yourself. How do we know who we are unless we engage with issues? What do I believe in? What am I prepared to fight for? When I look at myself in the mirror, what sort of person is looking back at me?

And it's not just about duty. I think we should never under-estimate the rewards that come from being part of a larger picture. Fulfilment in our personal lives is fundamental but there is also a magic that lights up other moments. For example, when I look back on my time in Brussels, I will never forget that intoxicating midnight on 1 May last year when we celebrated the moment of EU enlargement. As I drank champagne in the Grand Place with colleagues from the new Member States, the cliché about feeling the hand of history never felt more apt. As EU Presidency, Ireland had a particular role in the drama – to be even the smallest bit player in such a drama felt like an extraordinary privilege.

Our individual influence may be modest in the big scheme of things. But don't make it smaller then it need be; don't settle for, in the words of WH Auden "a safer life then we can bear". On the threshold of the life that lies ahead, look up, look out, look around.

And finally, I said I would tell you why – despite some misgivings – I said yes to this invitation. Of course I was honoured to be invited. More importantly, during my daughter Claire's time as a pupil here, I developed a deep respect for what St. John's stands for. I think it is a school that truly understands what education means: drawing forth the potential that lies within each individual.

But most of all I feel privileged to share with you these special moments of pride, celebration and transition. Pride in all the hard work and achievement that brought you to these wonderful results today. Celebration with the friends who have grown so close over your years together, and with your families and teachers who have supported you all along the way. And the special significance of this moment of transition as you look back with affection and forward with anticipation.

Particularly facing my own moment of transition as I leave Brussels in a few weeks time to take up my new life as Ambassador in Paris, I like to contemplate your more radical transition – to independence, adulthood, wider horizons and all that sparkling future that lies ahead.

All of us here have so much confidence in this class of 2005 and we wish you so much joy. In the words of the Irish blessing: *Go n-eirí an bothar libh*: May the road rise with you.

Reception for the Washington Ireland Program, Irish Embassy Residence, Washington DC
27ᵗʰ July 2015

It is always a special moment, at this point of summer, to celebrate the Washington Ireland Program and to convey our warmest wishes to this year's participants.

The Program is now in its twenty-first year. Over 500 alumni are making their mark across all walks of Irish society, in all parts of our island and further afield. WIP is a wonderful programme, whose promise is being richly fulfilled.

I know that this year's group of 30 students have had a summer they will never forget – broadening your horizons, making new friendships, challenging yourselves in every way. Our deep appreciation goes to the WIP sponsors and supporters; to all those who have offered internship opportunities; and most especially to the host families who have opened your homes and hearts with such great generosity of spirit.

In celebrating WIP tonight, and in greeting our program participants, I would like to take a moment to talk about some of the wider experiences of this summer.

I have always believed that the young people of Ireland are our greatest asset – your inquiring minds, adventurous spirits, and deep-down decency, represent our hope and our future.

Over the past six weeks, in circumstances sorrowful and joyful, that faith and confidence have been vindicated and fortified.

The six weeks began with the heartbreak of Berkeley, and are rounded out with tonight's reception for the WIP participants. In the interim, my travels have brought me to Alaska and, in the past few days, to the opening of the Special Olympics in Los Angeles.

I want to share with you some of what I have experienced and witnessed during those weeks.

411

For all of us, the tragedy of the balcony collapse in Berkeley cast a deep shadow over the summer. I joined others in San Francisco in the immediate aftermath, and the sorrow was unspeakable. Six bright and beautiful lives so prematurely ended; seven young people having to deal with the challenge of rebuilding their futures.

Amidst the sadness, something that shone through – and that has been recognised so fulsomely by the families – was the solidarity of the friends and fellow J1s of the Berkeley victims. These young people showed their love for their lost and injured friends in countless different ways – so many acts of comfort and support and tenderness. They have proven themselves such steadfast friends: "genuine heroes" as they were described in the statement issued yesterday by four of the families.

I went to Alaska in the days after Berkeley, in particular to help celebrate the 20th anniversary of the Hope Irish Partnership. Hope is an organisation which provides services throughout Alaska to support people with disabilities in leading full and meaningful lives. Over the past twenty years, hundreds of young Irish people – mostly from the Institutes of Technology in Waterford and Tralee, but from other Institutes and Universities also – have spent periods working as volunteers in the Programme. Their impact has been enormous. The head of Hope has described "the joy and beauty of twenty years of selfless giving by 1400 young people from Ireland".

"Joy" and "beauty" also characterised the past few days at the Special Olympics in Los Angeles. We felt so much pride in Team Ireland, so much respect for their achievements. Our 88 Irish athletes span all ages but the majority are young, close in age to the WIP participants here tonight. Their talent and tenacity, their grit and determination, make them role models for us all. And indeed the Special Olympics motto is one we might all adopt: "Let me win, but if I cannot win, let me show courage in the attempt."

Separately, while in Los Angeles, I had the opportunity to meet – and hear eloquent speeches from – young Irish law students participating in the annual summer programme with the Irish American Bar Association.

Throughout these past weeks, I was reminded of the breadth and depth of connection between Ireland and America, and particularly of the linkages involving our young people. I was also reminded of how often, and how naturally, we operate on an all-island basis: the Washington Ireland Program of course, but also Team Ireland at the Special Olympics, and the legal training programme in California.

But above all, this mosaic of experiences has allowed me to witness the qualities of our young people. I cannot imagine an Ambassador of any country who could feel more proud of her or his young compatriots.

To our WIP participants I would say this: you are part of, and representatives of, a great generation. You have so much to contribute, such boundless potential. As our country heads into a period of renewal, we urgently need that contribution; we need your empathy and your energy, your vision and your moral compass.

It has been a summer of sorrow, but also a summer of grace. For our WIP students, I hope it will prove to have been a life-changing and life-enhancing summer. Above all, I hope it will have reinforced your determination to seize life's opportunities – to go out and make a difference in our island and our world.

Again, to all who work so hard to make WIP the program it is, our appreciation and gratitude.

"The Conduct of Public Discourse: A Test for Democracies" Trinity College Dublin Historical Society Gold Medal Award 19th February 2018

I feel truly honoured and very privileged to receive this award. I am conscious of the long and distinguished history of this Society. Your founder members were among the most brilliant practitioners of public discourse in their time. Your Society has helped keep their legacy alive throughout the intervening two and a half centuries, and your role today remains as necessary and as relevant as ever. I am also particularly conscious that in receiving this award, I join a roll call of figures, both Irish and international, whom I greatly respect and admire.

As I reflected on the purpose of this medal, and what it honours, I began to ponder the very term public discourse, and how vital it is to any functioning democracy. Today I think we have grounds for concern, with challenges to the very basis on which public discourse is built. And so I decided to speak this evening about how societies create space for public discourse, and the circumstances in which it is put at risk. I am conscious of how large and challenging a topic this is, and I don't aspire to address it in a comprehensive way in the time allotted this evening. However, I would propose to explore some of the relevant issues, drawing in particular on my recent experience in the US, and touching also on the situations in Europe and here in Ireland.

At a the outset, a word about definitions. I am not sure what working definition of "public discourse" your Society applies. But I see it as rational, reasoned debate around key issues of the day, conducted in public fora and - at least in my sense of the term - it also implies a degree of civility in the exchanges, a readiness to respect and allow space for other viewpoints.

Let me say quite bluntly that, after my four years in Washington which finished in July of last year, I am left with considerable concern about the eroding space for public discourse.

My time as Ambassador there spanned the final years of the Obama Presidency, the 2016 Presidential election campaign, and the early months of the Trump Presidency. President Obama was a skilled practitioner of the art of public discourse: cerebral, with a passion for ideas; a gifted orator with a mastery of pace and cadence. Indeed his critics accused him of being too cerebral, too pedagogic, too much the Harvard Law School graduate.

I need hardly spell out the contrast with his successor, President Trump. Even if he has described himself (perhaps tongue in cheek) as a genius, I do not believe President Trump would lay claim - or would want anyone to lay claim on his behalf - to the terms cerebral or intellectual. His vocabulary quite consciously veers towards the basic and repetitive, and he does not shrink from crudeness, whether in the nicknames he attaches to his political opponents, or the taunting on Twitter, or the language he reportedly used in the Oval Office meeting in January that gave such deep offence to Caribbean and African countries.

It is important to make a clear distinction here. Effective public discourse does not require sophistication of language. Indeed plain speaking can help us all know where we stand. But there is a very legitimate discussion about tenor and style - what is or is not appropriate to a holder of high office, and what is the cost to society if all constraints of civility are abandoned.

But beyond any questions of style, public discourse requires respect for certain ground rules. Chief among these is that it should be fact based and evidence based. It renders it extraordinarily difficult, for example, to have what could be considered as genuine public discourse about climate change unless all protagonists accept proven scientific facts. Of course there can be robust argument about the burden of action today to safeguard our tomorrows, how that burden should be distributed, the trade - offs that might or might not be workable. But a wilful rejection of the science makes it almost impossible to get to first base.

Any analysis of the increasingly difficult climate for public discourse in America goes well beyond the personality of President Trump and some of the features of the current Administration.

In political terms, America is an increasingly divided country. The common frame of reference which provides the environment for public discourse is fraying. You all know the basics of the picture: coastal America which backed Hillary Clinton and flyover America which backed Donald Trump. Many of you will have read J.D. Vance's " Hillbilly Elegy" and Caitriona Perry's "Travels in Trump's America." One America prospers while the other languishes, with stalled incomes, sub-standard education, an opioid crisis. As so often in fractured societies, the places left behind offer fertile ground for demagoguery. It is all too easy to provide the scapegoats: immigrants, globalisation, the other.

To a significant extent, the shaping of public discourse has tended to be seen as the role and responsibility of the political class. Politicians of course are not the only actors: big debates on headline issues are also framed by the media, by public intellectuals, writers, think tanks and thought leaders of various descriptions. But the political arena is particularly important, because it is in that arena one expects the major debates to be played out. In a sense, it acts as a model: the tenor of the discourse there influences the tenor of exchanges elsewhere.

Throughout my time in the US, I observed the growing distrust in the political class - a sense that they are remote, self -interested, failing to provide leadership. As a candidate, a fundamental part of Mr. Trump's appeal was that he presented himself as the outsider, the anti-politician, the person who would take on Washington. The "drain the swamp" chant became a staple of his campaign rallies. And indeed his Inauguration speech as President was striking in the degree to which it took direct aim at the Washington establishment.

This distrust of politicians is strongly related to, and reflective of, the dysfunctionality of the US Congress. And in turn, the most significant causal factor of this dysfunctionality is the breakdown in bipartisanship.

My first posting to DC, back in the mid '80s, coincided with the years when Ronald Reagan was President and Tip O'Neill was Speaker. It was a time of fierce partisanship, a true clash of ideologies (and also I might note that President Reagan, like President Trump, would never have aspired to or wanted the label of intellectual.) It was nevertheless a time of robust public discourse, with views vigorously articulated and defended, but generally with a respect for civilities and ultimately a readiness to come together to achieve results. There were giants of Congress - people like Ted Kennedy, the "Last Lion"- who built monumental legislative legacies as a result of their willingness to trade across the aisle.

Today, bipartisanship seems to be regarded as a kind of betrayal. One of the more frustrating aspects of my four years as Ambassador was the failure to achieve outcomes in relation to immigration reform, including a way forward for the tens of thousands of Irish undocumented. The frustration was all the greater because it was obvious that, at least at one point, the numbers were there for a bipartisan compromise. What was lacking was the leadership, the courage to craft and stand over such an outcome - instead there was a stubborn insistence that legislation be delivered with a republican majority.

In recent months, a major tax reform has been pushed through by the Republicans in Congress without a single Democratic vote.

There is wide agreement that the US tax code was in need of reform, and there are certainly some passionate advocates of what has been achieved. But the legislation going on the books is fiercely contested and as of now at least, does not command the support of the majority of Americans. How much more persuasive the reform might have been had there been openness to a bipartisan approach.

Again, it is important to be clear. Public discourse as I said thrives on a robust give and take of ideas, a confident assertion of belief and position. But it does not and cannot thrive if positions one disagrees with are labelled treasonous, if building coalitions is seen as a sell-out, if closed-mindedness is allowed to parade as purity of ideology.

Political dysfunction is not the only ground for concern in today's America. The extent to which the US media increasingly functions in silos undoubtedly is a further factor in impairing the quality of public discourse. Most of you will be familiar with the general picture: the Republicans tuning into Sean Hannity on Fox News and the Democrats tuning into Rachel Maddow on MSNBC.

It is all too easy to live in an echo chamber, with a constant reinforcement of ones own views and a filtering out, or demonisation, of opposing viewpoints. Chat shows and panel discussions seem ubiquitous on American television today. With a relentless race after ratings, who is interested in wishy washy panellists who recognise both sides of of a debate? Instead, there is a premium on those who offer colour, certainty, hyperbole.

The effect of social media on public discourse, while of course not something confined to the US, also deserves brief mention. Does it widen the dialogue or dumb it down, or both? And to what extent is that a necessary or worthwhile trade - off? The importance to politicians and public figures of projecting through social media is obvious: it humanises them and extends their reach. But 140, or 280, characters shared on Twitter, or images flashed around on

Instagram, clearly cannot substitute for in depth analysis. If social media can usher people through the door, act as a kind of a teaser for further debate, then that is a bonus. But if it means shortened attention spans, feeding only or largely on the personal and inconsequential, then there is an enormous loss to the quality of public debate.

Especially since I am addressing you this evening in one of Ireland's foremost educational institutions, it is important to underline the role of universities as promoters and custodians of public discourse.There are question marks as to how some of America's leading universities are discharging this role.

Way back in 1987, when I was finishing my first posting in the US, I recall publication of a best selling book by American philosopher Allan Bloom entitled: "The Closing of the American Mind." Bloom was strongly critical of the American university system and what he saw as its excessive emphasis on relativism which was leaving students adrift, rudderless, unanchored in any value system. I am not close enough to the American university milieu to judge whether this criticism was, or is today, justified.

But the title of Bloom's book often came to mind over my last four years in the US. Time and again one read of campus warfare over controversial figures being invited, and sometimes subsequently disinvited, to speak. Safe spaces were constantly being created to protect student sensitivities in one context or another. Some of this may be justified, and obviously in no circumstances should institutions offer a platform for hate-speak. But there needs to be a willingness to listen to controversial and contrarian viewpoints, if responsibly expressed. Education is about opening minds, and what a grievous loss if universities too were to become echo chambers, insulating their students from the crossfire of ideological debate.

Europe

As I said, none of these concerns are confined to the US and one can easily trace a read-across in Europe. Brexit provides a prime example. I happen to be a very strong advocate of the European Union and I would regret the British decision to leave no matter the circumstances in which it was taken. But it was particularly disappointing to witness the terms on which the debate was conducted.

Of course there is scope for reasoned discussion. It is perfectly possible and defensible to take a view that Britain does not naturally belong within the European family, that it is in Britain's long term interest to leave, and that the unmooring was bound to come sooner rather than later. But the debate as it unfolded at times came close to travesty, with preposterous claims being made by some politicians and a daily assault on the facts in the tabloid media. It was an example of public discourse at its most impoverished.

Brexit has its own distinctive features and we should not over-extrapolate. But one can see the parallels with what is happening elsewhere in Europe. The Brexit referendum came about because David Cameron felt himself under pressure from extremists within his own party. There are similar developments across a range of European countries: a pulling of centrist parties to the right, alongside an "anti-party" sentiment which manifests itself as a rejection of mainstream parties in favour of newer parties that portray themselves as anti-elitist, anti-establishment, free of historical baggage, ready to refashion the political landscape. (You will readily recognise the same set of sentiments which helped propel Donald Trump to the White House.)

In an ideal world, one might be able to look on this as a time of renewal in Europe, introducing vigorous new ideas that will freshen and strengthen public discourse. And this is arguably the case in France, where President Macron and his movement "En Marche" have swept aside establishment parties and have begun to make good on their promise of renewing French politics, shaking it out of years of political and economic atrophy. Emmanuel Macron is clearly someone who engages with ideas, has a clear vision and is skilled in articulating and projecting that vision. And thankfully he is proving himself capable of arresting the momentum of Marie Le Pen and the Front National.

But France stands out more as the exception than representative of what is happening elsewhere in Europe. Developments in Germany are not reassuring. Although the CDU and SPD are finally cobbling together a Grand Coalition, it is clear from last year's election results that voters are becoming disenchanted with centrist politics and some are ready to dabble with unsavoury alternatives. Election results in Austria equally give rise to disquiet. And what is happening in Hungary and Poland is deeply troubling, at odds with the principles and ideals on which Europe is founded.

Once again, it is important to come back to a sense of what public discourse does and does not imply. Of course it can include a readiness to challenge the status quo and to think radically - indeed that is a hallmark of some of the most enlivening and enriching public debate. But there is always the issue of basic ground rules to be applied: we need reasoned, informed debate that respects fact and evidence, not sloganeering and irresponsible stoking of prejudice, chipping away at the foundations on which our democracies are built.

Ireland

Finally, a few comments on the state of public discourse in Ireland. Our inheritance in this regard I would suggest is something of a mixed bag. Our PR electoral system brings many benefits and it certainly ensures that TDs remain firmly rooted in their constituencies. But there is an opportunity cost: the primacy of constituency obligations has meant that political engagement on the big issues of the day has all too often been seen as a dispensable luxury. Additionally, for most of the span since the foundation of the State, the power and dominance of the Catholic Church, and its confident insistence on being the interpreter and arbiter of right and wrong in so many spheres, was a stifling influence on public debate.

On the more positive side, Irish people have legendary verbal skills - discourse is our natural medium. Even if we do not have a well-established tradition of "public intellectuals", we have an extraordinarily rich history of writers who have often, and tellingly, taken on big issues of the day. Our media is undoubtedly less silo'ed than the US - even today, RTE maintains a dominant position - and, insofar as I can judge, our universities do not seek to wrap their students in cotton wool to the same extent as can happen in the US.

In the political sphere, the Seanad - although of course it trails Dail Eireann by a long way in the hierarchy of power - has always provided a more hospitable environment for public discourse. I would like to interpret the referendum vote against abolition of the Senate as a statement by the Irish people of the value they attach to such discourse.

I also believe that the requirement to effect constitutional change by referendum has been an important catalyst for meaningful public debate. Think for example of the debates on European issues we had around the referenda on the Nice Treaty and the Lisbon Treaty. And the impassioned debates on the issues of divorce, abortion, marriage equality when those issues were subject to referenda.

I understand the concern that a referendum can be a blunt instrument to deal with what are often complex issues and choices.

And Brexit, as I said earlier, seems a textbook example of the risks associated with referenda. Indeed some of our own experiences, notably around our various referenda on abortion, did us no credit in terms of the tenor and quality of the debate.

But overall I think the referendum experience has been a positive one, and we have learned along the way. The defeats in the first Nice and first Lisbon referenda brought home the need for continual dialogue and communication on European issues. If a referendum takes place in a knowledge vacuum, then one can hardly be surprised if voters are disinclined to answer the specific question posed. And so we have had a range of public listening and learning exercise on Europe: important exercises in democratic engagement, and creating an environment for more informed voter choices.

Equally, it is very positive that the forthcoming referendum on the Eighth Amendment is built on the discussions and recommendations of the Citizens Assembly. It gives ground for hope that the debate this time round will take us beyond the vitriol that characterised some of the exchanges surrounding our earlier abortion referenda. The debate over the coming months undoubtedly will be vigorous and passionate, but one hopes within the bounds of reason and rationality, with respect for the convictions and motivation of those on the opposing side.

More generally, I think we have arrived at a time in Ireland which allows us to do some stocktaking of the quality of our public discourse. The next general election will be an important test. The country has come through boom and bust and we are now back on our feet again. With the 1916 centenary behind us, and the centenary of the Irish State approaching, we can describe ourselves as a mature nation. And a mature nation is ready for mature debate and mature choices. Do we want a Republic of Opportunity? Or a Republic of Conscience? Can we blend both without too high a level of compromise? How do we see ourselves in changed international circumstances and in the new Europe that will take shape in the aftermath of Brexit?

As we outgrow the structures and mindsets inherited from Civil War politics, and seek to mature and modernise our politics, it is vital that we stay grounded, maintain our moral compass, and beware of a populism that offers facile and false solutions.

To conclude: let me sum up the issues I have been talking about this evening. Public discourse is not an ornament in our societies - it forms part of the lifeblood of democracies, and indeed the state of public discourse is a good barometer of the overall health of a democracy. In today's circumstances, there is no basis for complacency and significant grounds for concern. America remains - in that time honoured phrase - the leader of the free world, and what unfolds there has consequences for us all. Europe manifestly matters to us: we are members of the European family and the overall health and strength of the family is dependent on the political, economic, and yes - moral - health of the individual members. And so we need to be alert to the risks emerging on both continents.

In Ireland, even if our legacy in relation to public discourse is a mixed one, there are factors which have helped build resilience and maintain a healthy space for such discourse. But we need that 'eternal vigilance' that John Philpot Curran first spoke about. Threats and risks to public discourse are not going to be confined within national borders and Ireland is not immune. As Stephen Collins put it in an op-ed piece in the Irish Times last week: "We take the survival of our democracy for granted but history shows that no people have an automatic right to a healthy democracy". And so we need to take conscious steps: valuing public discourse, creating the conditions in which it will flourish, protecting it against those who would debase the currency.

And that of course is part of the mission of your Society - an almost two hundred and fifty year old mission which you continue to discharge so well. And that is why I am honoured to receive your Gold Medal; I cannot think of a more important role and responsibility than contribution to Public Discourse. Thank you for this honour, and for your presence here this evening.

ACKNOWLEDGEMENTS

One of the early chapters of this collection includes a speech I gave shortly after retirement, accepting a Lifetime Achievement Award from the American Chamber of Commerce Ireland. I dedicated that award to "all my colleagues in the Irish foreign service: a band of skilled and dedicated men and women, true patriots, unstinting in their devotion and service to our country."I meant every word. My Departmental colleagues have been my extended family over many decades, and my admiration and affection go deep. I particularly thank those colleagues - both diplomatic and locally recruited staff - with whom I served in various Embassies and Missions abroad. Whatever we accomplished was as a team, and these teams were fuelled by hard work, good humour, kindness and mutual support.

A few of the speeches give glimpses of my father and mother, Tom and Margaret Anderson; it was their love and sacrifice that laid the foundations on which their children built. My siblings - my sisters Helen and Mary and my brother Robert - remain a strong and grounding presence in my life, and it says a lot about our bond that we still enjoy great nights out as a foursome.

My life is immensely enriched by a circle of steadfast friends. Some of the closest and most indestructible friendships go back almost fifty years. Others have been formed over the intervening decades: within the Department, during my postings abroad, and more recently in New York. To all my dear friends, for all the generosity and kindness over the years, for everything I have learned from them, my heartfelt thanks.

My ex-husband, Martin Wheeler, makes a brief appearance in these pages. Martin was a true helpmate throughout the early decades as we gained our sea-legs in diplomacy; we share many good memories and some never-to-be forgotten anecdotes from the early postings in Geneva and Washington.

The first dedication in this book is to my daughter Claire. From the very beginning, and throughout the past thirty-five years, Claire has brought a glow of sunshine to my life. Her warmth, grace and laughter brighten the space around her. The quality I most admire - and which I recognise in the dedication - is her unerring moral compass. Claire was with me throughout much of the hard work and great joy of my diplomatic career, and remains a wonderful companion in our shared world of words and ideas. (Let me also attest that, without Claire's expert help at every turn, this book would never have come together).

The book is also dedicated with love and gratitude to Frank Lowe, my partner of almost nine years. Frank is quite simply a "mensch"; he is also a life force, who helps me experience life in technicolour. Together, Frank and I shared the adventures of my final postings in New York and Washington, where Frank quickly became a beloved figure in the Irish American community. I thank him for his unfailing support, and am impatient for our continued shared adventures.